SEARCHING
FOR A
BETTER SOCIETY

John Sheahan

SEARCHING FOR A BETTER SOCIETY

The Peruvian Economy from 1950

The Pennsylvania State University Press
University Park, Pennsylvania

Library of Congress Cataloging-in-Publication Data

Sheahan, John, 1923–
    Searching for a better society : the Peruvian economy from 1950 / John Sheahan.
        p.   cm.
    Includes bibliographical references and index.
    ISBN 0-271-01872-0 (cloth : alk. paper)
    ISBN 0-271-01873-9 (pbk. : alk. paper)
    1. Peru—Economic policy.   2. Peru—Economic conditions—1918–
    3. Peru—Economic conditions—1968–   I. Title.
HC227.S435   1999
338.985   DC21   98-39335
                                                                                     CIP

Copyright © 1999 The Pennsylvania State University
All rights reserved
Printed in the United States of America
Published by The Pennsylvania State University Press,
University Park, PA 16802-1003

It is the policy of The Pennsylvania State University Press to use acid-free paper for the first printing of all clothbound books. Publications on uncoated stock satisfy the minimum requirements of American National Standard for Information Sciences—Permanence of Paper for Printed Library Materials, ANSI Z39.48–1992.

Contents

	List of Tables and Figures	vi
	Preface	ix
1	Peru and Latin America: Five Difficult Decades	1
2	Human Resources and Political Evolution	17
3	Changing Structures of Production and Trade	39
4	Agriculture, Rural Incomes, and Violence	57
5	Industrialization, Employment, and the Informal Sector	81
6	Poverty and Inequality	105
7	State-Led Development, 1963–1990	131
8	The 1990s: Reversion to a Relatively Open Economy	153
9	Interactions: Goals, Structure, and Strategy	173
	References	193
	Index	207

Tables and Figures

Tables

1.1. Economic and social indicators, Peru and Latin America, 1960, 1970, 1980, and 1992.	5
1.2. Gini coefficients of inequality in the distribution of income: Peru in 1971 and 1981; Latin America, East Asia, and the industrialized countries in the 1970s.	6
1.3. Summary of changes in governments and economic policy orientation, 1950–1998.	9
2.1. Regional shares of national population, percentage of region's households with indigenous maternal language, and percentage in poverty, 1994.	18
3.1. Distribution of the labor force by sector, 1950, 1980, 1990, and 1994.	47
3.2. Sector origins of gross domestic product, 1950–1995, estimated at constant market prices of 1979.	47
3.3. Growth rates by sector 1970–1995, and sector composition of GDP in 1995, estimated in constant dollars of 1990.	48
3.4. Structure of exports, 1970–1997.	52
4.1. Agricultural labor force and supply of arable land, Peru and South America, 1965–1994.	60
4.2. Indexes of output per capita of the agricultural sector and of food, 1965–1996.	65
5.1. Value added in manufacturing as a share of GDP, and rates of growth of manufacturing output by selected subperiods, 1950–1997.	83
5.2. Degrees of industrial sector protection against imports as measured by effective protection and by number of tariff positions for which imports were prohibited, 1955–1991.	84

5.3. Structure of employment in Lima, 1970, 1990, and 1995.	89
5.4. Open unemployment in urban areas, selected years from 1980 to 1997.	92
5.5. Index of real wages in manufacturing 1965–1980, and two alternative indexes for wages of hourly paid workers in the private sector 1980–1990.	93
5.6. Estimates of the percentages of workers in the informal sector and of domestic workers, Lima, 1970–1996.	98
6.1. Estimates of the shares of Peruvian households in poverty, indigence, and chronic poverty, 1970–1994.	108
6.2. Inequalities in rates of infant mortality among departments in Peru, 1981 and 1996.	109
6.3. Illiteracy rates for people over fifteen years old, in Lima and five departments in the sierra, 1993.	110
6.4. Estimates of the incidence of poverty and extreme poverty by major regions, 1985–1994.	112
6.5. Economic activities of people in extreme poverty, 1994.	113
6.6. Characteristics of heads of households for families in poverty and extreme poverty, 1994.	114
6.7. Estimates of the distribution of income in Peru, 1961 through 1994.	118
6.8. Social expenditures relative to GDP and to government spending, Peru and Latin America, 1990–1995.	126
7.1. Index of GDP per capita and rates of inflation for selected years, 1963–1990.	133
7.2. Comparative rates of inflation in 1980 and in 1989, and changes in GDP per capita, for seven Latin American countries.	144
7.3. External debt, public and total, 1970–1990.	148
8.1. Index of the real exchange rate, 1990–1997.	160
8.2. Inflation, changes in GDP per capita and gross investment, direct foreign investment, and external debt, 1990–1997.	161
8.3. External trade and current account deficits, 1990–1997.	164

Figures

1.1. Annual rates of change of GDP per capita, Peru and Latin America, by subperiods from 1950 to 1996.	7

2.1. Public expenditures for current functioning of the educational system, 1970–1994. 22
3.1. Share of manufacturing in GDP as a function of GDP per capita, fifteen Latin American countries, 1960. 50
4.1. Traditional and nontraditional agricultural exports, 1980–1997. 71
5.1. Indexes of real wages for hourly paid workers in Lima, for firms with ten or more employees, and of the real minimum wage, 1990–1997. 94
7.1. Balance of payments on current account, 1970–1990. 147

Preface

This study began in one of the most deeply troubled periods in Peru's history, 1989–91. Rural areas were being ravaged by the joint violence of *Sendero Luminoso* (Shining Path) and the military, blackouts and bombs in Lima seemed unstoppable, production and incomes kept falling, inflation ran out of control, and the structure of public order verged on disintegration. It was easy to see why many people were trying to leave the country; harder to see how most could go on with their daily lives, many doing their best to help one another as conditions grew ever more difficult. Lima's communal kitchens, run by volunteers, fed more than six hundred thousand people a day in 1991, one-tenth of the population of the metropolitan area.

Research for this study was originally an attempt to understand why things had gone so badly in Peru, especially why poverty, inflation, and violence had increased so persistently. The inquiry began with a focus on the 1970s and 1980s, went back to the beginning of the postwar period, and then farther back to the factors that shaped the postwar context. In the process, the similarities to and differences from other Latin American countries became touchstones of the possible, of what might have been and of the factors that determined different sequences and outcomes. Examining Peruvian experience in this way became a special window into Latin America: into the reasons that similar hopes and strains worked out in various countries in ways that have many parallels but that were sometimes strikingly different.

As in most of the rest of Latin America, Peruvian economic strategy has gone in something of a circle, from a long-established orientation toward an open economy with minimal state intervention to a period of state-led development, then back again to what looks much like the starting point. Most of the other countries adopted various forms of state-led development in response to the depression of the 1930s, but the political balance in Peru blocked change in that period. As soon as the Peruvian people got their first real chance to make a democratic choice between continuation or change of the country's open-economy orientation, in the 1960s, they chose to reject it. That choice was not provoked by any economic crisis: the economy had been growing well, with low inflation and no problem of external financing. The pressures for change came from rising antagonism to the long-established domination of the society by a privileged minority, extreme rural poverty combined with high concentration of land ownership, unequal access to education and economic opportunity, structures of production and trade adverse to adequate growth of opportunities for productive employment, domination of the main export sector—mining—and of the oil industry by foreign firms, and a general conviction of being left behind by the modern world. The majority of Peruvians were seeking objectives more fundamental than economic growth. They were, with conflicting visions but many good reasons, "searching for a better society."

This study examines the factors involved in these issues and the consequences of the new economic orientation intended to resolve them. Many things went wrong, to say the least. Some positive accomplishments have been important, too, but failures were frequent enough to lead the country back to a market-determined economic system in 1990. The final set of problems concerns the consequences of this return to the earlier economic strategy in a considerably different structural context and the steps that might be taken to shape the process of development—in Peru and in Latin America generally—toward less unfair societies.

I would like to think of this book as a complement to the thorough investigation of Peruvian economic history published by Rosemary Thorp and Geoffrey Bertram in 1978 . . . a complement in the sense of an extension of the period considered through an additional two dramatic decades and, more fundamentally, in the central direction of attention. Their book emphasizes problems of international trade and foreign investment, which have certainly been important for Peru. This study includes considerable discussion of international trade and finance, but it explains more of the country's problems in terms of internal divisions, inequity and social conflict, and implications of domestic policy decisions. It may give too little weight to external influences. Both sides matter greatly.

I owe many thanks to Rosemary Thorp for sharing her lively ideas in conferences and individual discussions with the vigor and keen interest in Latin America that she always communicates. I would especially like to thank two other economists who read early versions of several chapters of this manuscript and made invaluable suggestions: Ann Helwege of Tufts University and Efraín Gonzales de Olarte of the Instituto de Estudios Peruanos in Lima. Ideal critics both: with helpfully different angles of vision, patience most of the time, and shared concerns.

Many other people have taken time to discuss these issues, send helpful information and studies of their own, or simply explain their ideas about Peru and Latin America: Adolfo Figueroa, Javier Iguíñiz, José Távara, Mario Tello, and Jorge Vega in the Department of Economics at the Catholic University; Francisco Verdera at the Instituto de Estudios Peruanos; Jürgen Schuldt and Bruno Seminario at the Universidad del Pacífico; Marcia Koth de Paredes at the Fulbright Commission; Patricia McLauchlan de Arregui and Jaime Saavedra at GRADE; Jaime Galvez and Gilberto Moncada at Instituto Cuánto; Saúl Paredes and Renzo Rossini at the Banco Central de Reserva del Perú; James Rudolph as an adviser for promotion of exports by microenterprise producers; Bolívar Patiño as a rare contact with a (probably untypical) industrialist and exporter; and Elena Alverez, Ray Bromley, Shane Hunt, Daniel Schydlowsky, and Richard Webb in both Peru and the United States.

The great good fortune to meet helpful Peruvian people going about their work with remarkable calm in the face of the strains of life in Lima made an enormous difference: Olga Samanez coping with the endless operational demands of the Hostal El Patio, friendly haven through many visits; Fabiola Castillo going beyond the duties of a good librarian to locate material about the economy in her two successive libraries, at the Instituto de Estudios Peruanos and the Instituto Peruano de Administración de Empresas; and most especially Olga Chamorro, professor of mathematics at the Catholic University, enlightening interpreter of Peruvian ways, and among the most valiant and generous-spirited people one could ever hope to meet.

At Penn State Press, Sandy Thatcher's personal encouragement and interest in Latin America, and Cherene Holland's cooperative management of the editorial process, helped resolve uncertainties and improve the book. At home, Denise's sympathy for people in poverty and strong sense of fairness were never-failing guides.

Recent research studies by Peruvian economists and other social scientists have been a great help. Naturally, interpretations of causation remain very much open to debate. Many of the people cited here would disagree with my interpretations and with one another's as well. We all do our best to understand; reality always has yet another dimension.

1

PERU AND LATIN AMERICA

Five Difficult Decades

This book is centered on the goals, the conflicts, the economic strategies, and the process of change in Peru in the second half of the twentieth century. This period has not, for the most part, been a happy one. Conflicts and strains are normal for all societies in this unfair and frustrating world, but at times they can become explosive. For many Peruvians, and Latin Americans generally, the postwar period started with exceptionally high tensions between goals and reality.

Growing awareness of the extent and depth of poverty, inequality, and blocked life opportunities for most people heightened impatience with institutional and political structures geared mainly to protect privilege. Growing frustration with the sense of falling ever farther behind the modern world, of being caught in economic structures adverse to any self-determined course of development, opposed the constraints of technological dominance by the industrialized countries, scarce skills and weak innovative capacity at home, and resistance to change by the influential minority best able to gain from existing economic structures.

Impatience with resistance to change fed multiple reactions. One was an increasing appeal to revolutionary violence, with its counterpart of increasing support for repression from the conservative side. In Peru, revolutionary violence (as distinct from rural movements aimed mainly at seizures of land) flared up in the 1960s. It was quickly repressed in that period, only to return in far more drastic form, with much wider support, in the 1980s. Nonviolent leftist movements gained considerable strength by the 1980s as well, although their support decreased in the later part of the decade.[1] For the many Peruvians who disavowed both violence and communism but urgently wanted change, the alternative that came to dominate in the early postwar decades was state-led development: mainly public investment and protection against import competition, to foster industrialization, modernization, and capacity for independent development.

This last possibility, a partial turning away from the world economy toward internally oriented development, had always been favored by an active minority of intellectual and social leaders. Paul Gootenberg's *Imagining Development* brings out in illuminating detail the complex evolution of nineteenth-century debates in Peru, not just between conflicting economic interests but between concepts of growth through trade as opposed to arguments in favor of managing trade to promote self-determined development (Gootenberg 1993). The debate never stopped, but the liberal protrade side won the day in Peru and throughout the region until the international trading system broke down in the depression of the 1930s. The collapse of world markets and finance hit Latin America with such force that the orientation toward open economies lost acceptance almost everywhere. Many countries, although not Peru in the first instance, turned to rising protection and other measures to promote industrialization and recovery (Thorp 1984).

Peru did not join this process until the 1960s, just as some of the early leaders were beginning to turn away from it. As if to make up for the belated start, a surprisingly reform-oriented military government began from 1968 an aggressive strategy of nationalization, state investment, land reform, worker participation in industrial ownership, and an impressive variety of new social programs. The reforms created many

---

1. The APRA party, founded by Víctor Haya de la Torre early in the 1930s, offered a distinctively Peruvian anti–imperialist, prolabor, antioligarchic radicalism that was virulently anticommunist at the same time. It had a sad fate as a political force, as discussed in Chapter 2.

problems, and most were reversed by subsequent governments, but they produced fundamental changes in Peru.

The first years of the military government were successful in several ways, but economic policies generated increasing strains depressingly familiar throughout the region: rising inflation and external deficits, followed by forced contractions worsening unemployment and poverty, followed once again by even worse inflation and external deficits on the next round. As the economy went downhill and violence grew, successive governments reversed the policies of their predecessors in futile attempts to find solutions to problems that always proved more difficult than expected.

Throughout the 1980s, the most pressing questions about the economy and society centered on the causes of what seemed to be an inexorable process of deterioration: falling production, accelerating inflation, increasing poverty, and worsening violence. The first half of the 1990s brought considerable relief and hope, with much lower inflation and less violence, and with a recovery of production, although without any clear change in the degree of chronic poverty. Seeking the causes of these troubles is crucial for understanding the past and for overcoming possible obstacles in the future. Can economic growth be built on a more sustainable basis, can the gains of growth be more widely distributed, and can the process be shaped in ways that pull the society together instead of tearing it apart? These questions are acute for Peru and common to the rest of Latin America as well.

The Country and the Region: Similarities and Differences

Many of Peru's problems have been shared by the other Latin American countries as well as by developing countries in other regions. The causal factors at work clearly reach beyond Peru itself, partly to the specific historical heritage of Latin American society and partly to economic and political pressures acting on the entire developing world. To study Peru in detail can illuminate problems common to the region and the world; to place that study in the wider external context can clarify many of the issues facing Peru.

Of the many dimensions of Latin America's heritage relevant to this study, two strands are particularly important. The first is the common context of internal social division and high inequality: division between dominant minorities of European descent and majorities of indigenous and mixed descent in Peru as in most countries or of Black people in Brazil and the Caribbean (Chapter 2). The second is the region's failure to keep up with northern countries in the processes of innovation and structural change that began to differentiate them so markedly in the nineteenth century. That relative weakness left Latin America in the role of a supplier of primary products to the industrialized countries, dependent for growth on external markets and finance, through most of the twentieth century (Chapter 3). In turn, this structure of production and trade impeded efforts to overcome the underlying technological weaknesses.

The first strand, of profound inequality in social participation as well as in income, remained as marked at the beginning of the postwar period as it had been for centuries preceding: rural majorities were for the most part left out, disdained, or actively repressed by national leaders. Education was for the minority, not for everyone. In Peru in 1940, 45 percent of the men over age fifteen, and 69 percent of the women, were illiterate (Instituto Cuánto 1991, 153). The failure of most Latin American countries to incorporate the rural population in the process of development—to give them access to "human capital" in the sense of education, skills, and economic mobility—can be seen as the most important single cause of great inequality and weak capacity for economic transformation (Sheahan and Iglesias 1998).

The second common strand, weak technological change and prolonged dependence on primary exports, has long been recognized but has been interpreted in contradictory ways. The view associated with dependency theory emphasizes the self-perpetuating characteristics of trade patterns. Export earnings that favor primary products pull resources and new investment in their direction and raise the incomes and political influence of the groups opposing change. On the import side, competition from new products developed in industrialized countries discourages domestic investment in industries characterized by high rates of technological change.

This concept of self-reinforcing blockage has much logic and evidence in its favor but is incomplete. It leaves out the possibility that appropriate economic and social policies if they include widely distributed investment in human capital can change structures of trade and production in ways helpful for employment and for technological progress. Questions of how these contrasting concepts relate to each other and how structures of trade and production can be changed are among the most important

Table 1.1. Economic and social indicators, Peru and Latin America, 1960, 1970, 1980, 1992

	1960	1970	1980	1992
GDP per capita (constant 1988 dollars)				
Peru	1,293	1,656	1,788	1,287
Median for Latin America[a]	1,032	1,296	1,497	1,486
Ratio, Peru to median	1.25	1.28	1.19	0.87
Infant mortality (per 1,000 live births)				
Peru	142	—	—	64
Median for Latin America	115	—	—	40
Poverty (percentage of households below poverty line defined by ECLAC)				
Peru	—	50	46	—
Median for Latin America[b]	—	34	35	—

SOURCES: GDP per capita from IDB 1990, 4; 1994, 239. Infant mortality from UNDP 1995, 162–63. Poverty rates from ECLAC 1996, 145–46; 1997, 193–94.
[a] Median for nineteen countries.
[b] 1970 median for the nine countries reported in source; 1980 for ten countries in or near that year (1979 for Brazil and Peru; 1981 for Costa Rica and Uruguay; 1984 for Mexico).

issues facing Peru, and all of Latin America. They run through this whole book and play a central role in Chapters 3 through 5.

Economic Growth and Inequality

Peru had a comparatively good record of economic growth through the 1950s and reached a level of income distinctly above the median for Latin America.[2] Growth slowed in the next two decades, and output per capita fell drastically in the 1980s, then began to recover from 1993 on. Inequality and poverty have been exceptionally high, even compared with the rest of Latin America, but they have not been invariant. Both inequality and poverty decreased somewhat in the 1970s, and poverty rose painfully in the late 1980s.

Table 1.1 shows three summary indicators of income and aspects of inequality for Peru and Latin America from 1960 to 1992. As of 1960,

---
2. Comparisons with Latin America refer, whenever possible, to the twenty countries for which English is not the primary language; they exclude the Anglophone countries of the Caribbean except where otherwise noted. They necessarily omit Cuba when comparable data are unavailable.

Table 1.2. Gini coefficients of inequality in the distribution of income: Peru in 1971 and 1981; Latin America, East Asia, and the industrialized countries in the 1970s

Peru		
Estimate for 1971	.55	
Estimate for 1981	.49	
Average for 1971 and 1981		.52
Regional averages for the 1970s		
Latin America and the Caribbean		.49
East Asia and the Pacific		.40
Industrialized countries		.35

SOURCE: Deininger and Squire 1996a, 41; 1996b, 584.
NOTE: Averages include only the particular estimates of income distribution accepted as valid in the source. The earliest estimate accepted for Peru is for 1971, the next is for 1981.

Peru was among the higher-income countries of the region: its gross domestic product (GDP) per capita was 25 percent above the median. Despite that, infant mortality, which normally falls at higher levels of income, was 23 percent above the regional median. High levels of infant mortality relative to levels of income reflect a multitude of factors, including inequality of income and of provision of public services, notably for health and education. Traditional Peruvian society failed its poor people more seriously than did countries with lower levels of income.

Measures of the percentages of households below the poverty line for 1970 indicate a much higher share in Peru, fully one-half of all families, than for the median of the nine countries for which comparable estimates are available. The poverty head count in Peru came down moderately by the end of the 1970s but remained well above the median for the region. The widespread poverty, despite per capita income above the median for the region, is a strong indication of continuing exceptional inequality.

Direct estimates of inequality in the distribution of income always raise severe problems, especially in cross-country comparison, but a database compiled by researchers for the World Bank has helped to establish useful standards of acceptability (Deininger and Squire 1996b). Table 1.2 gives Gini coefficients, measuring the degree of concentration of income, calculated for Peru in 1971 and 1981, compared with averages for the decade of the 1970s in Latin America, East Asia, and the industrialized countries. Inequality can be considered high in all of them: the industrialized countries do not provide a benchmark of the ideal. Still, the Gini coefficients make clear that poverty is considerably higher in Latin America than in either the industrialized countries or the developing countries of East Asia. The coefficient for Peru was markedly higher than the average for the region in 1971 but came down to equal the average in 1981.

The main structural factors underlying persistent poverty and inequality are examined in Chapter 6. The most evident factors have been a deeply rooted pattern of neglect of the rural poor population in allocations of public-sector services in education and health, combined with market forces that pull private investment and employment opportunities toward the cities rather than the rural areas. This self-reinforcing pattern would have maintained high levels of poverty and inequality even if economic growth had been sustained throughout the postwar years.

From 1913 to 1950, the GDP per capita for Peru and Latin America as a whole increased faster than the average for industrialized countries (Hunt 1996). Peru continued to do well through the first half of the 1960s: GDP per capita increased 2.9 percent a year in the decade of the 1950s and 3.2 percent a year in the first half of the 1960s, compared with the regional growth average of 2.0 percent for these fifteen years. From then on, things went much less well. Peru's growth rate fell far below that of the region from 1965 to 1980 and turned steeply negative through the 1980s (Fig. 1.1). Although GDP per capita fell for the whole region during the debt crisis of that decade, the fall in Peru was three times as deep as that for the region. By 1992, output per capita had fallen all the way back to the level of 1960 (Table 1.1 and Fig. 1.1).

Fig. 1.1. Annual rates of growth of GDP per capita, Peru and Latin America, by subperiods from 1950 to 1996.

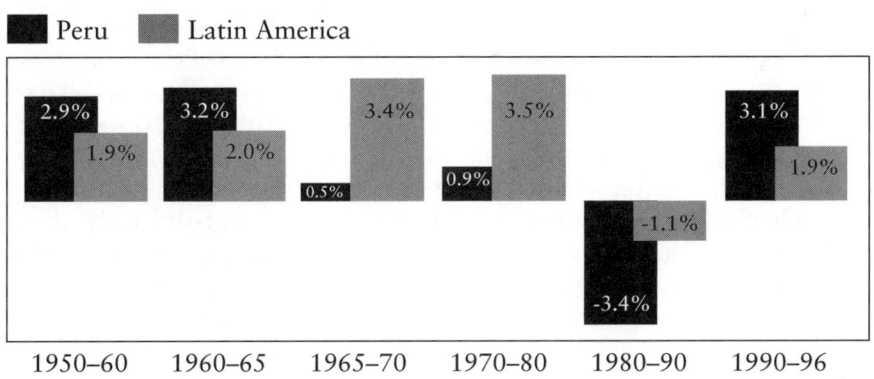

NOTE: 1950–70 at constant 1973 prices; 1970–96 in constant 1990 dollars; regional data include English-speaking countries in the Caribbean.
SOURCES: World Bank 1983, 486–88 for 1950–70; IDB 1997, 221, for 1970–96.

The first half of the 1990s brought marked changes for the better throughout the region. In terms of output per capita, Peru came out of the ghastly 1980s with a much more pronounced recovery than the region as a whole. At the same time, inflation fell far below the heights of the 1980s. Violence also decreased greatly after 1992 in Peru, and everywhere else except Colombia. Renewed growth and lessened violence brought new promise, although poverty and inequality remained stubbornly high.

Changes in Economic and Political Orientation

From a broad and partially misleading perspective, the major changes in rates of economic growth shown for Peru in Figure 1.1 may be related to corresponding evolutions of political balance and basic policy orientation. The positive growth rates of 1950–65 and 1990–96 were associated with conservative governments that mainly left the economy up to market forces; the slowdown and then reversal of economic growth from 1965 to 1990 were associated with erratic forms of state-led intervention. Still, any such generalization needs a great deal of qualification: many different governments and policies were involved, and many other factors came into play.

Table 1.3 summarizes the main changes in governments and policy orientation from 1950. What stands out is the back-and-forth efforts of postwar Peruvian society to find its way. The conservative governments in power until 1962 were interested in development but not in distancing Peru from the world economy. On the contrary, they considered foreign investment the most promising path toward modernization and shaped tax policies to favor it. They backed favors for foreign investors with considerable public investment in infrastructure and adopted moderate increases in protection while rejecting any strong version of state intervention. They kept down inflation and external debt but did little about rural poverty or highly concentrated land ownership; they repressed labor organization, and they left the country's growth largely dependent on exports of primary products and on foreign investment.

The break with this orientation under the government of Fernando Belaúnde Terry from 1963 was moderate, not to say ineffective, to the point of severely limiting its consequences either for good or ill. The government of General Juan Velasco Alvarado, who seized power in 1968, was a very different story, in terms of extensive structural intervention, nationalization and greatly increased roles for public firms, intensified protection, and rising fiscal deficits financed by heavy external borrowing.

Table 1.3. Summary of changes in governments and economic policy orientation, 1950–1998

	Governments	Economic Policy Orientation
1950–62	Conservative: first military (General Manuel Odría), then civilian (Manuel Prado)	Relatively open economy with tax favors for foreign investors; public investment limited to infrastructure
1962	Intervention by reformist military	Localized and modest land reform; creation of planning department
1963–68	Democratic election of promotional-reformist government (Fernando Belaúnde Terry)	Increased public investment and protection; political impasse over proposed land reform and foreign domination of the oil industry
1968–75	Radical reformist military (General Juan Velasco Alvarado)	Greatly increased state intervention and protection; nationalizations and state firms; thorough land reform; rising fiscal deficits and heavy foreign borrowing
1975–80	Much more conservative military government (General Francisco Morales Bermudez)	Partial reversal of Velasco reforms though continued extensive public ownership and high protection
1980–85	Democracy restored with Belaúnde back, now more conservative and weakened by rise of *Sendero luminoso*	Initial "neoliberal" changes; somewhat reduced protection but continued high public investment; excess spending and forced contraction
1985–90	All-out populism (Alan García)	Intervention in all directions at once; heterodox program to promote expansion while blocking inflation by direct controls; intense conflict with private sector over attempted nationalization of financial system
1990–	Neoliberal reforms combined with strand of authoritarianism (Alberto Fujimori)	Thorough reversal of state-led intervention; protection greatly reduced, and foreign investors welcomed back; extensive privatizations

That government created Peru's external debt burden and set up the country's debt crisis long before the general breakdown of international lending in the 1980s.

The following military government and the second administration of Belaúnde after restoration of democracy in 1980 were both much more conservative than the Velasco government. They reversed most of the latter's structural reforms, stopped expansion of the state firms, and made some reductions in protection. They did not sweep away state intervention and protection; they kept the general orientation of state-led development and import substitution while moving back toward a market-determined system.

The downturn in economic growth shown in Figure 1.1 became pronounced in this period of conservative governments, which failed to get the economy going again on any sustainable basis. The return to intensive intervention under the government of Alan García Pérez from 1985 to 1990 was no great help: after two initially euphoric years, its policies drove the economy downward with a vengeance. Disregard of macroeconomic balance would have been harmful enough, but an aborted attempt to nationalize the financial system created such intense conflict with the private sector that private investment plunged. These costly years turned the political balance strongly against activist intervention and created a context that favored movement back to a highly conservative economic orientation.

Structural Issues

Underneath the maze of contradictory economic policies tried out in postwar Peru and throughout Latin America, a shared set of structural factors acted to limit the possibilities of sustained, widely shared development. Such considerations were in the forefront of economic analysis of developing countries in the early postwar period but have had little intellectual standing in recent years.

The traumatic experiences of open-market economic systems in the depression of the 1930s and the postwar wave of independence for countries with undeniably weak productive capacities had helped to direct attention to the negative consequences of market forces and had stimulated new ideas about the problems of development. Structural obstacles were seen, rightly, to require corrective action for any well-sustained development to occur. As attention focused on these obstacles, more prosaic issues of incentives, efficiency, and macroeconomic balance were often downgraded as minor irritants that diverted attention from fundamentals. The costs in terms of mistakes and missed opportunities proved high for the region and especially for Peru.

In reaction, the pendulum has now swung the other way. Timeless truth—universally applicable logical principles and universally desirable economic liberalism—has temporarily come to dominate both economic analysis and the strategies of Latin American governments. Structural differences are not so much denied as ignored: to pay too much attention to them can and did lead to a dead-end economic strategy. But the opposite extreme is no better. The world offers more possibilities than either the version of state-led development that worked so badly in Peru or the particular model of liberalization that has, for the time being, replaced it. This fundamental set of issues is examined from many different angles in the last four chapters of this book.

The particular structural factors most relevant to Peruvian experience involve interactions between internal and external characteristics. Internally, a central factor has been the country's rapid growth of population and labor force relative to arable land and to opportunities for productive employment (Chapters 4 and 5). High rates of rural to urban migration have aggravated weak employment conditions in urban activities but have not been sufficient to prevent continuing increases in the ratio of the agricultural labor force to the supply of arable land. In such conditions, market forces work persistently against rising incomes for both rural and urban workers. Movement into informal sector activities has been the major outlet: it helps people survive, although mostly at productivity levels that make it difficult to escape poverty. Highly unequal access to education and skills, combined with concentrated ownership of assets, has worked in the same direction: to hold down opportunities for much of the labor force while giving special advantages to a few.

Higher rates of innovation, technical progress, saving, and investment by Peruvian firms might have helped to open up opportunities for productive employment, especially if they had led to diversified exports of labor-intensive products. In practice, Peruvian exports and economic growth were dominated by traditional agriculture and mining, with a good deal of low-productivity labor in the former sector but with highly capital-intensive methods in the latter. The industrial sector achieved reasonably good rates of economic growth during periods of success for primary exports but collapsed quickly whenever markets for the country's raw material exports weakened.

In one sense, Peru was unusually fortunate in its wealth of natural resources, and in another sense less so. The high rate of growth during much of its early history was due mainly to success in progressively diversifying the country's range of primary exports: from gold and silver to guano to copper and oil, to cotton, rubber, sugar, and—spectacularly in the 1950s—fish meal. Viewed in terms of national economic growth, the country's ability to develop such diverse primary product exports has been highly positive. The negative side was that the growth of employment opportunities in industrial and other nontraditional activities was to some extent suppressed by the country's ready access to foreign exchange to finance competing imports. The mining sector provided good exports but not much employment, the industrial sector failed to build up any capacity to compete in export markets, technical progress remained exceedingly slow, and the whole economy had to undergo repeated contractions whenever external demand for primary products weakened.

No one can be sure what would have happened if Peru had kept an open-economy orientation throughout the postwar period, but it is painfully clear that abandoning it in favor of inward-oriented development in the 1960s was followed by badly deteriorating economic performance (Chapter 7). How were the changes to an activist economic strategy and the breakdown of the growth process connected to each other? It is difficult to argue that they were not connected, but changes in many other dimensions could have dominated the effects of the redirection of economic strategy. The society's underlying strains associated with inequality, poverty, and pressures for truly radical change may have grown too strong to be successfully countered by either the country's traditionally liberal orientation or the versions of state-led development attempted from the early 1960s to 1990.

Economic Strategy, Social Goals, and Violence

Questions of economic strategy should be guided by some sense of where societies want to go. The starting point of this study is the belief that, from the 1930s through the early postwar decades, many if not most people of Latin America wanted to change their societies in significant ways: to escape their long-established orientations toward market-determined and relatively open economies that had worked so disproportionately in favor of privileged minorities.

On the internal side, the problems for Peru included widespread poverty, inadequate opportunities for productive employment, unequal access to education and skills, concentrated ownership and incomes, and pervasive discrimination holding down opportunities for much of the population (Chapters 2 and 6). In relation to the outside world, the problems included dependence on external demand for the country's primary exports, frustration from inability to compete in world markets for industrial products, dependence on external capital for investment, and growing resentment of extensive foreign ownership (Chapter 3). An understandable sense that the society was unfair and that an open economy made things worse built up pressure for economic and social change.

Against any concept that social objectives can shape national policies, current economic analysis usually emphasizes the side of competition among selective interests. *Rent seeking* and similar terms point toward individual interests as the dominant force shaping policy choice. In this view, it is not so much that Latin Americans were seeking better societies: the forces at work were mainly the struggles of industrialists, the traditional elite, the rising class of educated people without established positions, and the military to ensure gains for themselves.

These two ways of looking at history emerge clearly in the contrasting analyses of postwar Peru by Daniel Schydlowsky and Jürgen Schuldt (1996). For Schydlowsky, postwar state activism was a conscious effort to deal with specific economic and social problems. For Schuldt, this picture of Peru is totally inaccurate. "Perceived in this way, this is a country unknown to me. I have always believed that our economy is ruled by the law of the jungle, even if wrapped in gloves of silk" (Schuldt 1996, 65).[3]

Schuldt's interpretation has the appeal of realism, but it is an incomplete version of reality. While individual interests are always ready to take advantage of any opening they can find, societies can in some periods achieve a strong enough consensus on their goals to impose a higher level of direction. Societies are capable of varied behavior and sometimes even of constructive balances among competing goals. Shared social objectives and equitable societies have been more the norm in postwar Scandinavia than in Latin America or the United States. Social objectives were hardly notice-

---

3. Schuldt's statement sounds better in his original Spanish than in my translation: "Siempre creí que nuestra economía se regía por la ley de la selva, si bien envuelta en guantes de seda."

able in the policies of the United States in the 1920s; they became vastly more significant in the next two decades and somewhat so again in the 1960s, only to fade into near oblivion in the 1980s. Priorities change, as do problems. Even in the best of cases, shared goals never guarantee genuine social progress: misdirected methods and selective distortion can always block progress, as Peru and all of Latin America learned.

Peru's combination of persistent poverty, inequality, and worsening macroeconomic conditions in the 1980s did a great deal to discourage support for democracy and to feed rapidly growing violence. The country's violence has had many different strands (Chapter 4). One is the long history of unresolved rural conflict, involving not only struggles over land and power but also racial and ethnic discrimination and episodes of resurgent Indian resistance to domination (Chapters 2 and 6).[4] These conflicts can blend with, although they are not the same as, violence used as an instrument of ideological struggle, fiercely embodied by *Sendero Luminoso* (Shining Path) and the Movimento Revolucionario Túpac Amaru (MRTA). Neither movement was formed or led by indigenous people, although *Sendero Luminoso* effectively mobilized support based on their long-standing grievances (Degregori 1990 and 1992; Palmer 1992).

The drug trade is yet another strand of violence; it involves extensive corruption as well as direct conflict but also provides an important source of rural income. Still another form of violence common in most countries but not in Peru until the 1980s is pervasive urban crime associated with poverty, unemployment, and individual desperation. In the face of such strains, the government's ability to maintain order, even to prevent the police and the army from preying on the public, deteriorated badly. "The economic crisis has led to a crisis of the State, weakening progressively its authority, its capacity to arbitrate conflicts and even its capacity to maintain a minimum of social order . . . social behavior loses even minimal ethical standards" (Gonzales de Olarte 1991, 18–19).

These varied conflicts can by no means be blamed entirely on economic problems or readily cured by improved economic management. Still, worsening poverty and employment conditions, with repeated failures of many

---

4. An enormous literature on rural conflict includes illuminating analyses by Julio Cotler (1978a), Adolfo Figueroa (1984), and *Resistance, Rebellion . . .* , a collection of studies edited by Steve J. Stern (1987). Ciro Alegría's powerful novel *El mundo es ancho y ajeno* dramatically portrays rural conflict in terms of destructive pressures on indigenous communities (Alegría 1967).

different governments to find solutions, have seriously undermined political institutions as well as public willingness to negotiate and compromise for the sake of shared gains.

Redirection in the 1990s: To What Ends?

Does public support of the return to liberalized economies throughout Latin America constitute rejection of the social goals that fostered state-led development in the first place? Does it point instead to a change in understanding how these goals might best be realized? The redirection is probably in large part a matter of changing priorities as objective conditions changed: to increased concern for security and stability after the strains of the 1980s, to increased interest in production and living standards relative to questions of fairness and participation. Social goals may be less rejected than temporarily displaced. On other hand, many people have learned that attention to macroeconomic balance, efficiency, and incentives is essential for a reasonably well-functioning economy whether a particular government is trying to address social questions or not.

The underlying premise of this study is that successful economic strategy must be guided *both* by careful attention to methods and by the goals of the particular society. The strategy may and should include four sets of objectives, some widely shared and some in the nature of conflicts that require never-ending negotiation. Perhaps the most widely accepted goals are classic economic objectives: growth of production and income, restraint of inflation, and sustainable external balance. A second set that one would like to think of as widely accepted, although not one that everyone would support by agreeing to raise taxes, is to shape economic and social policies in ways likely to reduce poverty and inequality, to improve life opportunities for everyone.

A third objective, very much a matter of debate among conflicting interests, is to promote competitive industry and modern services, not just to achieve faster growth but to foster learning, innovation, and greater national autonomy. This objective could run counter to the economic logic of efficiency and comparative advantage. It could, but need not, degenerate into defensive separatism. On the positive side, it could enable a country to increase its capacity for self-determination through an ability to compete in the world economy.

The fourth and perhaps the most elusive objective is to build a common understanding of the possibilities of gain through negotiation among conflicting interests, by using economic strategies that take multiple goals into account: to create a growth process that can be supported by informed majorities because they can see that it helps most of them most of the time. That objective requires at the very least a more meaningful form of democracy than Peru has at present, with access to improved education for the whole country, with effective taxation of high incomes and asset holdings, and with a host of other institutional changes. Economic strategy is only one strand among many. The present economic strategy in Peru, and in most other Latin American countries, is not causing as much damage as did earlier strategies, but it is not particularly egalitarian or responsive to the true diversity of social interests. Peru has a long way to go. So have we all.

2
HUMAN RESOURCES AND POLITICAL EVOLUTION

Division and inequality, outweighing forces toward integration, have always been fundamental characteristics of Peruvian society: division among ethnic groups and regions and between social classes, inequalities in opportunities for education, earnings, and political voice. Such divisions and inequalities have been notable features of nearly all Latin American societies, perhaps more so in Peru than in the Southern Cone or Costa Rica but shared in similar ways by the other Andean countries. The last four decades have seen considerable progress in reducing barriers among groups, possibly more so than in previous Peruvian history, but the divisions remain strong, and inequalities remain high.

The discussion of human resources in this chapter refers to questions of demography, ethnic and regional differences, and *human capital* in the sense of capacities for production, responses to new opportunities, and innovation. The first section summarizes changes in population and differences among regions. The second brings out the very mixed picture of progress and the frustration in improving access to education. The third

Table 2.1. Regional shares of national population, percentage of region's households with indigenous maternal language, and percentage in poverty, 1994

	Percentage of National Population	Percentage of Households	
		Maternal Language Indigenous	Below Poverty Line
Metropolitan Lima	28.1	7.7	37.6
Coastal region			
Urban	19.5	2.4	48.9
Rural	4.1	4.4	66.3
Sierra			
Urban	16.7	18.4	41.6
Rural	19.7	46.8	68.3
Selva			
Urban	6.3	5.0	38.9
Rural	5.7	19.4	69.7

SOURCE: Instituto Cuánto and UNICEF 1995, 22, 24, 33.

section is concerned with the closely related questions of discrimination, motivation, and capacity for innovation. The fourth section reviews the main changes in governments and the political system of Peru from the 1930s, and the last section the troublesome question of the relations between democracy and economic performance.

Population and Regions

Peru has much poverty everywhere but especially in the rural areas of the sierra, the selva, and the nonirrigated desert zones in the coastal region. Table 2.1 shows the distribution of population by regions in 1994, with the percentages of each region's households in which the maternal language was reported to be Quechua, Aymara, or another indigenous language, and with estimates of the percentages of poverty in that year.

The clearest contrasts in degrees of poverty shown in Table 2.1 are between rural and urban areas in all regions. Two-thirds of all rural households were below the poverty line in 1994. The rural sierra, with one-fifth of the national population, stands out both for the greatest concentration of families in poverty and for the proportion in which the maternal language is indigenous: close to one-half of all households.

The population of the coast (including Lima and the great majority of the urban population), grew from 34 percent of the national total in 1940 to 52 percent by 1994. In the same period, the population of the sierra fell from 60 percent of the country's population to 36 percent. The population of the selva—historically very poor but now sharing to some degree in the income from coca production and processing—increased from 6 percent of the country's population in 1940 to 12 percent by 1994.

A high degree of rural poverty, a common characteristic of developing countries everywhere, is especially marked in Peru because of prolonged delay in providing opportunities for education in rural areas, an exceptionally low ratio of arable land to families depending on agriculture, and neglect of public support to raise agricultural productivity (Caballero 1981; Alberts 1983; Figueroa 1984). That neglect of the rural population reflected a general disregard by the European-descent minority for its indigenous people.

The proportion of people of indigenous descent in the population was estimated at 55 to 58 percent as of 1876. It fell to 46 percent by 1940 (Gootenberg 1991, 140; Instituto Cuánto 1991, 116). Subsequent censuses discontinued questions that provided comparable measures. In 1994, only 17 percent of the national population, although 47 percent in the rural sierra, reported indigenous maternal languages (Instituto Cuánto and UNICEF 1995, 24). These may be understatements: "[I]ndigenous languages have low status" (MacIsaac and Patrinos 1995, 220).

The total population did not begin to grow greatly until the second half of the nineteenth century, and even then at what has come to seem a modest annual rate of 1.4 percent. Growth speeded up in the twentieth century: the total reached 13.2 million by 1970 and 23.9 million by 1995. The rate of growth peaked at 3 percent a year for the decade 1960–70 and then, slightly more slowly than the rest of Latin America, began to fall. Fertility rates began to decrease for middle and upper income groups in the 1950s, but the great social distance between them and the rural poor delayed any significant change for the latter until the 1970s. The fertility rate, the number of children per woman of childbearing age, fell from 6.6 for the period 1965–70 to 3.2 by 1995 (Ferrando and Aramburú 1996, 414–36; World Bank 1997, 225). The rate of population growth came down from its peak of 3 percent for the decade of the 1960s to 2.1 percent a year for the first half of the 1990s (IDB 1996, 357).

Until the 1920s, the main economic activity of the population was overwhelmingly agricultural. As of 1876, Lima was the only city with more than 100,000 people, which was just 4 percent of the population.

At that time, the share of the population living in cities of more than 100,000 was 17 percent in Argentina, 14 percent in Chile, and 29 in Uruguay: Peru, like the rest of the Andean countries, remained far less urbanized than the Southern Cone (Sánchez-Albornoz 1974, 178–79). As of 1950, 59 percent of the Peruvian labor force was still engaged in agriculture and fishing. By 1990, this share had fallen to 34 percent, but the absolute total in agriculture and fishing continued to increase by 81 percent in this period (Instituto Cuánto 1991, 303).

Through most of its history until well into the twentieth century, the economy was characterized more by shortage of labor for new activities than by its modern problem of insufficient opportunities for productive employment. Difficulties in finding workers for haciendas and mines could have generated rising wages if employment had been based on voluntary demand and supply. The Spanish response, perpetuated long after independence, was to devise methods to tie workers to owners by law and force rather than by wages (Flores Galindo 1987; Tandeter 1993; Bulmer-Thomas 1994, 85–92). The strong preference of most indigenous groups to stay together in communal life and production rather than to seek outside employment was continuously attacked (Mallon 1983). Many indigenous communities managed to hold onto considerable independence despite such forces, and some still do, but growing population pressure in the twentieth century encouraged a rising flow of emigration from rural areas toward the cities. The first pronounced wave of migration into Lima came in the 1920s, a decade of prosperity and greatly increased employment in construction. The flow eased off in the 1930s, then resumed without stopping with the recovery of the economy in the 1940s.

Human Resources

If a large fraction of a country's population is illiterate and the minority who have access to both education and capital are strongly adverse to changes that might undermine their advantages, national responses to economic opportunities are not likely to be outstandingly dynamic. This expectation assumes no lack of human potential in the society, only the possibility that this potential can be wasted. In Peru's case, much of its people's potential has been wasted throughout much of the country's history.

The national census of 1940 reported that 58 percent of Peruvians over age 15 were illiterate: 45 percent of the men and 69 percent of the women (Instituto Cuánto 1991, 153). For the rural areas and for many of the urban poor, opportunities for education were abysmally low until well into the years after World War II. As of 1970, 47 percent of the labor force had less than three years of schooling (ECLA 1984, 113). For children, on the other hand, the picture was beginning to change for the better. As of 1993, the illiteracy rate for people over age 65 was 38 percent, for those in their thirties it was down to 9 percent, and for those from 15 to 19 it was only 4 percent (Instituto Cuánto 1995, 264). The proportion of the secondary school age group actually in school climbed from 25 percent in 1965 to 65 percent by 1987 (World Bank 1990, 234). For Lima as of 1985, 61 percent of the heads of households had at least some secondary or higher education. The rural sierra continued to lag behind: its proportion was still only 11 percent and that of the rural selva 9 percent (Glewwe 1988, 14).

Public expenditures on education increased rapidly in the 1950s and 1960s at a rate of over 11 percent a year in real terms. But through the next quarter century, the worsening conditions of the economy fed back into a much poorer record of support for education. Expenditures began to oscillate widely in response to changes in economic conditions, and longer term growth practically stopped (Fig. 2.1). Spending for teaching and current operations reached brief peaks in 1975 under the Velasco government and in 1987 under Alan García, but by 1990 it was one-fifth lower than in 1975. It started to increase again with the revival of the economy in the first half of the 1990s, although by 1994 it had barely reached the level of 1975 (Saavedra, Melzi, and Miranda 1997, 9, 55).

With the rapid growth of population and increases in the number of students, the lack of growth in current spending on education after 1970 meant a severe downtrend in expenditures per pupil: for 1990–94, despite the beginnings of recovery in these years, spending per pupil averaged barely half as high as in 1970. In that falling average for the country as a whole, the distribution of public spending by departments was systematically biased against support for education in departments with greater poverty (Saavedra, Melzi, and Miranda 1997, 17–23, 35–49).

Private spending on education has been an important complement to public spending, for contrasting reasons at higher and lower income levels. For high-income groups and for families with established social positions if not necessarily high incomes, private schools have been essential. Their quality is rightly seen as superior, with expenditures per pupil 2.5 times as high as in public schools at the primary level and 52 percent higher at the secondary. In addition to concern for the content of the education, private schools are seen by some families as a means to protect their

Fig. 2.1. Public expenditures for current functioning of the educational system, 1970–94.

Index: 1970 = 100

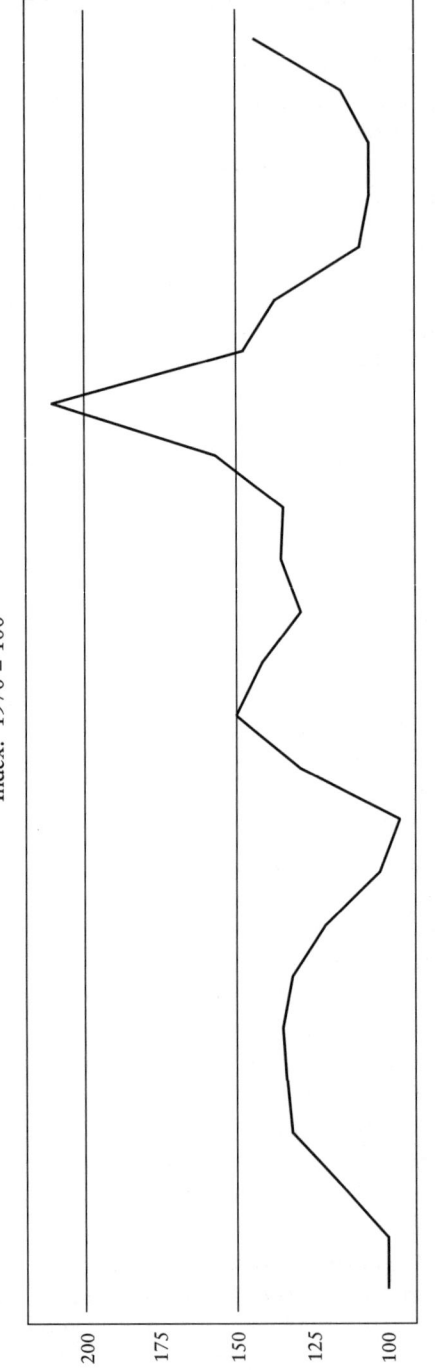

NOTE: Expenditures are in real terms, at constant 1979 dollars, deflated by the GRADE "geometric" price index explained in the source.
SOURCE: Saavedra, Melzi, and Miranda 1997, annex table A-1.

children from association with children from low-income families. At the same time, even low-income families have been forced, by the long downtrend of public support per pupil, into increasing personal expenditures for fees and school supplies required in the nominally "free" public system. Although only about 15 percent of all students were in private schools in 1994, private spending on education for all reasons was two-thirds as high as total public spending. These private expenditures were, of course, even more closely correlated with higher income regions—more steeply unequal—than the pattern of public expenditures (Saavedra, Melzi, and Miranda 1997, 33, 35, 45).

The tight squeeze on educational spending after 1975 had its direct counterpart in a drastic reduction of real earnings of teachers. By the beginning of the 1990s, their earnings had been driven down to about one-eighth of the 1975 level (Saavedra, Melzi and Miranda 1997, 14). By discouraging people from entering the profession and disheartening those unable to find alternatives, that process must have contributed to the many problems of quality in public education. High rates of dropouts, repetitions of grades, long delays in graduating at every level, poor training of teachers, miserable salaries that make it difficult to draw promising people into the field, and a centralized administration of public education that has itself proved adverse to innovation give evidence of an educational system that has yet to find a successful path (Arregui 1995, 217–31).

Although these problems are common to all Latin American countries, differences among them, and progress in some, suggest scope for possible corrective action. For the costly and discouraging problem of grade repetition, Peru has been on the high side. In 1972, 44 percent of children had to repeat the first grade; by 1984, the rate had risen to 47 percent (Schiefelbein 1997, 40). In a nine-country comparison, the median rate was 30 percent; Peru stood second highest. In contrast to the increase in this rate of grade repetitions, two-thirds of the countries in this sample show a downtrend for this twelve-year period.

Possibilities for improvement, on this and many other accounts, are suggested by Colombia's innovative primary school program, the *Multigrade escuela nueva*, now used in about 20,000 schools. The results of comparative test scores indicate greatly improved achievements. Compared with traditional rural schools, their pupils score far higher on tests both for skills in mathematics and languages and for measures of personal self-confidence and civic awareness (Schiefelbein 1997, 51–56). The methods are sensible and familiar: demonstration schools for teachers to promote emphasis on student participation, teaching writing as a means of promoting ideas, individual consultation, and similar concepts. All familiar enough; just not common, so far, in Latin American public schools.

Discrimination and Motivation

Low levels of rural education were common to much of Latin America up to the 1960s, although five countries had much better results: Argentina, Chile, Costa Rica, Cuba, and Uruguay. As of 1960, the median rate of adult illiteracy for the region was 39 percent; these five countries were in a different world, with rates ranging from 9 to 16 percent for the Southern Cone countries in 1960 and for Costa Rica and Cuba in 1970 (World Bank 1983, individual country pages). Why the great difference? For all except Cuba, the main factor was that higher literacy rates were identified with countries in which there was no sharp ethnic separation between urban and rural populations.[1] Where ethnic and racial divisions have been important for large shares of the population—everywhere, not just in Latin America—they have systematically been associated with relative disregard of rural welfare by urban elites and high degrees of inequality in terms of income (Papanek and Kyn 1987). For most Latin American countries, such separation has been central to their histories: predominantly separation between European-descent and indigenous people in the Andes and Central America and between White and Black people in Brazil and the Caribbean (Engerman and Sokoloff 1997). In the absence of such dualism, educational policies included rural areas on much the same terms as urban; in its presence, they did not.

From the earliest years of independence, a series of Peruvian political and intellectual leaders tried repeatedly to introduce legislation and institutional changes aimed at better treatment of the indigenous population, by provision of public education, protection of their access to land, and protection against abuse from large landholders. The problem, as so often in Latin American history, was that laws meant little when they ran against deeply entrenched resistance by opposing groups with political weight. The large landholders in the sierra paid little attention to legislation intended to limit their local dominance, efforts to extend education met either outright resistance or neglect, and governments that tried to help

---

1. For Cuba, the explanation is more a matter of deliberately changed national policies after its revolution: universal literacy was one of the revolutionary government's first goals.

invariably found their attention diverted by more pressing concerns (Davies 1974). The will to help was often there but it was not strong enough to overcome resistance by those who profited from the existing situation or feared what might happen if the indigenous people gained education and political voice.

In terms of the treatment of its rural labor force, Peru in the first decades after independence resembled the U.S. South during the same period. Dependence on slavery in the South and on repressed indigenous labor in Peru meant in both cases that the great majority of the rural population was held to subsistence levels of living, with little or no education, restricted personal mobility, and no political voice. In the contrasting case of the northern United States, with access to land relatively open, with agriculture characterized by independent small farmers able to raise incomes through their own productive efforts and to insist on opportunities for education, the rural sector played an active role in the process of economic change. Relative equality of income favored development of broad markets, economic mobility, technological change, and broad political participation (Engerman and Sokoloff 1997). Correspondingly, early industrialization and inventive activity in the United States centered in the North, whereas industry remained almost nonexistent in the South until well into the twentieth century (Meyer 1983, 157–60; Krugman 1991, 10–22).

In addition to this basic retarding factor, innovative activity may have been held back by characteristics common to Spain and Portugal during the colonial period and passed on to their colonies. Southern Europe had been in the forefront of economic strength and scientific discovery through the sixteenth century, but by the eighteenth it had sunk into a relative backwater both economically and intellectually (Trevor-Roper 1967, 1–45, 193–236; Vicens Vives 1965, 301–427). Political and religious diversification in Northern Europe stimulated change in all dimensions, while centralized authoritarianism in Spain went the other way. The Spanish church and state, with the crusading fervor that had driven out Islamic occupation in the fifteenth century and with the sudden wealth gained from conquests in the Americas, were both determined and able to shield Southern Europe from the materialistic individualism characteristic of the early industrial revolution. The countervalues of tradition, order, and spiritual concerns maintained more weight in social preferences and were passed on with full force to Latin America. These values might have made for more humane societies in the North if given greater weight there, but the different balance in Southern Europe and Latin America may well have restrained innovation and structural change.

Research and innovation require social values that support them and gain considerably from a community of scientists. Before World War II, it would have been difficult to create such a community in Peru in any case: as of 1940, less than 1 percent of the population had any postsecondary education in any field (Arregui 1995, 10). In addition to that fundamental lack, sciences ranked low in priority. The only private university at the time, the Catholic University of Peru, was founded in 1917; it did not establish a department of sciences until 1966.

Higher education has grown explosively in Peru in the postwar period, and the wider classes of students coming in have changed the balance of studies away from emphasis on law and humanities to many new fields. The proportion of the population over age 15 who acquired at least some postsecondary education shot up from 2 percent in 1961 to 20 percent by 1993 (Arregui 1994, 10–12). The number of universities increased from nine in 1960 to fifty-six by 1992. The upsurge in university education has included a strong increase in engineering studies, although not as strong a rise in basic sciences. As of 1972, a country of 14 million could count just 202 people classified as physicists (most with titles approximately equivalent to masters' degrees) and slightly over 800 with degrees in each of biology and chemistry. By 1989, the numbers of both chemists and physicists approximately doubled, to bring the ratio of chemists to total population in Peru up to 15 percent of the ratio in the United States (Arregui 1994, 35). In the same period, a fourfold rise in the number of people with engineering degrees brought the ratio of engineers to population up to 37 percent of that in the United States.

The rapid spread of access to education at all levels has opened up improved possibilities for personal mobility and for technological progress, although many doubts remain about quality, inequity, and motivation. The severe problems of quality in the public system may owe more to organizational weaknesses and institutional resistance to change than to matters of economics and financing, but they must have been aggravated by the tight squeeze on educational spending in the 1970s and 1980s. Perhaps one of the highest costs of the weakness of the economy is that, by putting downward pressure on educational spending per pupil, it held down the potential of Peru's children. Expenditures have risen along with national product in the 1990s, but the system remains deeply unequal, in two dimensions: in the much greater resources available per student in private schools than in public and in the bias of public educational spending toward regions with higher incomes.

The weak record of grade repetitions and early dropouts suggests that problems of motivation may be at least as important as problems of financing. Erratic motivation may be due to a large extent to doubts, for the poor and near-poor, that the education available to their children offers promising possibilities of economic and social mobility, even if they do persevere to higher levels. The performance of the economy and in particular the pace of structural change opening up new possibilities of employment could play an important role in improving motivation for education. The decisions of the society to supply resources to the educational system, the capacity of the system itself to stimulate learning and raise the personal confidence and flexibility of students, and the operation of the economy all come together to determine the scope for change.

The Political System in Relation to Economic Strategy

In common with many other Latin American countries, Peru started the twentieth century with the forms of democracy but with its political system under firm control by a small minority of traditional interests. The state served to protect these interests rather than to promote or guide change in the economy or the society. Again in common with much of the rest of the region, this seemingly stable system began to unravel in the interwar period under pressure from new industrial and professional interests, a growing urban labor force, and activist-intellectual demands for change. The key periods of political reorientation for many other countries were the 1930s and 1940s, in reaction to both the economic turmoil of the depression and the heightened appeal of democracy associated with World War II. Peru's political system proved to be more resistant to change in these years. It began to show more strains but stayed almost continuously under traditional control up to the 1960s.

The period from 1895 to 1930 is known as the *República aristocratica*, with elections reduced to contests between conservative parties, each controlled by a narrow elite group. The majority of the population was largely disenfranchised by direct manipulation of votes, by property requirements, and in some periods by literacy requirements in a context of extremely weak public education (Cotler 1978a; Stein, 1980).[2] With one brief exception, the governments of this period were consistently oriented toward an open economy favoring export and financial interests, foreign investment, wage restraint, and varied forms of forced labor in agriculture and in public-sector construction.

For the upper income groups and even for many of the rest of the urban population, this was something of a golden time. Life in the cities was for the most part safe and peaceful beyond anything imaginable today. A relative prosperity provided openings for jobs and investment, Peruvian literature flourished, and an enormous program of urban improvement in the 1920s made it possible to characterize Lima as "one of the most modern and beautiful capitals in South America" (Stein 1980, 56). That judgment for the time is still believable now in the broad avenues, parks, and plazas that remain, but walking with caution through Lima in the 1990s brings home a powerful sense of loss.

Very different political voices gathered strength in the interwar period, as rapid migration into the cities and increasing industrial employment provided a base for expression of mass interests. That was when Víctor Raúl Haya de la Torre entered political life, first as a student leader pointing the way toward a student activism almost unknown until then in Peru. In 1919, he seized the opportunity of a strike by textile workers to take on their cause and become their effective spokesperson. By helping them win their demands and then going on to promote organization and worker education, he became a leading voice for labor in the political process. Forced into exile in the mid-1920s, he returned in 1930 to form Peru's first mass-based political party: APRA, the *Alianza popular revolucionaria Américana* (Stein 1980; Graham 1992; Cotler 1995).

This period was also the time in which José Carlos Mariátegui created his alternative vision of a new world for Peru, an Andean Marxism linked to the country's indigenous traditions. Mariátegui was an original thinker, with enduring influence in Peru and throughout Latin America, more interested than Haya de la Torre in ideas but less in political organization (Flores Galindo 1987, 283–84). In direct conflict for control of the workers' movement, Haya de la Torre won and put APRA together as a tight political party with a long life ahead of it. He "brought the issues of social justice, structural change, and national integration to the fore of the nation's politics" (Graham 1992, 23).

---

2. In the election of 1895, when the population was 2.7 million, only 4,310 people voted (Cotler 1995, 324).

Accidents, or at any rate events outside the control and intentions of political leaders, have had dramatic impacts on Peruvian history. The system of political control that seemed so well entrenched from 1895 into the 1920s suddenly lost support from all sides. For the conservative elite, the problem was that the president elected in 1919, Augusto Leguía, turned himself into a dictator and broke down the established party system. For many Peruvians, the impact of the depression destroyed confidence in an open economy, discredited the government, and made clear the need for change. Haya de la Torre seemed perfectly placed to lead the way, but another accident intervened: someone else moved first. An army officer from the provinces, Luis M. Sánchez Cerro, led an easy coup, sent Leguía into exile, and offered his own brand of populist government.

With Leguía gone and the conservative side of the country in temporary disgrace, a presidential election in 1931 offered something wholly new: a choice between two populist alternatives. Haya de la Torre stood for violent opposition to the traditional elite and to foreign imperialism, for state control of the economy, and for a coalition between workers and the middle class. Sánchez Cerro's version of populism promised special favors to the poor, although not for organized labor. In his brief period of control before the election, he gained great support from the rural poor by eliminating Leguía's aggressive practice of the *conscripción vial*. This was a system of forced labor for construction of roads and other public works in rural areas, imposed to get labor without needing tax revenue to pay adequate wages to hire willing workers. Forced labor for the indigenous poor, with many deaths from mistreatment and unattended accidents, made it possible to hold down taxes on higher income people (Davies 1974, 82–94). Sánchez Cerro stopped the practice and gained the gratitude that may have made the difference in the following election. According to the official election results, he won.

Haya de la Torre refused to accept the possibility that the election was fair and began a series of attempted coups.[3] The coups were invariably suppressed, although Sánchez Cerro himself was killed by an APRA supporter in 1933. Haya's own chances for the presidency went out the window in the struggle: one of the APRA uprisings led to a massacre of army officers captured in the attempt and to a determination by the

---

3. Stein (1980) considers the evidence for and against fraud in this election and concludes that there is no strong ground to doubt the validity of the result. Fredrick Pike (1967, 256) insists that the APRA protest had no foundation. James Rudolph (1991, 39–40) takes the opposite position: Haya de la Torre lost "only on account of massive official fraud."

military never to allow him to become president. The two populist rivals managed to cancel each other out. A conservative government committed mainly to order, efficiency, and the open economy took over in their stead.

The frustrated pressures for change in the 1930s left the country with no opening toward the kind of state-led development starting in many other Latin American countries in this period. Among the other consequences, the military began to intervene more aggressively in the political process, and the left–activist side of the political spectrum was handicapped for years to come by identification with violence. APRA worked against other reformist movements as well as Marxist activism and eventually joined the most conservative forces of the society to block proposed reforms in the 1960s. The military played a complementary role in blocking Haya de la Torre; between the two of them, a major share of the potential forces for change in the society was held to the sidelines.

The next opportunity for possible reorientation of economic strategy was opened up by the election of 1945. A National Democratic Front brought together interests of industrialists, urban workers, and the APRA political machine. Haya de la Torre remained excluded as a presidential candidate, but the two preceding presidents negotiated compromises allowing APRA to take part in the election at the congressional level. For president, they were able to influence the choice of a nonpolitical attorney and academic, José Luis Bustamente y Rivero. The Front won the election, and APRA won control of the congress. It quickly used that control to initiate what were to become familiar populist economic policies: expansion of public-sector employment, legislated wage increases, price controls, and direct controls over both imports and foreign exchange. That mixture produced its usual results. Inflation set in despite the price controls, incentives to export were undercut, the import controls disrupted supplies of equipment and inputs for production, and investment began to fall. The conservative faction of the society easily gained support for military intervention to overturn the government in 1948 (Thorp and Bertram 1978, 187–90).

The confusion and costs of the 1945–48 period might be explained as a heritage of the country's long reliance on a noninterventionist state: Peru had little in the way of an administrative structure to implement economic reforms or people with technical expertise to evaluate the likely consequences of policy alternatives. In that view, the country's quick reversion to a noninterventionist system prevented learning and adjustment and left the future open to repetition of similar confusion (Thorp and Bertram 1978, 190). This interpretation has Rosemary Thorp's generosity of spirit to recommend it, but it can deflect attention from the general character of the problems. The policies that failed to work have failed too often, in too many countries, to be understandable simply in terms of a particular country's learning process. When repeated under both the military government of 1968–75 and the García government of 1985–90, they gave similarly hopeless results.

The overturn of the Bustamente administration in 1948 left the conservatives in control of the government until 1962, first under the dictatorship of General Manuel Odría and then under his chosen successor Manuel Prado. Their position was strengthened by a high rate of economic growth through the 1950s, based on successful exports, high rates of domestic and foreign investment, and showcase government spending. In a move to gain popular appeal, the conservatives negotiated a *convivencia* with APRA in 1956 and brought its now totally domesticated leadership into a coalition for Prado's election (Cotler 1978a, 295–305). That move delayed, but did not stay, the pressure for change. The growing middle class, seeking more influence for itself as well as state support for industrialization, along with growing antagonism to foreign influence and increasing awareness of extreme inequality, all worked strongly against continued acceptance of the country's traditional economic strategy.

A new populist party appealing to these concerns, Fernando Belaúnde Terry's *Acción popular,* made a strong showing against the Prado-APRA coalition in 1956 and tried again in the election of 1962. At that point, the conservatives at last allowed Haya de la Torre, now their ally, to run for president. In the three-way contest among Haya, Belaúnde, and the former dictator Odría, Haya de la Torre came in first in the popular vote, although barely ahead of Belaúnde. Under Peruvian law, Haya de la Torre's share of the votes was too low for direct election: the decision was left up to the congress. He concluded that the unforgiving military would not allow him to take office in any case and accepted a deal throwing APRA support in the congress to Odría. At that point, the military leadership moved in a new direction, to favor the possibilities of change by blocking Odría's return to power.

The head of the joint chiefs of staff, General Pérez Godoy, announced that a new election would be held the next year and made clear that at least a significant fraction of the military had come to the conclusion that the old system of political and economic management had to go. In his brief tenure, General Pérez created a national planning commission as well as a new bank and housing agency to stimulate low-cost housing. In response to an upsurge of peasant protests and land occupations in the sierra, he initiated trial land reform projects in the area most affected (Pike 1967, 300–301; Flores Galindo 1987, 304–13). Other military officers intervened to depose Pérez Godoy in his turn, but they allowed a new election in 1963, and Belaúnde won the presidency.

Belaúnde promised land reform, protection and other aid for industrialization, more control over foreign investment, renegotiation with the International Petroleum Company to limit its domination of the oil industry, and large-scale public housing. His favorite individual project, a highway to open up access to new land on the eastern slopes of the Andes, was presented as an antidote to the flood of migration into Lima and to growing inadequacy of the national supply of food. The rural poor of the sierra were to be encouraged to stop coming to the coast and to go the other way, to clear the jungles on the eastern slopes of the Andes to raise both their own living standards and the supply of food. The idea had wide public appeal in a period not yet greatly concerned with environmental damage or with the fact that indigenous communities lived as they had for centuries in the jungles that were to be cleared. In any event, neither environmentalists nor the indigenous people need have worried. Belaúnde got practically nowhere.

Tariffs were raised to promote import substitution, but land reform was effectively blocked by the combined resistance of landowners and APRA. A new source of economic aid from the United States became available through the Alliance for Progress, offering support for land reform, but the aid was made contingent on continued acceptance of foreign investment. This proviso conflicted with the highly charged issue of renegotiation with the International Petroleum Company, promised by Belaúnde and widely supported by the country. Whether for that or other reasons, Belaúnde, under confusing circumstances that made it look as if he had sold out, backed down from his promise to reduce the company's privileges. The reformist wing of the military stopped waiting. General Juan Velasco Alvarado deposed Belaúnde and initiated much the kind of populist reform program that Haya de la Torre had advocated forty years earlier, including extensive direct controls over trade and foreign investment (Lowenthal 1975; McClintock and Lowenthal 1983; Graham 1992, 37–91).

The economic content and consequences of Velasco's military populism are discussed in Chapter 7. For the political system, the changes included the disappearance of the old landowning elite as a major force, with greatly broadened and intensified politicization of the country as a whole. Labor and community organizations proliferated, new political parties entered the election process, and lower income people began to confront public authority much more aggressively (Stevens 1983; Stokes 1991).

The intensified awareness and activism of the whole society offered promise for a meaningful democracy when the military relinquished power at the end of the 1970s. An elected assembly drafted a new constitution in 1979, and Belaúnde returned as president in 1980. The enthusiasm of the moment seemed well founded, but then everything went downhill, in two traumatic dimensions that reinforced each other: rising violence and drastic deterioration of the economy (Gonzales de Olarte 1991; Gonzales de Olarte and Samamé 1994).

Rural violence has a long history in Peru, but the kind that broke out in 1980 was something new. *Sendero luminoso* was a university-based Marxist splinter group at first, in a provincial university where the students were outside the mainstream of national leadership and personally close to rural poverty (Degregori 1990; Palmer 1992; Starn 1995). During the 1970s, the movement spread to the surrounding area by careful organization and with no overt violence. The first act of violence that brought it to national attention was a protest against the election of 1980. From that year it spread rapidly, with increasingly murderous methods. A great many Peruvians proved ready to use systematic terror to destroy the existing society.

Both the Belaúnde administration of 1980–85 and the APRA administration of Alan García in the following five years turned much of the country over to control by the military in their futile efforts to stop *Sendero* (Roberts and Peceny 1997). The legal leftist parties split between those that condemned violence in favor of negotiation and the election process and those more disposed to consider even *Sendero*'s extremes as an acceptable part of the struggle to change the society (Pásara 1989, 15–17). These divisions in the left practically eliminated it as a political force by the time of the election of 1990.

The Belaúnde and the García administrations were both singularly unsuccessful in dealing with the economy (Chapter 7). Peru seemed to be losing much of its capacity to produce; incomes fell drastically, employment conditions worsened, and inflation accelerated. The deterioration of the economy, in turn, deepened public discouragement about the country's likely future and fostered widening acceptance of *Sendero* among the young. That disheartening process, closely associated in García's case with APRA's vision of state-led development, greatly weakened public support both for that economic strategy and for democracy (Graham 1992, 203–19).

Economic strategy became a central issue in the elections of 1990, although the general direction of likely change was clear from the start. The main question was the choice between an all-out shock program of liberalization promised by the leading candidate, Mario Vargas Llosa, and the gradualist, partial liberalization advocated by Alberto Fujimori. The latter's victory was credited by many to public fear of the more drastic alternative, although it perhaps owed at least as much to Vargas Llosa's suicidal self-presentation as a cosmopolitan intellectual in contrast to Fujimori's as a down-to-earth engineer, free of any identification with the traditional Hispanic elite. More of Peru's population is nonelite than elite, and they have learned to vote.

Fujimori may have truly intended to adopt the gradualist economic program that he advocated during the campaign, but trips to Washington and Tokyo immediately after his election apparently convinced him that Vargas Llosa had been right in the first place. The economic consequences of the liberalization program are discussed in Chapter 8. In the political arena, the business community, which had for the most part opposed him in the election, switched sides enthusiastically to support him once he opted for economic liberalization. It also reacted with evident approval, along with the majority of the country, when the president responded to congressional criticism by turning to military support to close down the congress in April 1992 (Cotler 1995, 350–51; Cameron 1997). Democracy seemed to be dispensable to the president, the business community, and to many although by no means all the Peruvian people.

Democracy and Economic Liberalization

In the 1970s, economic liberalization in the Southern Cone was closely associated with intense political repression. The association was no accident. The conservative side in each of these countries, allied with a ruthless military, imposed neoliberal economic systems as the core of vengeful crusades to remake these societies in their favor (Foxley 1983; Ramos 1986; Sheahan 1980a). In this period, the relation of market-oriented economic systems to political freedom, often thought to be positive, proved to be strongly negative in the only Latin American countries that adopted them.

Subsequently, as the Mexican governments of the 1980s chose to liberalize the economy while taking steps toward democracy rather than through military repression and as many other Latin American countries followed suit, they demonstrated that the region can combine market-oriented economic strategies with democratic institutions. The great underlying change was that the debt crisis and the accompanying economic setbacks throughout the region had greatly diminished public confidence in state economic management: a choice of liberalization no longer needed to be imposed or protected by repression. That change seemed true in Peru as well in 1990–91, but the president's decision to call on the military to close the congress in the following year put the connection back in question again.

Peru adopted its liberalization strategy under an elected government, in the third presidential election in a row successfully managed by the country's newly recovered democracy. It is true that the voters chose the candidate who promised a gradual adjustment program, as opposed to any sudden leap to full economic liberalization. He did not follow the gradualist path he promised, but Peruvian realism more or less accepted that as one of the breaks of the game. The public clearly agreed on the need for a major change in economic orientation. In that sense, the new economic strategy was a democratic choice.

The all-out version of liberalization adopted in 1990–91, perhaps above all its convincing attack on inflation, won acceptance from the poor as well as strong support from leaders of the private sector. Many people attacked its harsh quality, with good reason, but for the general public and the private sector the traumatic consequences of erratic state intervention under the García government had destroyed confidence in state activism. That experience gravely weakened "[t]he burning desire for democracy and social justice which had captured the Peruvian electorate in 1980" (Kay 1997, 86). Peru had reached a point at which economic liberalization was readily acceptable.

Why then did Fujimori turn to the military to close congress and purge the judiciary? One possibility is that he genuinely feared that his ability to control events was threatened by congressional attacks. Another possibility is that he simply could not stand being criticized: a personal characteristic of impatience with any democratic process of discussion and compromise. Neither of these considerations can be ruled out but perhaps the dominant factor, convincingly explained by Carlos Iván Degregori, was Fujimori's relation to the military. The military leadership was resentful toward, and fearful of, threatened congressional inquiry into abuses of human rights (Degregori 1994). Fujimori shared that concern, possibly because of the need to rely on the military in the then uncertain struggle against *Sendero luminoso,* possibly because of a more general goal to keep the military on his side. In that interpretation, the orientation of the economy was not the main issue, at least for the president and the military.

The economic orientation was probably the central issue—more important than democracy—for the private sector (Durand 1997, 171–72; Roberts and Peceny 1997). Relations between democratic institutions and liberal economic policies have always been ambivalent. Leaders of the private sector have learned to distrust military governments, but they may not object to nondemocratic actions of a civilian government that is convincingly opposed to interference with the economy (Conaghan and Malloy 1994, 203–31). Correspondingly, presidents committed to economic liberalization, either from their own preferences or from a perceived need to reassure investors, may be willing to suppress channels of opposition when they seem to threaten that strategy. Economic liberalization may be consistent with democracy, but the wish to protect it can be a stimulus to repression.

The Fujimori government remains formally democratic in the sense that it was elected and re-elected and goes through the motions of democratic process, but its human rights record and its manipulation of congress and the judiciary do not make it a happy example. For many people, its economic record has outweighed such questions. The more clearly democratic governments of the 1980s make a sorry contrast for economic performance, as did the National Democratic Front in the 1940s. Is there, or has there been, something systematic about Peru that makes successful economic performance under democracy exceptionally difficult?

Three factors are likely candidates for a possible explanation. One is an institutional characteristic of the political system, the second a historically passing framework of understanding, and the third a fundamental problem of economic structure. The institutional characteristic is that Peruvian democracy, like that of many other Latin American countries, has been consistently characterized by weakness of restraints on arbitrary actions by the executive. The Peruvian people clearly value democracy in the sense of the right to vote, but they have not demonstrated serious concern for anything like the Madisonian concept of checks and balances among the executive, the legislature, and the judiciary (Carrión 1994).[4] Checks

---

4. Carrión's interpretation is based on analysis of public opinion polls in the early 1990s, not on a historical review of actual practice. It certainly fits a good deal of the country's history, under civilian presidents as well as military.

and balances have their costs—they can obstruct desirable changes—but human rights, equitable treatment, and economic performance as well can be badly damaged when they are weak.

Alan García's out-of-the-blue attempt to nationalize the banks and insurance firms in 1987 was a major factor in the disastrous turn of the economy during his administration. Fujimori's attack on congress and the judiciary in 1992 had exactly the same arbitrary character, although directed to a different end. In this case, the main costs were in weakened protection of human rights, but the scope for arbitrary action can hardly be promising for long-term economic performance. "The construction of a market economy goes hand in hand with the formation of a culture of respect for the rules of the game. . . . The authorities weaken their legitimacy for demands to respect the law, when they simultaneously violate the rules themselves, in particular those that regulate how the rules can be changed" (Távara 1996, 55).

The second factor, now much less of an issue, is that democratic governments were particularly prone to economic problems through the last half century because they were trying to respond to popular preferences for change under a dysfunctional model of thought. The evidence that market-oriented economic policies had generated highly unequal societies supported widely held convictions that any escape from this trap required rejection of market forces and of economic leadership by the private sector. In the early postwar years, very few Latin American countries escaped the common populist strands of disregard for domestic and external macroeconomic balance, efficiency, and incentives. Peru started the process of intervention later than most of the other countries and was correspondingly late in learning the possible costs. By the 1970s and 1980s, democratic governments in Colombia provided a sharp contrast in terms of coherent economic management and achieved both above-average growth and some reduction of inequality while Peru was still wandering in the wilderness (Thorp 1991; Londoño 1995). By 1990, most Peruvians were ready, perhaps too ready, to go back to a more conservative economic orientation. The balance changed from one extreme to the other: from overly generalized hostility toward a market-determined economic system to insufficiently selective acceptance.

An economic orientation as conservative as that established in the early 1990s is not a promising answer to the third problem: under the structural conditions of the Peruvian economy, any all-out version of economic liberalism is more likely to worsen than to resolve the strains of profound inequality. Extreme inequality intensifies impatience with the balances and restraints needed for a well-functioning economy. That tension can be answered only by finding an inclusionary style of economic growth. It does not require any relapse into populism: what it requires is a new consensus on how to reshape the functioning of an open economy without damaging it in the process.

In the second half of the 1990s, Peru is back once more in a context in which political authority is used to support an economic strategy that relies on private enterprise and market forces and to limit channels of opposition to this approach. Is this strategy essentially a return to the *República aristocratica,* changed only in the sense of being run by a nonaristocrat? In some ways, yes, although perhaps more in the nature of a new "neoliberal populism" (Cotler 1995; Roberts 1995; Kay 1997). It contrasts with traditional populism by deregulation and macroeconomic restraint, but at the same time it involves extensive intervention to reinforce personal power, with systematic weakening of public institutions: political parties, labor organizations, and the independence of congress and the judiciary.

The Fujimori government responded successfully to the dominant concerns of the society at the beginning of the 1990s: to stop the growth of violence and of inflation, to restore some sense of order and control. With the survival of the society seriously in question and personal insecurity a constant problem, the immediate issues were no longer centered on social reform or democracy. After the considerable gains in terms of public order and reduced economic instability in the 1990s, the emphasis seems likely to change again. Persistent underlying problems—the deep unfairness of the society and the need for greater protection of human rights—may regain the importance they deserve.

3

CHANGING STRUCTURES OF PRODUCTION AND TRADE

Peru's wealth of natural resources helped make Spain the richest country in the world in the sixteenth century and contributed significantly to Peruvian exports and national income ever after. It is doubtful that this form of wealth has done much for the majority of the Peruvian people. It may well have slowed the country's process of diversification, development of entrepreneurship, technological change, and growth of opportunities for productive employment. Because of concentrated ownership of both land and mines up to the late 1960s, it also contributed to the country's high degree of inequality.

The countering forces of broadening access to education in the last half century, of both private and public investment adding new productive capacity, of land reform, and of a more aware and more mobile population looking for new opportunities have kept the economy moving slowly toward a more promising structure of production and trade. Specific economic policies intended to promote structural change have had highly contradictory effects, often negative, but in one critical period a new policy orientation favorable to export diversification began to bring that promise to life. That reorientation came with considerable cost in the first instance and has not been followed up in the 1990s for fear of possible conflict with the strategy of economic liberalization. It does not come free, the problems are real, but when it is resumed, it could still become a key component of change toward a more equitable and progressive economy.

Although the main concern of this book is with the developments of the last half century and the question of what alternatives are open for the future, the first section of this chapter goes much farther back in Peruvian history to bring out the trends of production and trade that shaped the context of the period after World War II. The second section focuses on underlying factor proportions—relations among labor, land, and capital—and the closely related question of why Peru, and Latin America as a whole, fell so far behind Northern Europe and the United States in rates of technological change. The third section reviews the evolution of the structures of employment and production in the postwar period, with emphasis on their striking divergences. The last section examines the emergence and trend of nontraditional exports, in particular, the crucial issue of the competitive capacity of the industrial sector.

International Trade and Structural Change

Peru's economic growth has historically been linked to the development of primary product exports in an economic system that remained relatively open to trade from the middle of the nineteenth century until the 1960s. That pattern, shared with the region as a whole until the 1930s, left Peru far behind Europe and the United States in terms of industrialization and per capita income. Compared with other Latin American countries, its economic growth was reasonably good: income per capita reached 25 percent above the median for the region as of 1960 (Table 1.1). Its exceptional ability to develop new primary exports as older exports ran into difficulties was a major factor in this relative success. In the 1950s, it was also helped by a surge of foreign investment that gave the country one of its best periods of economic growth, although at the cost of intensifying inequality and social conflict (Gonzales de Olarte 1996b).

In the early years after the Spanish conquest, Peru was almost a synonym for an unlimited wealth of gold. Despite intensive exploration and mining during all the centuries since, gold remains an important product in the 1990s. Silver became the main export in the late colonial and early postindependence period, followed by the less glamorous export of guano starting in the 1830s. When Europe discovered that the large natural deposits of guano in Peru could be used to yield greatly increased agricultural output, its export rose rapidly and continued at high levels up to the 1870s.

When the guano ran out, the Peruvian economy ran down, but it did not stay down. Growth resumed, based partly on a turn toward development of the domestic market but also on diversified exports of silver, cotton, rubber, sugar, and wool. As of 1890, silver provided one-third of all export earnings, sugar 28 percent, and cotton, rubber, and wool collectively 37 percent (Thorp and Bertram 1978, 40). Copper became important from the beginning of the twentieth century, followed by petroleum from 1915. In addition to these traditional products, fish meal from anchoveta caught off the Peruvian coast became an important new export in the 1950s and 1960s. Industrial products are notably absent from this list. As late as 1960, manufactured products constituted only 1 percent of total exports (World Bank 1981, 150–51).

Primary exports can be consistent with reasonably good rates of economic growth and were in Peru up to the 1960s, but they can be adverse for industrialization and diversification of the economy (Diamand 1973). Although earnings from such exports can raise domestic demand and help finance investment, they also raise relative returns on investment for production of primary exports: they make investment possible, but can pull it away from industrialization. This conflict, between positive contributions to current income and negative implications for the capacity to enter new activities, has been a universal problem for developing countries and can be important for industrialized nations as well. Its current name, the *Dutch disease,* refers to the role of natural gas discoveries in the Netherlands in weakening the country's competitive position for industrial exports.[1] For the Netherlands, the problem was temporary; for Peru in the 1990s, it remains highly relevant in distinctive ways (Schuldt 1994).

The guano export boom in the nineteenth century was a fascinating example of such conflicts. The new exports raised national income, stimulated rapid growth, and by giving new resources and influence to the

---

1. The many-sided aspects of Dutch disease, macroeconomic as well as structural, are brought together particularly well in W. M. Corden's analysis (Corden 1984).

previously feeble central government did much to convert Peru from a geographical area run by feuding regional caudillos into a country with a meaningful government. As in many other cases of wealth based on natural resources rather than human productivity, these exports also pulled the society away from the efforts needed for long-term progress. The export earnings financed such easy access to imports that Peruvian industry and urban employment were set back. Taxes bearing on upper income groups were reduced. The mixed pattern of government spending based on the new revenue included measures helpful for poor people but for the most part went in directions that helped concentrate wealth (Hunt 1985; Berry 1990, 36–39). The whole episode reinforced a sense that wealth comes when it comes and goes when it goes: it is not a matter of hard, well-directed work but a gamble in which the external world holds most of the cards.

Growth resumed on a sustained basis in the 1890s, in a different and healthier way. The key cause of change was a fall in the world price of silver, then the base of Peru's currency as well as its most important export. With a silver-based currency, falling world prices meant in effect that Peru's currency was devalued by market forces. The value of other exports in terms of Peruvian currency increased, and this increase provided the incentive for markedly increasing exports. Similarly, prices of imports relative to domestic costs of production went up considerably and stimulated investment in production for the home market. Without any overt change in national policies, Peru entered a process of import substitution combined with continuing incentives for exports. Domestic entrepreneurs responded successfully, and the economy began to show promising signs of diversified and autonomous growth (Thorp and Bertram 1978, 26–71).

That hopeful evidence of national capacity for economic change, led by domestic producers, was undercut by a deliberate change in economic strategy in 1898, combined with a shift toward foreign ownership in many activities. The change in economic strategy was the government's decision to adopt that ultimate in conservative financial commitments, the gold standard. The decision was in part a response to a real problem of relying on silver: the prolonged decrease in its value exerted upward pressure on the domestic price level by making imports more expensive and by pulling productive capacity toward exports. Concern for inflation argued for the new economic strategy, even if it hurt exporters. Perhaps the decisive pressure to make the change came precisely from the internal conflict of interests involved in the issue. For exporters and new industrialists, a falling currency value was a powerful stimulus; for importers and the financial community, it was either directly harmful or a source of the instability that financial interests detest (Quiroz 1993, 43–89). The government in power responded to the latter interests and set the stage for new external problems as a direct consequence of internal conflict.

Adoption of the gold standard did not immediately affect the prosperous context of the economy, but it paved the way for increasing trouble. From then on through the 1920s, successive governments did everything they could to keep the commitment to a fixed exchange rate despite increases in domestic prices relative to those in the outside world. The fixed price of foreign exchange, combined with low tariff rates, made it increasingly difficult to find profitable investments in domestic industry (Thorp and Bertram 1978, 112–44). This policy could not have been sustained in the absence of new sources of foreign exchange, but for better or worse new sources did turn up. Both copper and oil exports added to earnings in the period before World War I, and then the wartime commodity boom took over. Negative effects of the fixed exchange rate on production and the trade balance began to show up severely in the 1920s, but the exceptionally ready supply of international lending in that decade permitted the government to borrow heavily and thereby to keep the exchange rate fixed despite weakening exports and increasing dependence on imports.

Foreign ownership had not played any great role in the nineteenth century but began to gain importance rapidly in the twentieth. The two fields that it entered most aggressively were precisely the two most significant new exports: copper and oil. Shortly after 1900, U.S. firms began an aggressive program of buying up all but the smallest Peruvian copper mines. Similarly, the International Petroleum Company established practically complete control of oil production by buying the restricted rights needed to work the main oil fields. Foreign investment also moved into sugar production and exports, textiles and to a lesser degree other industries, finance, and public utilities. The main activity of foreign investors remained in export fields: by the end of the 1920s, foreign-owned firms produced over 60 percent of Peru's exports. The depression of the 1930s both brought new foreign investment to a halt and drove down the prices of the products exported by foreign firms (especially copper), much more than those exported by Peruvian producers. The share of exports by foreign firms fell to about 30 percent by the end of the 1940s (Thorp and Bertram 1978, 153).

For many Latin American countries, the depression of the 1930s stimulated efforts to find a new, more independent path of development. In the face of collapsing export earnings, many governments added deliberate programs of public-sector spending to help shore up demand and production, combined with protection to drive demand toward domestic products. Brazil, the Southern Cone, and Colombia and Mexico to more moderate degrees, managed to respond by such methods with early recovery and then exceptionally fast growth of their industrial sectors. This period proved to be a critical turning point for these countries, with many problems ahead but with significantly changed economic structures. The Peruvian reaction went in the opposite direction, toward greater restraint on government spending, with early reversal of currency depreciation and very little recourse to protection. In contrast to most of South America, although parallel with the Central American countries, Peru stayed amazingly faithful to its pre-1930s economic orientation (Díaz Alejandro 1984).

Peru's nonactivist response to the depression might be explained as a consequence of the country's rapid political return to a conservative government in the early 1930s, after the violent confrontations between the APRA and the elected government of Sánchez Cerro (Chapter 2). In general terms, the response was a result of the country's relatively low degree of industrialization and urbanization and of the correspondingly low weight of industrial and professional interests in the political system. Market forces worked in the same direction: although export earning went steeply downhill for copper, world demand trends and prices proved relatively favorable for Peru's cotton and highly favorable for its gold. Its trade balance began to improve early in the 1930s, and its temporarily devalued currency began to appreciate. External luck in this respect was not acting alone: the domestic policy option in favor of deflation rather than fiscal stimulus held down demand for imports and by this repression of demand helped the trade balance and favored currency appreciation (Thorp and Bertram 1978, 182–201).

As a consequence, apart from the brief experience of interventionism from 1945 to 1948, Peru remained an exceptionally open economy. In the late 1950s, its tariff rates for manufactured consumer goods remained far lower than those of Argentina, Brazil, Chile, and Colombia (Macario 1964, 75). With that continued option for open trade, Peru gained advantages of efficiency and avoided much of the economic trauma of Argentina and Brazil in the 1950s and 1960s. It also fell behind these countries' trends toward industrialization and diversification and then inherited many of their earlier problems in the 1970s and 1980s.

Factor Proportions and Technological Change

The basic balance among the country's factors of production—labor, land, and capital—changed greatly between the nineteenth century and the second half of the twentieth. In the earlier century, labor was scarce relative to land and other natural resources, as it was in the rest of Latin America and the United States as well. In the twentieth century, population growth accelerated, and the labor force increased rapidly relative to the supply of arable land and to employment opportunities outside agriculture: the basic context shifted from labor scarcity to a persistently excess supply of unskilled labor. Skilled workers remained scarce relative to unskilled, in a society with limited access to education, although even people with completed secondary and higher education began to experience increasing difficulties in finding employment and suffered steeply falling real earnings in the severely depressed conditions of the 1980s and early 1990s (Arregui 1994).

Exactly as would be expected from basic principles of international trade theory, conditions of labor scarcity and natural resource abundance in the nineteenth century made Peru, the rest of Latin America, and the United States as well exporters of primary products in exchange for imports of manufactures.[2] That pattern of trade economized on the scarce resource, labor, and raised the relative incomes of owners of land and other natural resources. In both North and South America, it raised national incomes but also increased inequality (Williamson 1996, 15–19, and table 2).

Although the conventional Heckscher–Ohlin principles of comparative advantage account reasonably well for these patterns of trade up to the early twentieth century, they do not account readily for the striking contrast between changes in the United States and lack of change in Latin America. Innovation in the northern United States gradually built up strong competitive positions for industrial exports, but Latin America scarcely made any move at all in that direction until the 1960s. The most evident background factor bearing on these differences was the contrast in development of human capital discussed in Chapter 2: widespread

---

2. The exports of the United States were almost but not quite exclusively primary products at the beginning of the nineteenth century. "Finished manufactures" constituted 6 percent of total exports by 1820, 13 percent by 1850, and 24 percent by 1900 (Bureau of the Census 1975, 890).

access to education and widely dispersed industrialization in the northern United States favored innovation and change, but restricted access to education and limited social mobility kept Latin America tied down much longer to a pattern of trade dominated by primary exports. Inevitably, that pattern proved self-reinforcing: weakness in technological progress in the nineteenth century and the first half of the twentieth left Latin American industry, as it developed more strongly in the second half of the twentieth century, constantly behind in technical skills, research capacity, and ability to compete in industries characterized by rapid change.

Factor proportions in a narrowly defined sense show Peru in a particularly weak position in basic sciences as of the early 1970s, and still at the end of the 1980s (Chapter 2). For the decade of the 1980s, just 2 percent of the bachelor's degrees awarded in the country were in the sciences: the lowest share of any country in Latin America for which Patricia Arregui was able to find comparable data (Arregui 1994, 21–23). Still, the country's supply of engineers began to rise rapidly and multiplied four times between 1972 and 1989. As Arregui suggests, the workers of the country are now much better prepared to implement technological change, although "we could be condemned, in the best of cases, to be good at selecting technology, but not at generating it" (Arregui 1994, 21, n. 7).

Sector Differences in Production and Employment

Despite the country's low level of protection up to the mid-1960s, the manufacturing sector proved able to grow in response to helpful factors of demand and supply. On the demand side, rising private investment and incomes fostered growing markets, and firms responded by raising production for domestic sales (Tello 1990; Gonzales de Olarte 1996a). On the supply side, gradually improving access to education helped raise the supply of labor readily able to respond to opportunities for industrial employment and to learn on the job. At levels of technical and university education, increasing numbers of people were preparing to take on or initiate professional activities. Although the economy continued to depend heavily on traditional exports to finance imports of supplies and equipment, it began, at long last, to diversify reasonably well.

If viewed in terms of occupations, Peru remained in 1950 predominantly agricultural. In that year, 59 percent of the labor force was still in agriculture or fishing (Table 3.1). If viewed in terms of sector contributions

Table 3.1. Distribution of the labor force by sector, 1950, 1980, 1990, 1994

	Percentages			
	1950	1980	1990	1994
Agriculture and fishing	59	40	34	31
Mining	2	2	2	1
Manufacturing	13	12	11	13
Construction	3	4	4	4
Services	23	42	49	51

SOURCES: For 1950, Thorp and Bertram 1978, 259; for later years, Instituto Cuánto 1990, 203; 1992, 483; 1996, 485.

Table 3.2 Sector origins of gross domestic product, 1950–1995, estimated at constant market prices of 1979[a] (percent of GDP)

	1950	1970	1980	1990	1995
Agriculture and fishing	24.4	16.6	10.7	13.6	13.3
Mining	7.7	9.4	13.2	12.3	10.8
Manufacturing	19.4	25.7	24.5	21.7	21.9
Construction	6.0	5.5	5.7	6.4	9.3
Government	6.0	5.9	6.6	6.4	5.2
Other[b]	36.5	36.9	39.3	39.5	39.5

SOURCES: For 1950–1980, INE 1989, 93; for 1990 and 1995, BCRP 1996, 139.
[a] Data for 1950–80 from the Instituto Nacional de Estadística include import duties in estimates of GDP at market prices; calculations of sector percentages in this table subtract these duties.
[b] "Other" includes public utilities, housing, and all other private-sector services.

to national income, agriculture and fishing accounted for one-fourth of total output in 1950, less than half of their share of employment (Table 3.2). Manufacturing accounted for 19 percent of total product and used 13 percent of the labor force. Mining, the leading export sector, accounted for 8 percent of total output and used only 2 percent of the labor force.

Such measures of value added by sector at constant prices can be misleading, in that the estimated relations are highly sensitive to the particular year used as the base for the constant prices. For example, the 1979 base used in Table 3.2, the base currently used in reporting of national accounts by the Central Bank, gives manufacturing's share of national product in 1995 as 21.9 percent. An alternative measure published by the Inter-American Development Bank, based on dollar prices of 1990, gives a much higher share of 26.6 percent. Worse, the share of mining for 1995, given in Table 3.2 as 10.8 percent, turns out to be only 2.1 percent when estimated on the 1990 base (IDB 1996, 359–65). The problem is the logical impossibility of comparing output quantities over

Table 3.3. Growth rates by sector, 1970–1995, and sector composition of GDP in 1995, estimated in constant dollars of 1990

	Annual Rates of Growth of Value Added			Percentage of GDP in 1995
	1970–80	1980–90	1990–95	
Agriculture, forestry, and fishing	−0.6	2.2	5.1	7.0
Mining	7.4	−4.0	2.7	2.1
Manufacturing	3.3	−1.9	5.5	26.6
Construction	4.3	−0.5	13.5	11.6
Electricity, gas, water	10.0	2.7	4.2	0.5
Services	4.1	−1.3	4.8	52.1
GDP	3.7	−1.2	5.8	

SOURCE: IDB 1996, 359–63.

long periods in which the composition of output and the relative values of different products keep changing. All the estimates have the same problem, although in general the 1979 base in Table 3.2 is probably preferable for the earlier years, and the 1990 base for the later. Table 3.3 uses the 1990 base for an alternative picture of change among sectors for the period 1970–95.

Perhaps the most striking feature of the sector growth rates in Table 3.3 is their extreme variability. The mining sector took a spectacular dive in the 1980s, from a growth rate of 7.4 percent a year in the 1970s to an annual rate of decrease of 4.0 percent. Even manufacturing output fell during the 1980s. Agriculture and fishing proved to be the only sector that did better in the 1980s than in the 1970s and then followed with an extraordinarily high rate of growth in the first half of the 1990s, probably its highest for any five-year period in the last half century.

Comparisons among these tables give a suggestive picture of disjunction between employment and output. Output from agriculture and fishing increased in the decade of the 1980s while the economy as a whole was falling, but nonetheless their share of employment fell from 40 to 34 percent. In the same decade, employment in services increased from 43 to 49 percent of the labor force even though output fell. The sector most important for exports, mining, has been the sector least helpful for employment. It accounted for only 2 percent of employment from 1950 to 1990 and only 1 percent by 1994. Manufacturing grew from 19.4 to 24.5 percent of total output between 1950 and 1980, as measured in

Table 3.2, but its share of employment in that period fell from 13 to 12 percent. Both manufacturing and mining were singularly unhelpful for provision of employment opportunities.

The agricultural labor force fell steadily as a proportion of the total labor force, from 59 percent in 1950 to 31 percent by 1994. Mining and manufacturing showed no offsetting increase: their combined share of employment also fell slightly. The net result was a drastic increase in employment in services, from 23 to 51 percent of the total. But that increase does not seem to have contributed much to national product. Combining government and private services in Table 3.2, their share of national product barely budged, from 42.5 to 44.7 percent.[3] With the share of the labor force in the service sector more than doubling in the face of such a slight rise in its apparent contribution to national income, it seems evident that much of the additional employment had very low productivity.

Manufacturing, Competitiveness, and Export Diversification

Peru's open-economy regime proved to be consistent with relatively successful development of the manufacturing sector in terms of its role in production, but not for its ability to compete in world markets. Manufacturing came to rely heavily on imports of supplies for production without being able to earn any significant share of the foreign exchange needed to pay for its imports. This imbalance can be seen as efficient in terms of resource allocation: if lower cost primary exports could pay for the growth of imported inputs, there was no need for the manufacturing sector to be the one that provided the exports. Still, its inability to do so was testimony to a failure to keep up with the rest of the world in terms of cost reduction, technological change, and product innovation. The economy remained dependent on the erratic course of traditional exports, and Peruvian

---

3. This comparison between the employment share and the output share of the services sector is subject to the special difficulties of measuring changes in production for this sector: for some services, measures of inputs provide the only basis for estimates of changes in output. The comparison is not intended to imply that the sector itself is unproductive: services are essential components of all economies. It is meant to direct attention to the role of the sector as a last resort for employment, often in activities of very low productivity, forced by weak growth of employment opportunities in the rest of the economy.

industry stayed out of contact with the pressures and stimuli of learning through active participation in world markets.

The industrial sector's continued lack of competitive strength in the 1940s and 1950s was certainly understandable because of its costs and technological weakness and the country's relative scarcity of skilled labor. With the gradual improvement of the educational base of the labor force in succeeding years, including that of company management, and the substantial scale of the manufacturing sector by 1960, it should have been possible to begin bringing industry into export competition. In fact, this change turned out to be perfectly feasible in the one period in which economic policies provided appropriate incentives; the great loss of opportunity so far is that there has been only one such period.

The scale of the manufacturing sector as of 1960 was not in any evident sense below normal for the country's level of income. Figure 3.1 relates shares of manufacturing in GDP at that time to levels of GDP per capita for the fifteen countries for which both estimates are available. The share of manufacturing in Peru was approximately one-fifth higher than the norm for the region at its level of income. Still, the industrial sector remained notably unable to compete in world markets. Its output was strongly oriented toward domestic consumption rather than toward exports, capital equipment, or technically advanced industries in general (Vega-Centeno 1989, 1993). The other leading Latin American countries were not doing much better at the time, but even those with much higher protection, and thereby a greater handicap to exporters, still managed to achieve slightly higher shares of manufacturing exports than Peru (Sheahan 1987, 91).

Nontraditional exports in total, including industrial, began at last to take on significance in the 1970s. They were only 3 percent of total exports at the beginning of the decade (Table 3.4). Although manufacturing accounted for one-fourth of GDP, it provided only 2 percent of total exports, but a new trend was about to get underway and has continued even through very difficult conditions since. From 1970 to 1990, the dollar value of nontraditional exports multiplied twenty-nine times. Exports of manufactures considered separately multiplied fifteen times over between 1975 and 1980.

These extraordinary rates of growth started from a very low level in 1970. After nearly a century and a half of the country's independence, exports of manufactures were still trivial. Then something changed to make them much less trivial. What caused the change?

Fig. 3.1. Share of manufacturing in GDP as a function of GDP per capita, fifteen Latin American countries, 1960.

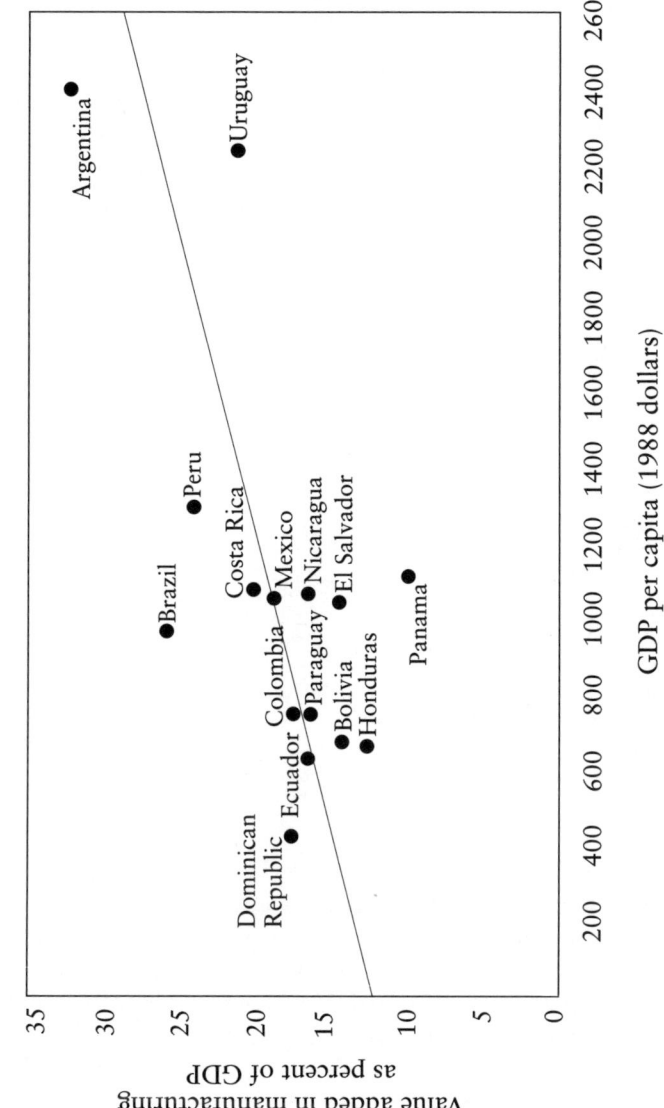

SOURCES: Manufacturing shares from World Bank 1983, 512; GDP per capita from IDB 1990, 4.

Table 3.4. Structure of exports, 1970–1997 (in millions of dollars)

	1970	1975	1980	1985	1990	1996	1997
Traditional, total	1,000	1,234	3,071	2,264	2,259	4,213	4,692
Mining	465	589	1,795	1,205	1,481	2,654	2,718
Petroleum	7	41	792	645	258	353	377
Agricultural	157	371	225	225	174	297	472
Fishing	303	168	195	118	345	909	1,126
Other	68	65	64	71	—	—	—
Nontraditional, total	34	96	845	714	989	1,590	2,043
Agriculture	8	12	72	93	119	323	340
Fishing	7	17	117	124	107	212	278
Textiles	1	12	224	244	364	454	571
Chemicals, dyes	6	10	90	46	90	167	206
Metals, and nonmetallic minerals	4	39	198	132	210	227	342
Other	8	6	144	75	99	206	308
[Manufactures]	16	38	553	342	510	NA	NA
Fishing permits, ship repair, miscellaneous					73	94	74
Percentages of Total Exports							
Nontraditional	3	7	22	24	30	27	30
Exclusive of agriculture and fishing	2	5	17	17	23	18	21
Manufactures	2	3	18	15	22	NA	NA

SOURCES: Instituto Cuánto 1991, 931; 1992, 1016; World Bank 1992, 486–87; BCRP 1998a, 166.

Three changes in basic institutions and economic structure, followed by a new economic policy, support one another in favoring the first real growth of industrial exports. One institutional change was the shock of land reform in 1969. As the large landowners were forced to turn to new fields, some shifted into industry and may have brought with them greater awareness of possible gains from entering export markets. Second, entry into the Andean Common Market, established in 1969, opened the way to new exports from Peru to the other countries in the region (Rudolph 1992, 57). The capacity to compete successfully was growing at the same time, through increases in semiskilled and skilled labor made possible by the extension of access to education. All three changes improved the chances of raising industrial exports.

The main economic variable that might have pushed producers in this direction, the exchange rate, was no help at all in the first half of the 1970s. The real exchange rate appreciated significantly, as the government of that period froze the nominal rate in the face of rising inflation (Sheahan 1980b). That effect was partially counteracted by application of a system of subsidies, through tax advantages, selectively applied to new exports: the Certex system (Schydlowsky, Hunt, and Mezzara 1983; Iguíñiz and Muñoz 1992, 125–30). The subsidies may have been wastefully misdirected to some degree: some of the new exports classified as manufactures were scarcely distinguishable from raw materials, with low degrees of industrial value added. They involved no significant changes in the character of Peruvian industry (Vega-Centeno 1988, 23–26). Still, an industrial sector with practically no previous interest in exporting began to pay some attention to the possibilities, at first in response to the subsidies and then to repeated devaluations.

When the fiscal and external deficits of the Velasco government led to a balance of payments crisis and forced correction in 1975, the stabilization program included both tighter fiscal restraint and devaluation of the currency to restore external balance (Chapter 7). This combination had a powerful effect on nontraditional exports. A study of structural change in the Peruvian economy brought out a striking "structural break" in the time series of the country's production and international trade in 1976 and identified devaluation as the main cause. Between 1975 and 1979, the real price of foreign exchange doubled (Seminario and Bouillon 1992, 13, 70–78.)

The sudden change in exchange rate policy, helped by a rising cycle of external demand, gave a strong stimulus to both traditional and nontraditional exports, especially the latter. Their potential was already present and could have been released earlier: the exchange rate finally moved in the right direction to release it.

No such dramatic change has appeared in any subsequent period, although both nontraditional and industrial exports have continued increasing. Nontraditional products rose from 22 percent of total exports in 1980 to 30 percent in 1990 and remained at 30 percent in 1997. Exports of nontraditional agricultural products, discussed in Chapter 4, grew to the point that they passed the total value of traditional agricultural exports by 1993, although the latter then grew faster through 1997. Industrial exports also rose relative to total exports in the course of the

1980s, from 18 to 22 percent. In the absence of a fully comparable measure for 1997, manufacturing exports might be approximated, as in Table 3.4, by subtracting agriculture and fishing from the total for all nontraditional products. This measure indicates continuing growth, from $763 million in 1990 to $1,425 million in 1997, although a decrease in their share of total exports from 23 to 21 percent. The return to an open-market economy in 1990 was accompanied by strongly growing exports, both traditional and nontraditional, but not by an increasing degree of diversification.

The period from 1975 to 1980 when the real exchange rate was raised so sharply and exports of manufactures rose swiftly as a share of total exports made the country briefly one of the leaders in the region's rapid change in this direction. For the region, manufactures increased from 11 percent of total exports in 1970 to 33 percent by 1990 (IDB 1992, 196). For Peru, this share went from just 2 percent in 1970 to 18 percent by 1980, then rose much more slowly to 22 percent by 1990. The country's share of the region's total manufacturing exports remained low, but it increased: from an average of 0.7 percent for 1970–75 to 1.2 percent for 1985–90 (IDB 1992, 262).

Textiles and clothing became the largest single group of manufactured exports from the late 1970s; they reached 16 percent of total exports by 1990, although they fell back to 12 percent in 1997 (Table 3.4). The skill- and capital-intensive groups of machinery and transport equipment provided only 2 percent of total exports as of 1990, but the growth rate for this category for the period 1970–90 was a high 17.5 percent, matching the growth rate of these exports for the region. Chemical products, led by explosives (!), dies, tanning, and coloring materials, rose at almost exactly the same rate.

This continuing growth of industrial exports is especially striking because, after the initial stimulus of devaluation in the second half of the 1970s, the real exchange rate has gone the wrong way ever since. In the first years of the 1980s, it was deliberately allowed to appreciate as a counterinflationary measure, although when an external crisis reappeared it was devalued again. Under the government of Alan García, from 1985 to 1990, the exchange rate was no longer used to promote exports. Nominal devaluations were held far below the rate of inflation: the real exchange rate, as measured by correcting the nominal rate for inflation, appreciated by a phenomenal 66 percent from 1985 to 1990 (IDB 1992, 157). That estimate for 1985–90 raises a host of problems, discussed in Chapter 7: it is an overstatement of the negative impact on incentives to export.[4] Even by more moderate alternative measures of the real exchange rate, export incentives clearly worsened in the 1980s; it is not surprising that total exports in 1990 were far lower than they had been ten years earlier.

Emphasis on the role of exchange rate policy in determining the growth of nontraditional exports runs into a difficulty in terms of econometric tests. The regression coefficient for the role of the real exchange rate in explaining year-to-year variations in nontraditional exports in the 1980s is close to zero and not statistically significant (Sheahan 1993). Part of the explanation may be that the learning process of gradual entry into export markets was dominant: once brought into exporting by the powerful incentives of the late 1970s, exporters kept trying and to some extent succeeding, despite adverse subsequent appreciation. In addition, the high and unstable levels of protection throughout this period—with accelerating inflation and particularly chaotic changes in relative prices in the late 1980s—may well have dampened the role of exchange rate incentives. Very preliminary tests for the effects of real exchange rates on nontraditional exports in the first years of the 1990s, with levels of protection and of inflation greatly lower, show a change toward a more systematic relation.[5]

It is surely more than a coincidence that the only five-year period in which the currency was drastically devalued in real terms is the only one in which all exports increased greatly, and nontraditional exports far more dramatically than traditional products. That experience points to the possibility of a real breakthrough in the structure and sustainability of Peruvian economic growth. More the pity that no government since has repeated the experience.

Conclusions

It took much longer than it should have, but Peru has managed to move a considerable distance from a premodern economy dependent for its

---

4. The real exchange rate can be measured in many different ways (Edwards 1989). The series reported by the IDB converts nominal exchange rates to real rates by correction for domestic and external inflation. An alternative measure that compares export prices to costs of production shows much less appreciation than shown by the IDB series for the period 1985–90 and for the early 1990s (Rossini 1991; Sheahan 1994, 913).

5. These tests use quarterly data for two different measures of real exchange rates (Sheahan 1993). They demonstrate statistically significant relations between both these measures of the

growth on exports from agriculture and mining with the main benefits of growth going to the owners of the land and mines. With the share of the labor force in agriculture and fishing down from 59 percent in 1950 to 31 percent in 1994 and the share of nontraditional exports up from 3 percent in 1970 to 30 percent by 1990, the basic structure of the economy has changed in ways more promising for the future.

Three major weaknesses of this transition remain serious problems: (1) the failure to provide adequate opportunities for productive employment for people moving out of agriculture and for those entering the labor force with more education than in the past; (2) the corresponding weakness of real wages and of real earnings from self-employment in the service sector, contributing to poverty and high inequality; (3) the slowness of the industrial sector in raising productivity, achieving technological change, and strengthening its capacity to compete in external markets. On all three counts, structural factors have made progress understandably difficult. In addition, many problems have been due at least as much to erratic, often unhelpful, orientations of national economic strategy. It should be possible to do better: better for creation of employment opportunities, for development of a more competitive industrial sector, and for a more equal society.

---

real exchange rate and nontraditional exports in the early 1990s, but the period covered was too short for high confidence in this behavioral pattern.

4

AGRICULTURE, RURAL INCOMES, AND VIOLENCE

Peruvian agriculture and rural society have gone through greater changes in the years after World War II than at any other time in the country's history, changes that have destroyed stubbornly rooted patterns of economic and social control. These changes may open the way to a dynamic process of productivity growth, but for the postwar period as a whole, the sector has been notoriously weak in terms of both production growth and rural incomes.

If production is considered the key issue, the main weakness in Peruvian agriculture up to the 1990s was its failure to keep up with the growth of population: per capita production of food and of agricultural output in total fell through most of the postwar period. If the focus is on incomes, the main problem is the extent and persistence of rural poverty. The fundamental constraint underlying both problems is that the growth of the rural population relative to the availability of arable land makes it very difficult for rural families either to produce enough to get out of poverty or to keep output growing as fast as the population as a whole.

Three additional factors have aggravated the effects of the scarcity of arable land. Until 1969, a highly concentrated structure of ownership worsened the scarcity of land for the mass of the rural poor. The land reform of that year changed this context greatly by turning the large haciendas into cooperatives consisting of their former workers, although it did little to improve access to land for the great majority of the rural poor: those who were not employed in the haciendas. A second severe constraint that has been partially but inadequately answered is that the rural population has had extremely limited access to education (Chapter 2). This deficiency has been both a handicap to increasing productivity in agriculture and a discouraging factor for any nonagricultural activities that might otherwise have been established in regions with high poverty. The third additional factor has been the scourge of rural violence that spread through the country and into the cities from 1980 to 1992. This problem too has lessened for the time being; the great question for the future is whether Peruvian society can succeed in reducing the inequalities that contributed so much to the willingness of young people to turn to violence in the recent past.

The first section of this chapter summarizes conditions of the agricultural labor force and its relations to the supply of arable land. The second section reviews issues of concentrated land ownership before the land reform of 1969 and the consequences of that reform. The third section centers on weakness in agricultural production; the fourth on trends in traditional and nontraditional agricultural exports. The fifth section is concerned with the special role of the illegal coca economy in recent years, and the final section with rural violence.

Rural Labor, Land, and Incomes

Poverty is omnipresent in Peru, but at its worst in rural areas. That is true for all regions, as summarized in Table 2.1. It has been particularly important in the rural sierra because of the great number of people involved: one-fifth of the national population, compared with 9 percent for the rural areas of the coast and the selva combined. It shows through clearly in terms of the percentage of households with incomes below the poverty line, and glaringly so for its consequences in terms of infant mortality. For the five lowest income departments of the sierra, infant mortality rates in 1993 averaged 3.5 times those of Lima (Instituto Cuánto 1994, 270; Table 6.2 following).

A natural reaction to such inequality between rural and urban incomes is that people move, if they can, toward urban areas in general but particularly away from dependence on agriculture. Rural Peruvians have done both, in large numbers, especially since the beginning of the 1940s. The largest net emigration has been from the poorest region, the sierra. The bulk of the migration has been to urban areas, roughly two-thirds to Lima, although it has also included net migration to higher income agriculture in coastal areas or, more recently, the selva. Emigration was not fast enough to fully offset the natural growth of the population in the sierra, but it was significant: in the intercensal period 1961–72, net emigration was equal to 18 people for every 100 births (Caballero 1981, 140–46). On the receiving side, 44 percent of the population of metropolitan Lima in 1991 consisted of immigrants, as did 41 percent of the population of the country's other urban areas (Instituto Cuánto 1993, 185). "Lima has been losing its physiognomy of a city of industry and governmental administration, to convert itself into a *ciudad bazar* . . . [the] rich and the middle classes have been reduced to an isolated situation in their residential barrios . . . in an urban regime conceived as a home for a *criolla* style of life and never thought of as a place to live for provincial populations" (Matos Mar 1984, 60, 76).

The share of the labor force in agriculture dropped from 59 percent in 1950 to 34 percent by 1990 (Table 3.1). Still, by one critical measure, the shift out of agriculture was too slow: it was not fast enough to reduce the ratio of labor to land to allow the remaining families in agriculture to use more land. The absolute number of agricultural workers increased from 1.7 million to 2.8 million between 1965 and 1994. The area of land classified as arable increased as well, although more slowly. Counting both fully arable land and land under permanent tree crops, the area increased by 52 percent between these years while the agricultural labor force was increasing by 62 percent (Table 4.1).

Peru has the blessing of a great deal of dramatically beautiful space, but most of it is of little use for agricultural production. The ratio of arable land to the agricultural labor force was only 1.56 hectares per worker in 1965 and fell to 1.46 by 1994. For comparison, the ratio for South America as a whole in 1994 was 3.74 hectares per worker. Peru's ratio of arable land to total population in that year was slightly below the ratio in India and only one-fourth that of the United States (FAO 1995, 8, 26–27). Desert, jungle, and mountain areas have slowly been

Table 4.1. Agricultural labor force and supply of arable land, Peru and South America, 1965–1994[a]

	Peru			South America
	Labor Force, 1,000s	Land 1,000 Hectares	Ratio Land/ Labor	Ratio Land/ Labor
1965	1,734	2,701	1.56	3.36
1979	1,939	3,470	1.79	4.00
1984	1,978	3,691	2.00	4.23
1989	2,417	2,730	1.54	4.55
1994	2,819	4,110	1.46	3.74

SOURCES: FAO 1967, 5; 1980, 66; 1984, 67–68; 1985, 67–68; 1990, 26; 1995, 8, 26–27.
[a] The labor force is intended to include self-employed small landowners and workers in indigenous communities, in addition to hired landless labor; land supply includes areas under permanent tree crops as well as cultivated land. All these inescapably uncertain estimates keep getting revised; the data in the table are taken whenever possible from the latest FAO reports that cover these years.

brought into cultivation at their margins, but the economics and ecology of going much further in this direction are dubious. Studies of costs in terms of capital investment and environmental degradation suggest that they jointly impose severe constraints on large-scale projects to add new land to cultivation, as distinct from investments aimed at improving productivity on existing cultivated areas (Caballero 1981, 61–91; Alberts 1983, 209–16).

Without intending to contradict this sensible conclusion, one should note that the extreme diversity of conditions among regions casts some doubt on generalizations about the room for expansion (Gonzales de Olarte 1994, 58–74). Water can be more important than land area, especially on the coast but in parts of the sierra as well. Where the coastal area has had access to water, it has had many successful plantations yielding good incomes. From 1976 to 1991, investment raised the area under irrigation by 11 percent, although that achievement looks modest compared with an increase of 32 percent for South America as a whole (FAO 1992, 17).

It is surely possible to continue expanding irrigation and to increase other agricultural inputs profitably, but it is doubtful that this will change the basic problem: the scarcity of arable land to work with, relative to the size of the agricultural labor force, makes it extremely difficult for the majority of people in the rural sector to produce enough to get out of poverty. With labor abundant and land not, the price system works strongly to keep rural incomes down. This factor is one of the most important, although not the only one, responsible for persistent rural poverty.

Control of Land: Before and After Land Reform

The distribution of land ownership has historically been another crucial consideration worsening poverty and inequality. Peruvian agriculture went through an almost continuous process of increasing ownership concentration in the haciendas of the highlands and the plantations of the coast from the mid-nineteenth century up to the 1920s, although the tide began to turn slowly against the haciendas from then on (Jacobsen 1993). In the early years after World War II, the large haciendas and plantations still held high shares of the land. Peru was by no means exceptional in this respect: concentration of land ownership was the rule in all Latin American countries in which the Spanish-speaking population dominated a large indigenous rural labor force. Gini coefficients of ownership concentration were as high as .96 in Mexico before its reforms of the 1930s and .94 in Bolivia in 1950 (Eckstein et al. 1978, 2). The corresponding estimate for Peru in 1950 was just above the regional median at .88. For comparison, the median and mode reported by this study for twenty-one developing countries in other regions were between .60 and .69.

Naturally, all such estimates have a host of problems, including that of variable land quality. The haciendas often held large areas that were poorly suited for production. An adjusted estimate of concentration in the sierra, taking into account differences in land quality and also the availability to campesinos of land on haciendas whose owners had abandoned control or on isolated holdings of the church that were not commercially exploited, indicated that large landholders held something on the order of 50 percent of the land under cultivation and 50 to 60 percent of that used for grazing (Caballero 1981, 92–109). Even on that corrected basis, a small number of families held half the usable land, while the great majority did not have enough to produce a minimally decent level of income.

In the early postwar years, about one-fifth of the rural population in the sierra lived on the haciendas, most of them as tenants under varied forms of crop sharing or exchange of labor for rights to use small plots or to graze cattle (Deere 1990). The rest of the agricultural labor force was divided between independent small landholdings and traditional indigenous communities. The communities held about one-fourth of the land as of 1969 and slightly more by 1985 (Gonzales de Olarte 1994, 46). They combined, in varying ways among areas, elements of both private and collective ownership. Individual families own the cultivated plots, with distinctly unequal holdings, but grazing land is usually held in common. Communal labor is required on community infrastructure projects. Families depend on one another for exchange of labor on a reciprocal basis, but individuals can—and most do because their incomes from agriculture are so low—work for wages either for others in the community or for outside employers. In general, the postwar trend has been toward increasing reliance on wage labor, with lessening participation in communal activities. The communities still provide the support of the group in dealing with the outside world and collective help for families with special difficulties, while allowing scope for differential earnings. As a social institution, they have helped the weak in a very unequal struggle (Figueroa 1984; Gonzales de Olarte 1994, 175-296).

The communities and the haciendas were in almost constant conflict when the haciendas were aggressively building up their holdings, from the 1850s to the 1920s. The hacienda owners sometimes acquired land and labor in open commercial transactions. Perhaps at least as often, they used deceit and debt to trap campesinos, or their control of local courts to take over land with invented claims, or simply direct force to seize what they wanted. They could usually count on local police and courts to discipline campesinos for any reason they wished; any signs of revolt from the campesinos quickly led to police or military suppression. The indigenous communities made great efforts to carry legal appeals to Lima and sometimes found responsive courts and government agencies, but the powerful influence of the hacienda owners usually dominated the results (Tullis 1970; Davies 1974; Cotler 1978a).[1]

This long-standing pattern began to change, from the 1920s onward, under the impact of adverse economic trends for the sector combined with rising social protest. The adverse trends included constraints on

---

1. Two classic Peruvian novels, Ciro Alegría's *El mundo es ancho y ajeno* (1967) and José María Arguedes' *Los ríos profundos* (1973), give compelling and appalling pictures of the injustice of rural society under this system of locally concentrated economic and political power. Their portrayals are consistent with historical evidence, but their *indigenista* orientation has been sharply criticized. Nils Jacobsen gives an unhappy account of a seminar at the Instituto de Estudios Peruanos, in 1965, at which Arguedes was attacked by younger sociologists for his failure to see that problems of caste, of the indigenous peoples, had been superseded by issues of class (Jacobsen 1993, 1-2).

supply imposed by natural resource limits, weakened export markets in the 1920s and 1930s, and increasingly restive rural labor. The comparative advantage Peru previously had in agriculture was gradually eroding.

For large landholders, economic incentives to take their capital out of agriculture were accompanied by powerful pressures from growing public awareness of extreme rural poverty and inequality, widening support for land reform, and direct seizures of land by rural activists. A wave of uprisings in the sierra from 1915 to 1924 and the bloody repressions that followed marked the beginnings of the downturn of hacienda dominance (Caballero 1981, 313–67; Jacobsen 1993, 331–56).

In the department with the highest percentage of the rural population living on haciendas, Cajamarca, modernizing landowners began to break up and sell large portions of their estates in the 1950s and 1960s to concentrate on dairy production. That change allowed them to enter a favorable market with production that required much less labor: economic incentives began to turn against dependence on large numbers of tenants to ensure their labor supply (Deere 1990, 147–209).

Land reform became an increasingly active political issue in the early postwar years; Fernando Belaúnde Terry made it one of his basic appeals for election as president in 1963. Although he succeeded in getting a reform bill passed by congress, it was so weakened by the opposition that it accomplished next to nothing (Cotler 1978a, 358–83; McClintock and Lowenthal 1983, 3–38). Belaúnde's failure to make any headway on either land reform or his proposals to restore national control of the oil industry cost him and democracy itself much public sympathy. An impatient military, under the leadership of General Velasco, removed him from office in 1968 and quickly adopted a land reform far more radical than Belaúnde's proposals.

The reform imposed by the Velasco government effectively eliminated all large private landholdings. In most of the sierra, it converted the haciendas into cooperatives owned by previous tenants and salaried workers on the estates. The intent was to destroy the basis of power of Peru's traditional elite and at the same time to foster a more cooperative society. Such social-political purposes apparently dominated questions of agricultural production or any planned changes in patterns of land use. It was as if the question of ownership was all that mattered, not the consequences for output or for rural poverty.

The reform included varied kinds of cooperative arrangements applied differently among regions. In the southern sierra, where indigenous communities were particularly important, many were allotted land from the former haciendas and allowed to divide it among families. In the department of Pasto, where peasant communities had controlled slightly less than one-fifth of the land area before the reform, their share increased to 30 percent (Hunefeldt 1997, 122–24). In the central highlands, the common pattern was to turn ownership over to former tenants and permanent workers on the haciendas, either on the original holding or in large units formed from several haciendas. Because the tenants and permanent workers on the estates were at most about one-fifth of the rural labor force, the great majority of the people in agriculture were simply left out (Caballero 1977, 146–59; McClintock 1981; Kay 1982).

On the modernized coastal estates, the workers included in the new cooperatives fared reasonably well; those in highland crop production mostly did not. One problem was that the previous owners decapitalized their properties as best they could when they saw that they were going to lose them. A second was that new administrators sent in by the government often lacked managerial and marketing experience. Perhaps most important, incentives for members of the cooperatives were not closely related to effort or efficiency: greater or lesser individual effort on the cooperative's land made little difference to the family's income.

By the end of the 1970s, many cooperatives were either bankrupt or close to becoming so (McClintock 1985; Lastarria-Cornheil 1989). It became common, although at first illegal, to subdivide them among their members. In 1980, such conversions were legalized by new legislation on condition that the majority of the cooperative members voted for such a breakup. In the course of the 1980s, most did, although some retained cooperative arrangements for equipment purchasing and marketing (Hunefeldt 1997, 125–32). The preferences of most of the people involved at that point were clearly for individual family ownership. The whole set of changes was not a reversion to the prereform agrarian structure. It left Peru with a much less unequal pattern of landownership than it had before the reform, with greater scope for family farming than ever before in its history.

Agricultural Output and the Supply of Food

One of the core weaknesses in Peruvian economic growth in the postwar period has been the failure of the agricultural sector to raise output fast enough to keep up with the growth of population. With brief exceptions,

Table 4.2. Indexes of output per capita of the agricultural sector and of food, 1965–96

	Volume Indexes, Base 100 for 1989–91[a]	
	Agricultural Production	Food Production
1965	127	117
1970	123	123
1975	111	114
1980	95	100
1985	100	98
1990	96	96
1991	98	99
1992	89	91
1993	94	97
1994	105	108
1995	111	113
1996	114	—

Sources: FAO 1975, 45, 47; 1980, 79, 81; 1990, 49, 51; 1995, 49, 51; BCRP 1997, 70.
[a] Estimates for 1985–95, from FAO 1995, are on the base 1989–91. Estimates for earlier years were constructed by chaining indexes from earlier FAO reports using different base years in each decade. The estimate for 1996 is derived from the reported change in agricultural production as evaluated at constant prices by the BCRP.

per capita output of food fell persistently until the early 1990s (Table 4.2). That trend both held down the possible growth of the economy and directly worsened poverty: when food supplies run short, it is the poor who eat less. For Latin America as a whole, the per capita supply of calories increased 9 percent between the mid-1960s and the mid-1980s as measured by the median percentage change; for Peru in the same period, the supply of calories per capita fell 5 percent (FAO 1985, 171; 1987, 291; World Bank 1988, 278).

Although measures of food production are notoriously uncertain, especially because of the considerable share of self-consumed output that does not pass through any markets, the diverse estimates available are reasonably consistent about the long-term trend. On one basis of estimation, total output of agriculture as measured by value added doubled in the thirty-five years from 1950 to 1985, but the population increase of 154 percent implied a 20 percent fall in output per capita (INE 1989, 93; Instituto Cuánto 1992, 173). Alternative measures reported by the Food and Agricultural Organization of the United Nations suggest that food production per capita fell 14 percent from the crop year 1952–53 to 1964–65 (FAO 1965, 33), then a further 18 percent from 1965 to 1990

(Table 4.2). For agricultural output in total as distinct from food, the estimates given in Table 4.2 suggest an even sharper decrease from 1965 to 1990. More fortunately for the country, and the poor, both agricultural output and food production per capita started rising impressively in the last years reported, 1993–96.

In a sense, the main factor underlying the long downtrend of production per capita has been the rapid growth of population rather than any dead end in agriculture itself. Slower growth of population would have made it easier for the agricultural sector to keep up. Other factors specific to the sector were important too, including erratic investment, delays in searching for possible openings for high-value products in export markets, extreme rural violence in the 1980s, and for a time—although probably no longer—adverse effects from land reform.

Investment in agriculture has long been more public than private and became overwhelmingly so in the early 1970s. The military government that carried out the land reform backed it up with a great increase in public investment from 1970 to 1975. By 1975, it was approximately six times as high as private investment in agriculture (Ministerio de Agricultura 1990, 9–10). From 1975 on, first as a result of the stabilization plan imposed in that year and then as a general policy under the Belaúnde administration, public investment in agriculture stopped growing. Private investment showed a slightly more positive trend, with an especially marked jump in 1986 under the impetus of the initially proagriculture policies of the García government. Then both private and public investment fell back steeply in the disintegrating economic conditions of the late 1980s and the fiscal tightening of the early 1990s (Gonzales de Olarte 1996a).

Differential trends of output and productivity for particular products suggest considerable scope for increasing output through incentives, technical assistance, and changes in production methods. With favorable support prices in the 1980s, output of rice increased at an annual rate of 7.9 percent for the decade. Although average land productivity showed practically no gain for corn or wheat from 1970 through 1989, output of rice per hectare increased by one-fifth. Similarly, supplies of chicken and eggs increased rapidly, at a rate of 6.5 percent a year for the 1980s, in this case as a result of changes in production techniques to reduce costs. The Ministry of Agriculture interprets these positive results as evidence of what could be generally accomplished with better incentives and improvement of agricultural techniques (Ministerio de Agricultura 1990, 20–32). That interpretation is reinforced by data for many crops that show wide variations in output per hectare even in similar conditions of land and water supply. The differences point to as-yet-unexploited possibilities for raising output if effective extension services could raise average productivity closer to the demonstrated results of the leading producers (Figueroa 1988).

The land reform of 1969 has sometimes been blamed for weakness of production in the 1970s and 1980s. The reform can hardly be the whole story, because output per capita had been on a downtrend long before that, but it clearly failed to improve the trend. For the decade of the 1970s, total agricultural output rose just enough, by 10 percent, to match the increase of the agricultural labor force: labor productivity failed to improve at all. The increase of 10 percent in total output in this decade was only one-fifth of that for South America as a whole (FAO 1981, 77).

The subsequent conversion of the cooperatives into individual holdings could have both positive and negative effects on production: positive through stronger incentives for personal effort but potentially negative, for very small landholdings, by loss of economies of scale (Carter and Alvarez 1989, 161–67). An econometric study of land productivity in north coast agriculture, tracing output from previous cooperatives through individual results with the same land in the 1980s, showed a variety of results rather than any great change in total. The individual holdings produced on average slightly more than the preceding cooperatives on the same land but not enough more to make a convincing case for their superiority. The authors of this study rightly emphasize that results in the 1980s cannot be adequately explained in terms of farming practices: they were adversely affected by the deterioration of the economic system as a whole (Melmed-Sanjak and Carter 1991, 190–210).

It did not help agricultural production at all that governments from the 1970s through the 1980s did their best to hold down agricultural prices by direct controls, by state-monopoly buying, and by subsidized imports of food. The purpose of such policies was in part to lower living costs for the urban sector and perhaps in larger part to limit the visible evidence of inflation. The most important consequence was to weaken incentives for producers and thereby to restrain the growth of output.

A revealing break in the general downtrend from 1985 to 1988 helped bring out the scope for improvement. This period was the first part of Alan García's government, in which it applied strongly proagricultural policies. They included directed credit on a massive scale, price support for major crops, and increased public investment in infrastructure. In addition, relative prices changed greatly in favor of agriculture. The change in relative prices was less a planned way to help the sector than it was the outcome of a breakdown in food price controls. The government's initial attempt to control practically all prices gave way quickly for food products, when it was faced with the near-impossibility of enforcing controls for food under conditions of strongly growing demand. Prices remained blocked for the many public services under government ownership and for those industrial products that could be controlled, and food prices rose sharply relative to other goods and services. For once, intervention in pricing worked in favor of agriculture rather than against it. With all these factors operating together, per capita output of food rose 10 percent between 1985 and 1988 (FAO 1992, 53).

This striking interruption of the downtrend in output per capita made clear the ability of the postreform agricultural sector's ability to respond to incentives, although the deterioration of the economy soon afterward also made clear that the particular set of policies of this period was not sustainable. The main problems were excess spending and fiscal deficits on the macroeconomic level and severely distorted relative prices on the microeconomic. Prices of government services and energy were held far below costs and fed inflation through the borrowing and monetary expansion used to make up the deficits of state firms. Prices of industrial products that could be controlled were held down to a degree that discouraged production in the first place and led to a leap in inflation when they were finally released (Paus 1991). Agricultural credit, provided almost without effective limit, played a major role in the acceleration of inflation. Credit had to be cut back sharply in the adjustment program of 1990, but even before that the disorganization of the inflation-ridden economy of the late 1980s had its counterpart in a new downturn of agricultural output per capita. By 1990, it was 7 percent below the level of 1981.

The extraordinary confusion of economic policies during the last years of the García administration makes it difficult to conclude whether the government was actually trying to help agriculture and to reduce rural poverty. Even while attempting in some sense to help, it was using exchange rate policies that made imported food supplies progressively cheaper relative to domestic costs of production. Beyond that, this government used direct subsidies for imported food as part of its hopeless effort to restrain inflation through direct intervention while increasing inflationary pressures by monetary and fiscal imbalance. The Ministry of Agriculture estimated that food imports were subsidized by nearly 50 percent of their value at the beginning of 1988 and 80 percent by September of that year (Ministerio de Agricultura 1990, 24).

The Fujimori government lost no time in eliminating most of the remaining price supports and subsidies to agriculture. It simply eliminated the Banco Agraria, the main source of agricultural credit under García. Its initially tight monetary and fiscal restraint also cut back greatly on infrastructure and social investment that might have been helpful to agriculture. On the positive side, it eliminated controls on the sector as on the whole economy and set up conditions for a favorable change in relative prices by its massive reduction of protection for industry. Beyond that, in direct contradiction of its open-market orientation, it adopted a nominally temporary "surtax" on agricultural imports to provide some protection to the sector (Gonzales de Olarte 1996a). Furthermore, this government made considerable headway against the ancient problem of unclear land titles, in the belief that settled ownership rights encouraged investment in land improvement. The number of titles cleared in 1992 and 1993 averaged nine thousand a year; that rate jumped to an average of seventy-three thousand a year for 1994–95 (Instituto Cuánto 1996, 569).[2]

These policy changes in the 1990s were complicated and partially contradictory; they did not at first stimulate agricultural growth. The sector's output per capita responded poorly from 1990 through 1992, but it then turned strongly positive from 1993 through 1996 (Table 4.2). What explains that upturn? Is it testimony to the power of the market-determined economic strategy or a matter of temporary luck, not likely to be maintained?

Any adequate explanation would require a major research project to sort out all the factors involved. They include the stimulus of rising domestic demand as the economy began to recover, a recovery that could be attributed in part to the new set of economic policies. Important extraneous factors were part of the picture too, including unusually good rainfall and, after 1992, greatly reduced violence. It is notable that output per capita plunged by 9 percent in 1992, *after* the adoption of the new economic strategy. That year was one of bad luck with climate, and also a peak period of violence, until the capture of the leaders of *Sendero luminoso* in September. The new set of policies needed help from other factors.

Perhaps the most clearly positive component has been the reduction of tariffs and quotas for imports of manufactures: this reduction helped hold down prices of domestic industrial producers as well as imports and

---

2. I owe this observation to Raúl Hopkins, who pointed out its importance for the long-term prospects of the sector. Gonzales de Olarte (1996a, 113) emphasizes that clearer land

led to a marked change in relative prices favorable for the agricultural sector. From 1990 to December 1995, wholesale prices of agricultural products increased 28 percent faster than did prices of domestic manufactures (Instituto Cuánto 1996, 521). Changes in transportation costs and commercial margins may have offset some of the change in relative prices, but the producers certainly have acted as if they considered expansion to be profitable.

A further implication of the positive trend for 1993–96 is that the more equal distribution of land holdings following land reform, which seemed to be negative in the 1970s, may by now have become a helpful factor. Small producers, with the benefit of experience and with direct personal incentives, may provide a more elastic and responsive sector than Peru has ever known. More nearly equal land holdings, combined with better relative prices, proved to be a highly positive combination.

Agricultural Exports, Particularly Nontraditional

The constraints on agricultural production turned the sector from a net exporter to a net importer in the 1980s, as its exports stopped growing (Ministerio de Agricultura 1990, 16). That impasse proved temporary rather than the end of the road: exports of traditional products recovered from their decrease in the 1980s, and those of nontraditional products grew very rapidly, under the more open trade regime of the 1990s (Table 3.4).

From 1948 to 1952, Peru exported 23 percent of its agricultural output; by 1976, the export share was down to 8 percent (Alvarez 1983, 47). As of the mid-1970s, agricultural exports were almost entirely traditional products: predominantly sugar, followed by cotton and coffee. Nontraditional exports were negligible at that time but rose swiftly in the second half of the decade, in that rare period in which the real exchange rate was significantly increased (Chapter 3). In the following decade, as traditional exports fell, those of nontraditional products increased by

---

titles give greater mobility to small landholders through improved access to capital, both for those who wish to invest in productivity improvements and those who prefer to move to nonagricultural activities.

Fig. 4.1. Traditional and nontraditional agricultural exports, 1970–97.

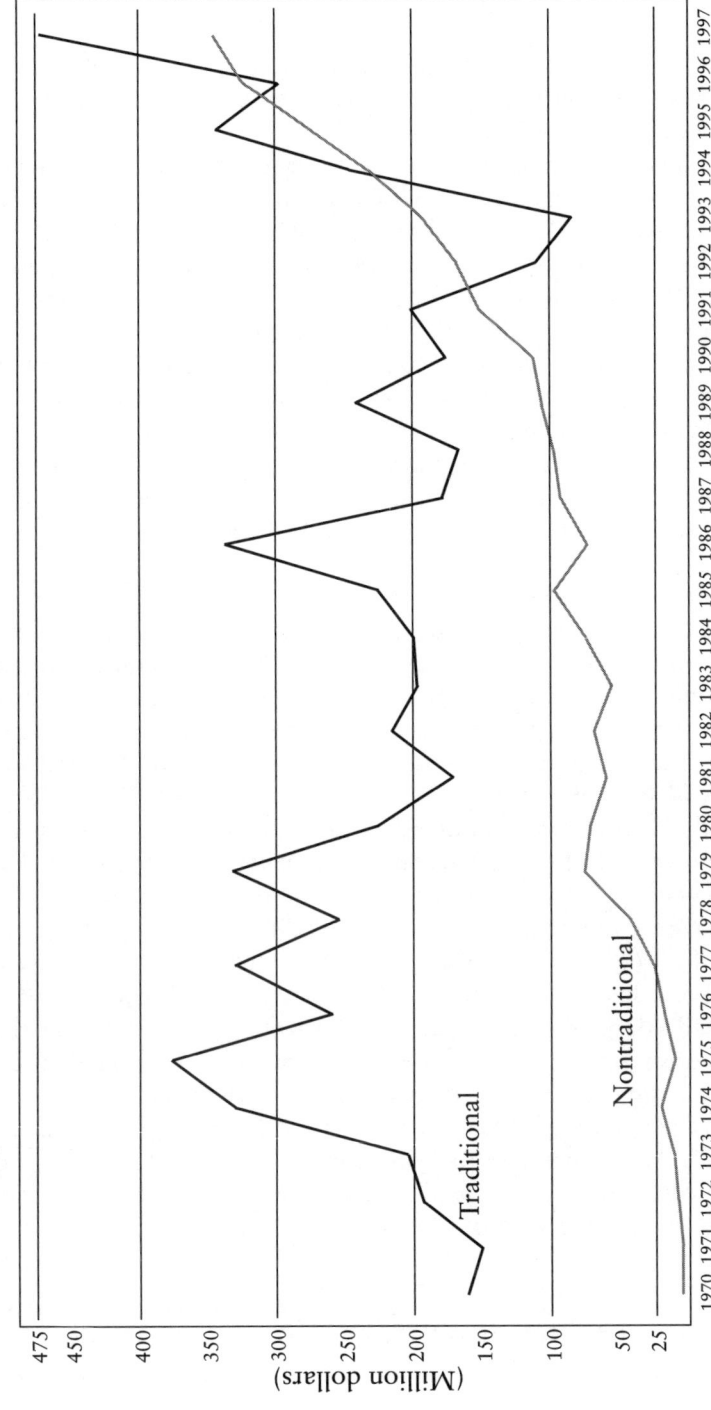

SOURCES: Gómez 1994, 120, for 1970–89; BCRP 1998a, 166, for 1990–97.

enough the keep the total practically constant. Then in the 1990s, while both sets of exports increased, nontraditional products exceeded the traditional exports in 1992–93 and again in 1996 (Fig. 4.1).

A growing number of Latin American countries have found a powerful way to raise agricultural earnings per hectare by creating or entering new, high-value export markets. Leading examples have been fresh flowers from Colombia, snow peas from Guatemala, and a wide range of fruit from Chile (Carter et al. 1993). These exports all have the advantage of being relatively labor intensive; they provide more employment per hectare than traditional crops and, in the case of Guatemala although not Chile, improved earnings for small producers. Peru found several such openings in the 1970s and 1980s, most importantly for exports of fresh and canned asparagus, primarily to Europe. These exports increased from $3 million in 1970 to $100 million by 1995. In the latter year, they were equal to 40 percent of all nontraditional agricultural exports (Instituto Cuánto 1996, 1021).

The other nontraditional agricultural exports have been overshadowed by those of asparagus, but as of 1996, four others earned more than $10 million each: cocoa, marigold, cochinilla,[3] and mangoes. In total, nontraditional agricultural exports were only $8 million in 1970 but then grew at an annual rate of 25 percent a year for this decade, 5 percent in the 1980s, and an impressive 18 percent from 1990 to 1996 (Gómez 1994, 120; BCRP 1997, 140).

The initial spurt of these nontraditional exports followed closely after the land reform of 1969. The haciendas had never been greatly interested in such innovative performance. The shake-up of ownership in the reform may well have facilitated the turn in this new direction, although the rapid growth of the 1970s certainly owed a great deal to the positive incentives to export provided by increasing real exchange rates in the second half of this decade (Chapter 3). Through the 1980s and 1990s to date, the movement of exchange rates has been adverse rather than promotional. Perhaps the basic explanation of growth in the face of this adverse factor is the power of learning. Once the gains from new exports were demonstrated in the course of the 1970s, exporting firms and associated agricultural producers found that it paid to continue building them up despite the adverse movement of the exchange rate. That process might well

---

3. Cochinilla is a natural dye with particularly valuable properties as an alternative to synthetics; it is extracted from an insect living off the nectar of cactus that grows wild in the sierra.

owe something to the land reform and subsequent deconcentration of ownership: greater numbers of independent producers almost surely raised the capacity to respond to new opportunities.

The Coca Economy

Production and exports of coca and its derivatives have many different effects on the Peruvian economy, all of them difficult to quantify because basic information cannot be checked in any dependable way. On the positive side, they add to the incomes of otherwise extremely poor peasant producers and to foreign exchange earnings that, at least in part, flow through to the legal economy. On the negative side, they pull human effort and land into production of coca at the expense of alternative food production, hold down the price of foreign currency and therefore the incentives for legal exports, impose ecological damage from the chemical residues used to process cocaine, increase violence and the costs to the society of trying to restrain it, and aggravate corruption in the military and in the civilian government (Alvarez 1993, 72–87). If coca production were to fall back to traditional levels of consumption by Andean peasants themselves, many Peruvians would lose income; if it continues at present levels or grows, the society as a whole will be the poorer in terms of competitive strength in legal markets and in terms of civil order.

Neither Peru's official national accounts nor its export data include any estimates for the value of coca leaf and its derivatives. Elena Alvarez, reviewing several unofficial estimates for the year 1988, suggests a wide range of possible values: from $0.5 to $1.2 billion value added and from $0.4 to $0.9 billion exports (Alvarez 1993, 81). A dependable private research organization, Instituto Cuánto, gives a slightly higher estimate of $1.4 billion for value added in 1988 and a much higher estimate of $1.7 billion for exports. According to these estimates, average coca exports were stable at $1.6 billion for both 1985–89 and 1990–93, and coca production added an average of 3.6 percent to officially reported GDP in these years. Subsequent estimates show pronounced decreases in value added by coca production from 1992 through 1995, down to no more than 1 percent of GDP in the latter year (Alvarez 1998, table 1).[4]

---

4. Elena Alvarez (1998, table 1) gives separate high and low estimates of value added by coca production for each year from 1992 through 1995. Both the high and the low values fell

For the agricultural sector separately, these estimates suggest that coca raised value added by about 13 percent for 1993. That extra income goes in unknown proportions to dealers and processors (mostly Colombians), to third parties providing protection, and to peasant producers. Even though the share going to peasant producers may not be high, their incomes from coca can be more than seven times as much per hectare of land as alternative earnings in the next most profitable legal crop. Growers in the main producing region, the upper Huallaga valley, earn about $4,500 per year for each hectare in coca, compared with about $600 in coffee, the best legal alternative (Alvarez 1993, 83). Such differentials are mainly a matter of the high market value of coca, but they also reflect the fact that this particular region of Peru is singularly favorable for coca and poorly suited to most alternative crops. Coca would be an ideal crop here, with low opportunity costs, if it were not for its negative human implications.

Government policies to restrain coca production and marketing have been focused more on police and military action than on economic incentives. One of the most appealing proposals has been to promote alternative crops through credit and technical assistance, with guaranteed purchasing at favorable prices. The two main problems limiting such efforts so far have been the difficulty of financing them and the enormous differentials between earnings from coca and those possible from alternatives. The approach would have much more of a chance for success if demand in the United States could be reduced significantly. Without such a change on the demand side, economic incentives in Peru work powerfully to keep up supply.

Violence

Peru has known many different kinds of violence, although none in the twentieth century as deadly and far-reaching as the struggle with *Sendero luminoso* became in the 1980s. That movement has been in serious disarray since the capture of its leader in September 1992: it maintains some strength but has lost its capacity for the continuous bombings and assassinations that seemed so unstoppable up to that point. The change has

---

by more than half in this period. Similarly, estimates of land use for coca production show a decrease from 268,000 acres in 1993 to 170,000 acres in 1997 (*New York Times*, 1 June

allowed the government, private business, and most of the people of Peru to breathe easier, feel safer, and look with more confidence to the future. It could be a mistake to see this respite as the end of such conflicts. *Sendero* has so far been the worst, but only one, of many kinds of violence. The inequalities that fueled them have not gone away.

At least four major strands have been involved, in different mixtures in different periods: (1) from far back in the colonial period through the eighteenth century, although no longer a realistic force in the twentieth, millenarian ideals envisaging the creation of a wholly new society to restore the integrity of the indigenous peoples, free of the subjugation that has so strongly marked Peruvian history; (2) from the 1920s, multiple versions of Marxism, also envisaging a new society but as an escape from capitalism and imperialism rather than an indigenous ideal; (3) in many periods but perhaps especially in the early postwar years, specific economic and social issues, not confined to Marxism, including access to land and to education, anger against entrenched inequality and special privilege, and lack of any realistic hope that one's children could ever escape poverty; (4) in all periods, fears from the conservative side, and often from the government, that the country will slide into chaos unless violence is used by the military and the police to repress whatever form of protest may be seen as a threat (Flores Galindo 1987; Stern 1987; Gonzales de Olarte 1991).[5]

Objective economic pressures, changing ideological forces, and a serious weakening of the state came together to heighten violence in the postwar years. The objective economic pressures arose from the continuing growth of population relative to land and to opportunities for productive employment, intensified from the mid-1970s by the generalized deterioration of the economy as a whole. Ideological forces, associated with many variants of Marxism, gained strength from the frustrations of an extremely unequal society, from the example of the Cuban revolution, and from the breakdown of attempts at noncommunist reform under the military government of 1968–75.

1998, A12).
5. Nils Jacobsen suggests that the provincial elite did its best to perpetuate an image that the indigenous people were driven by messianic ideals and eternally dangerous, long after they had realistically turned away from such visions toward issues of specific unfair treatment, rights to land, and opportunities for their children (Jacobsen 1993, 340–41, 354). Blaming them for an imagined atavism can still serve as support for repression.

Before the emergence of *Sendero luminoso,* the relative quiet of the first postwar years gave way to repeated outbreaks of rural violence in the sierra, chiefly over access to land, from 1958 to 1963. In 1965 a group of urban intellectuals started what they hoped would become a guerrilla war in the Andes, meant to follow the Castro model in Cuba but in this case quickly suppressed by the army (Brown and Fernández 1991). In urban areas, the MRTA added episodic violence, smaller in scale than *Sendero* but deadly from 1986 into the 1990s. Peru's traditional strongholds of civilized life, its major cities, began to turn into something like daily battlegrounds from the 1960s onward as the strains of massive population growth outran the existing social framework, the opportunities for productive employment, and the ability to maintain public order (Matos Mar 1984; Gonzales de Olarte 1991).

On the order of 21,000 people were killed as a result of political violence in the decade of the 1980s. At least 200,000 people were forced to flee their homes and became displaced persons in and around the major cities (Kirk 1991). In 1990, 44 percent of the victims were "presumed terrorists," and 13 percent were military or police. The others were civilians, victims of both sides (Instituto Cuánto 1992, 442–43; 1993, 254). Robin Kirk emphasizes that the majority of the civilian deaths were Quechua-speaking peasants. "In effect, the civilian population is itself the target in Peru. Its potential neutrality—neither for or against, steering the impossible course between collaboration and rebellion—is a threat to all sides" (Kirk 1991, 3).

Deaths of civilians have to be attributed in considerable measure to actions of the Peruvian military, not just to *Sendero luminoso.* Massacres of peasants by the military, particularly in villages believed to have sympathized with or helped *Sendero,* became frequent in the 1980s. In some of the rare cases in which investigations raised any threat of punishment for the military, witnesses were systematically killed (America's Watch 1992; Degregori 1994). Public protests and congressional investigations did little, except briefly at the beginning of the García administration, to protect human rights or lives.

Both government officials and the general public have been divided between those who oppose military violence against civilians and those who consider the fight against *Sendero* to require a free hand for the military to do whatever it believes to be necessary: divisions much like those in the United States during the Vietnam War. The balance of such pressures changed in significant ways in the 1990s. On the one hand, the Fujimori self-coup of April 1992, closing congress and purging the judiciary, reduced the scope for investigation and possible checks on the military. On the other hand, international pressure helped secure the right of the Red Cross to interview prisoners, the election of a new congress, and the investigation of an episode in 1992 in which a military unit abducted and killed a professor and nine students from the teacher-training university *La Cantuta*. The president displayed remarkable disinterest in that case, but public protests were so vehement that the military responded by sending tanks through the streets of Lima. Two years later, after a sudden change in the law governing judicial procedures made it possible to take the matter out of the hands of civilian courts, a military court held a closed trial and convicted nine officers and enlisted men, with no reported discussion of where their orders came from (Degregori 1994, 88, 98, note 10). The convicted military were released soon afterward under a general amnesty to cover all such cases.

After the Lima police captured the leader of *Sendero luminoso* in 1992, both its own violence and that of the military decreased greatly. That hopeful change still leaves many questions about what accounted for the extraordinary strength of *Sendero* from 1980 to 1992, and what factors might make likely, or prevent, any new version in the future.

Sendero luminoso developed in the 1970s in a part of the sierra that had always been intensely poor and that suffered further deterioration of living conditions in the economic recession of the second half of that decade (McClintock 1984). The movement was not a peasant revolt over land like those of the 1958–63 period. It was led by a university professor, Abamael Guzmán, his students, and some of his colleagues in a break from the conservative main branch of the Communist Party. They were not particularly concerned with issues of land ownership or peasant welfare: their goal was to make way for a wholly new society by destroying the existing one (Degregori 1989, 1990; Palmer 1992). Still, the economic context was a fundamental factor: the young people who were indoctrinated were the children of a stagnating provincial city and a desperately poor rural area. The movement's success grew from genuine misery and blocked futures in the existing society.

A second factor, emphasized by David Scott Palmer, is that the traditional repressive supervision exercised by the large landowners had weakened greatly in the postwar period and had largely disappeared after the land reform. As the old rulers of the rural areas left, nobody replaced them. The government followed its predecessors in leaving the poor rural areas almost entirely to their own fates, leaving the way open for revolutionary organization (Palmer 1992).

A third major factor or necessary condition was that the organizational capacity of the movement's leaders proved to be phenomenal. Much planning and training went into the creation of *Sendero luminoso*'s powerful base before it entered into violent action. The preparation began in the provincial university of Huamanga, at Ayucucho, itself recently reestablished as a part of the reforms of the Velasco government. The core adherents were university students: young people newly given a chance for higher education but in the confines of an extremely poor region and a deteriorating economy. The combination of their objectively dismal outlook with Guzmán's charismatic version of Maoism turned them into a zealous base for widened recruitment and violent action. "As children of the deceived, they are looking for truth. . . . At the root the revolution is perceived by Sendero militants as a means of social mobility" (Degregori 1992, 42–43).

A long tradition of revolutionary groups in Latin America, exemplified by Fidel Castro and Che Guevara, has relied on the conception that oppressed peasants are ready to revolt as soon as any effective leadership shows the way (McCormick 1992). It is up to the leaders to demonstrate by violent actions that repressive authorities can be successfully challenged. If they can do this, the downtrodden poor see that revolution is possible and rise up to follow. In that view, it is action that counts, not mass organization. *Sendero*'s concept was different. It built up support among the young of provincial towns and the surrounding countryside and indoctrinated its adherents with a belief in their own deep understanding of the real world as a precondition for success. Then it undertook a campaign with two sides: righting wrongs for poor communities that had been exploited by moneylenders or corrupt government officials, accompanied by an utterly ruthless use of terror and selective assassination to discourage opposition. Any notably independent and courageous community leader, labor leader, or teacher became a target to drive out or kill to prove that *Sendero* alone knew the way to the truth (McCormick 1992; Isbell 1992; Smith 1992).

Sendero could not have been stopped by economic recovery or generous social programs. It was not interested in such details. It had to be answered by force and by capture of its leaders. Its resulting decline does not change the basic conditions from which it and many other forms of violence have grown. The worst of them remain: extreme inequality, persistent poverty, and a weakened social order.

Conclusions

On one level, the causes of massive rural poverty and of falling food output per capita are evident and unified. The basic problem is a worsening imbalance between the growth of the agricultural labor force and the country's population, relative to the supply and productivity of land available for agriculture. Through the early postwar period, the structure of land ownership and of political control by large landowners made things worse: it aggravated the scarcity of arable land for the great majority of the rural labor force outside the haciendas and denied them education, judicial protection, and political voice. Changing economic and political conditions in the postwar years cleared away the old forms of domination by the large landowners but could not in themselves cure rural poverty: the basic scarcity of land and weakness of productivity remained to hold down rural incomes.

Questions of causation and of possible change go far beyond agriculture itself. Most important, successful management of the economy as a whole would help those people who want to move out of agriculture by providing faster growth of opportunities for productive employment in other activities. More directly, although not in any sense as alternatives, social programs to improve earnings potential and personal mobility, to be discussed in Chapter 6, could do a great deal to raise both incomes and production. Sustained reduction of poverty requires improvements in the quality of rural education, changes in the pattern of public investment, effective taxation to finance higher levels of investment without aggravating inflation, and a structure of incentives systematically favorable for labor-intensive industrial production. The "causes" of rural poverty include limitations and missed opportunities in all these respects, not just constraints in agriculture.

To reduce the number of people trying to make their living from agriculture need not mean increasing the flood of migrants to Lima. The great hope is to develop dynamic regional economies, able to generate income by industrial production and services and to provide new employment alternatives in regions that are now predominantly rural (Gonzales de Olarte 1994, 1996b; Schuldt 1995). Many Peruvians throughout the country's history have had this dream. It has been blocked on the demand side by weak regional markets and on the supply side by limited access to education and lack of skills in the rural labor force. It could be becoming a realistic possibility through broadening access to education and through rural social programs aimed at training for alternative activities.

Agricultural production and income have shown more sustained signs of growth in the 1990s than in any period in the last half century. The combination of reduced violence and improved incentives has clearly helped a great deal. That has helped to reduce rural poverty but needs to be accompanied by rapid growth of openings for productive employment outside agriculture itself. A successful growth pattern would include strong incentives for nontraditional agricultural exports but would almost necessarily emphasize developing new comparative advantages in the industrial sector.

The deadly knot of poverty favoring violence and violence in turn worsening poverty has been loosened to some degree by the capture of the leaders of *Sendero luminoso* and the MRTA. The question is whether the new economic strategy of the 1990s can be guided in ways that provide wide opportunities for productive employment and gradual escape from poverty. In an environment of deep poverty and inequality, improving macroeconomic performance cannot rule out recurrent violent movements (Figueroa 1993, 1997). Directing macroeconomic performance toward reduction of inequality might make all the difference in the world.

5

INDUSTRIALIZATION, EMPLOYMENT, AND THE INFORMAL SECTOR

The goal of industrialization took on something of a mystic character in early postwar Latin America, for both economic and social-political reasons. On the economic side, industrialization was seen as the essence of modernization, expected to change the structure of production toward markets with stronger potential for growth, to raise employment and productivity, to foster entrepreneurship, and to provide an escape from dependence on primary exports. On the social side, it was seen as a way to open up new opportunities for people coming from outside traditionally dominant groups, to strengthen workers and industrialists relative to landowners, and in general to weaken the forces opposed to change. On the crucial question of relationships between industrialists and workers, two very different visions came together to support industrialization: one of them aiming at greater scope for labor organization and political strength in the hope of radical change, the other believing that class conflict might be moderated by a "developmentalist alliance" between workers and industrialists, based on shared gains from the rising value of industrial production (O'Donnell 1973, 55–59).

The concept of industrialization as a goal in its own right, to be pursued by selectively favorable economic policies, naturally ran against the particular interests of landowners and others involved in international trade and finance and also ran contrary to basic ideas of economic efficiency. Efficiency criteria are not opposed to industrialization per se, but the classic vision of growth through an open economy rejected selective intervention to promote it. Industry should be expected to grow with development, but its structure and rate of growth should vary according to each country's resource base and pattern of comparative advantages. This view, of course, aims at ruling out selective intervention and avoids any explicit position on possible connections to social change.

Peru did not join the Latin American countries that adopted proindustrialization policies in the 1930s, but growing pressures in favor of change began to break through in the 1950s: even the conservative government in office at the end of that decade joined, cautiously, the region's "search for *deliberate industrialization*" (Vega-Centeno 1988, 13–14). Its *Ley de promoción industrial* in 1959 specified protection for that purpose, as distinct from use of tariffs for revenue. This legislation was soon followed by the election of Belaúnde on a platform promising stronger action to promote industrialization and then by the Velasco government's much more radical program. Succeeding governments rejected many of Velasco's reforms, and two of them retreated from high protection, but until 1990 none repudiated the idea of promoting industrialization. Again, as in Velasco's movement in the opposite direction, the Fujimori government went beyond the gradual stages and compromises of most other Latin American governments to an extreme version of the new approach. Nothing in its statements or actions so far hints of any special concern for industrialization.

The main questions in this chapter concern the consequences, for industry, for labor, and for the economy, of the country's long period of attempts to promote industry and of the subsequent reversal of that strategy in 1990. The first section focuses on the growth and problems of manufacturing, the second and third sections on employment and wages, the fourth section on organized labor, and the fifth section on the country's large informal sector.

Manufacturing: Trends and Problems

Peruvian manufacturing grew rapidly from 1950 to 1965 under conditions of relatively modest protection. As measured in Table 5.1, its share of

Table 5.1. Value added in manufacturing as a share of GDP, and rates of growth of manufacturing output by selected subperiods, 1950–1997

	Percentage of GDP at 1979 Prices	Annual Rates of Growth	
		Period	Percentage
1950	19.4		
		1950–65	7.7
1965	25.5		
		1965–80	3.7
1980	24.5		
		1980–90[a]	−(1.7)
1990	21.7		
		1990–97	5.4
1997	21.8		

SOURCES: For 1950 to 1980, INE 1989, 93; for growth rate 1980–90, Instituto Cuánto 1993, 368; for 1990–97, BCRP 1998, 151.
[a] 1980–90 growth rate measured at constant prices of 1986.

GDP increased from 19 percent in 1950 to 26 percent by 1965. As protection increased, its growth slowed, and its share of GDP fell. The negative association between protection and the pace of industrialization might be seen as little more than a coincidence: the erratic course of the economy as a whole dragged down the industrial sector, along with everything else, first in the forced contraction of the second half of the 1970s and then in the disastrous mismanagement of the second half of the 1980s (Chapter 7). On one level, this explanation is reasonable, but on another, it just opens up more questions. Was the poor performance of the economy as a whole partly caused or aggravated by the policies used to promote industrialization?[1]

Two indicators of degrees of protection are given for various years in Table 5.2: average effective protection for industry as calculated from tariff rates and the number of products for which imports were prohibited. In general, protection relied chiefly on tariff rates before the 1970s (when tariffs themselves were low), then much more heavily on quantitative restrictions in the 1970s and again from 1985 to 1990. In between, under the Belaúnde government from 1980 to 1985, tariff rates were cut considerably, and very few imports were prohibited, although effective protection still averaged much higher than before 1965.

Up to the late 1960s, the underlying factor governing changes in rates of industrial production was the course of earnings from primary exports.

---
1. Mario Tello explains and analyzes many alternative hypotheses in his study of Peruvian industry (Tello 1993, 25–98).

Table 5.2. Degrees of industrial sector protection against imports as measured by effective protection and by number of tariff positions for which imports were prohibited, 1955–1991

	Effective Tariff Protection, Percentage	Prohibited Imports as of December	
		Number of Tariff Positions	Percentage of All Tariff Positions
1955	31		
1963	22		
1973	118		
1978	—	1,852	40.0
1980	57	7	0.1
1985	87	525	10.0
1988	83	539	10.0
1991[a]	24	0	0.0

SOURCES: Tello 1993, 105–6, for all except 1991; Rossini 1991, 3, for June 1991.
[a] Measure for 1991 is for June, following the tariff reductions implemented in March.

Rising earnings from exports stimulated domestic demand, and the increasing availability of foreign exchange allowed firms to raise their imports of equipment and supplies to increase production (Tello 1990, 39–48). The counterpart was of course that periods of falling primary exports cut industrial growth as well. The industrial sector had no independent capacity to pay for its own foreign exchange requirements.

The change toward higher protection in the 1960s was in part intended to free industrial investment from such dependence on primary exports, and in fact it broke down their previously close positive relation. For the period 1970–87, the two variables show systematic negative rather than positive correlation. The basic reason was that expansionary policies of governments, rather than increases in exports, became the leading source of growth in demand.

Domestically induced expansion implied the need for increased imports, but without providing increased earnings from exports to pay for them. To make the imbalance worse, rising demand pulled into the domestic market supplies of primary products that could otherwise have gone into exports (Tello 1990). The solution attempted by the Velasco government in the 1970s was to turn to external borrowing on a large scale. That tactic worked as long as foreign lenders were not worried, but as soon as they called a halt to further credit, domestic expansion had to stop. Conditions of external credit, rather than the course of exports, became the key constraint.

External credit for Peru turned extremely tight by 1975, as the country's debts mounted but its export earnings did not. That loss of access to credit forced an adjustment program that included both domestic contraction and devaluation. Industrial growth slowed, but the devaluations stimulated industrial producers to turn to exports on a significant scale for the first time. Favorable trends of export demand for primary products in the same period led to an extraordinary rise in total exports and helped restore the confidence of foreign lenders. This combination permitted a new burst of growth, although for a shorter period this time, from 1979 to 1982. As soon as external balance was restored, the same process of rising deficits and expanding domestic credit was repeated from 1985 to 1987.

The imports used by the industrial sector consistently exceeded its exports. Its separate trade deficit rose from $0.4 billion in 1970 to a peak of $1.5 billion in 1975 during this relatively prolonged boom, then from $0.7 billion in 1979 to twice that level in 1982, and again from $0.6 billion in 1985 to $1.1 billion in 1987 (Caller and Chuecas 1989, 24). Some part of these deficits could be seen as a natural manifestation of comparative disadvantage: a country with a strong export surplus for its primary sectors can be expected to have an approximately equivalent deficit for its industrial sector. The problem is that, when growing import requirements for the industrial sector outrun exports, the Peruvian impasse is bound to return.

If Peruvian industry had been able to raise its own exports fast enough to keep pace with its production—in something even slightly like the East Asian pattern of expansion led by industrial exports—then the industrial sector itself and the whole economy could have maintained a high rate of growth. The positive performance of industrial exports from 1975 to 1980, discussed in Chapter 3, suggests that such a result was by no means impossible. Although exports of manufactures were almost insignificant up to 1975, they increased from $38 million in that year to $553 million five years later (Table 3.4).

The strikingly positive performance from 1975 to 1980 could be credited in part to the protectionist policies starting in the 1960s. These policies initially stimulated industrial investment and thereby created new potential to export, but that potential could not have been realized—it was not in fact realized—as long as the real exchange rate kept moving adversely for export incentives. When the adjustment program of 1975–79 combined rapid devaluation of the real exchange rate with some degree of restraint on domestic demand, the industrial sector turned seriously and successfully toward exports. Correspondingly, the paralysis of industrial export growth in the decade of the 1980s is hardly surprising in view of the combination of renewed appreciation of the real exchange rate with repeated bursts of excess domestic demand.

To place so much emphasis on the exchange rate as a determinant of export incentives is not meant to downgrade a more fundamental requirement: the ability of producers to reduce costs, improve quality, introduce new products, and establish contacts with export markets. For the East Asian countries that achieved such remarkable success with industrial exports, the exchange rate regime was an essential help, but it was not the key. Japan started its postwar export drive with an undervalued currency, and South Korea used devaluation when necessary to offset inflation, but the underlying determinants of success were rapid improvement of productivity and continuous introduction of new and higher quality export products (Amsden 1989, 1994).

Research on technological change in Peruvian industry has been consistent in finding that it has so far been relatively weak (Vega-Centeno 1989, 1993; Iguíñiz and Muñoz 1992, 163–70). Mario Tello adds the consideration that the industrial sector has been slow either to develop backward linkages to new domestic suppliers or to take advantage of economies of diversification (Tello 1993, 99–176). Such patterns of behavior are hardly unusual for developing countries: it takes a long time to develop the needed skills and the confidence to enter fields of rapid technological change. Peru's technical base, especially in the numbers of people with training in scientific research, has been decidedly weak (Chapter 2). Still, the numbers of engineers and even people in basic sciences began to rise rapidly in the 1970s; more might have been done to draw on this improving background, for at least modest increases in research and innovation. On that score, protection was not ideal.

A leading feature of protection is that firms can cover their costs by raising prices and can get by without great effort to improve quality, because they have little reason to fear any competition from outsiders. Innovative actions take effort. To create conditions under which innovation is unnecessary makes it less likely than it otherwise would have been. The contrasting behavior of so many producers in East Asia may well owe something to a strong work ethic, but it also owes a great deal to the deliberate efforts of governments to promote industrial sectors able to compete in export markets. Government help was available only for those firms able to maintain competitive quality and prices and to extend their markets through product innovation. Peruvian industrialization policies lacked the force of any such drive to export or of any effective substitute from competition in domestic markets.

The slowdown of industrial growth under protection was also due in part to a sharp decrease in foreign investment from the last years of the 1960s. Foreign investment had become important early in the twentieth century in minerals extraction, then gradually spread into domestic industry as well. One estimate of its extent is that firms under foreign control owned 46 percent of the fixed assets of all large manufacturing businesses by 1969 (FitzGerald 1979, 274).[2] In periods of particularly conservative governments, notably in the 1920s and again in the 1950s, everything possible was done to encourage foreign investment. In both these periods, it responded strongly—perhaps too strongly, from many points of view. Foreign investment helped to finance and fortify nondemocratic governments, it may have precluded potential Peruvian producers from developing entrepreneurial skills, it permitted foreign concerns to control the majority of the country's exports, and it held down the share of export earnings returned to Peru (Thorp and Bertram 1978). Still, whether it provided adequate offsetting value or not, foreign investment contributed to the high rate of industrial growth from 1950 to 1965, and its fall at the end of the decade slowed further industrialization.

At the end of the 1960s, Peruvian policy under the Velasco government turned strongly against foreign investment. Expropriations, state purchases of foreign-owned firms, and evident hostility to foreign investors in general set foreign investment on a downward path through the 1970s. After a modest revival in the first half of the 1980s, hostility from the government of Alan García drove foreign investment down again in the second half of the decade (Gonzales de Olarte 1996b, 15).

In the early 1990s, the Fujimori government reassured investors as well as everyone else by bringing down inflation and went out of its way to make foreign investment welcome once again. When the Lima police captured most of the leaders of *Sendero luminoso* in 1992, the reversal of basic conditions was practically complete. Investment and industrial production rose strongly: from 1990 to 1997, value added by manufacturing increased 5.4 percent a year (Table 5.1).

---

2. *Control* in this case is taken to mean ownership of more than 20 percent of the equity of the firms concerned.

Trade liberalization allowed imports of manufactures to rise greatly through the first half of the 1990s, but the increase in domestic demand pulled industrial production up as well. Liberalization did not set back the industrial sector in any absolute sense. On the contrary, its output grew much faster than in the 1970s and 1980s. Still, in a relative sense the sector lost ground: imports of manufactures increased more rapidly than domestic production. In addition, several lines of production were reduced in absolute terms. The hardest hit were automobiles, electrical equipment, and paper products (Saavedra 1997a, 43–44).

The increase in import coefficients and the setbacks to some specific products were not due exclusively to reduction of protection. Relative prices of imports and of tradable goods in general were reduced by allowing the exchange rate to rise in real terms. The industrial sector is not dead or dying, but it needs the help of a competitive exchange rate and, even more fundamentally, the help of an increased effort to improve productivity and product quality.

With so many different factors playing important roles, it is simplistic and inaccurate to conclude that the weakness of industrialization from 1965 to 1990 was caused by protection and the other measures of intervention intended to favor it. Still, the core systematic problem was the self-contradictory character of the industrialization strategy. Successful industrialization requires development of competitive industries able to restrain costs and keep up with technological change. Reliance on protection may provide some initial help to induce investment in new directions, but if it remains the central method it undermines the motivation vital for development of a strong industrial sector. A wish to restrain the pressures of the external world is certainly understandable, but a wish to create a dynamic industrial sector requires going in the opposite direction to find ways to participate in it actively.

Employment

Poverty and violence have been worse in the last three decades than they might otherwise have been because employment conditions have been miserable. Between 1970 and 1990, the number of people trying to survive by selling in the streets, the *vendedores ambulantes,* increased from 3 percent of Lima's active labor force to 13 percent (Table 5.3). In the same period, regular wage and salaried employees of private-sector businesses

Table 5.3. Structure of employment in Lima, 1970, 1990, and 1995

	Percentage of Labor Force			Growth Rate	
	1970	1990	1995	1970–90	1990–95
Private sector companies					
Wage workers					
Unionized	12.4	4.8	2.4	0.5	−8.6
Nonunionized	14.0	15.9	17.5	6.1	7.1
Salaried workers					
Professionals[a]	1.7	4.6	6.4	10.8	12.2
Nonuniversity	18.0	13.7	18.3	4.0	11.3
Total private sector	46.1	39.0	44.6	4.5	7.9
Public sector					
Professionals[a]	2.2	4.7	3.7	9.5	0.1
Nonuniversity	10.2	10.5	6.4	5.6	−4.9
Total public sector	12.4	15.2	10.1	6.5	−3.3
Informal sector					
Independent nonprofessional	15.7	14.9	15.0	5.1	5.2
Street vendors	2.5	13.1	11.6	14.5	2.5
Owners of microenterprise and others[b]	13.4	12.7	15.0	5.1	8.6
Total informal	31.6	40.7	41.6	6.8	5.5
Household workers	9.8	5.1	4.7	2.0	3.3
Total active labor force				5.4	5.0

SOURCE: Adapted from Verdera 1994, 21, for 1970–90; information for 1990–95 supplied by Verdera from work in progress.
[a] Professionals identified as university graduates.
[b] "Others" includes independent drivers of taxis and buses, independent professionals, and unpaid family labor.

fell from 46 to 39 percent of Lima's labor force. Real earnings of workers fell greatly, although problems of measurement have led to widely different estimates of the degree.

From 1970 to 1990, the active labor force in Lima increased at a rate of 5.4 percent a year. Salaried employment in the (formal) private sector grew more slowly at 4.5 percent a year. The difference was made up by rising employment in the public sector, which grew at 6.5 percent a year, and by an even faster growth of employment in the informal sector. These relations improved in the first half of the 1990s, both because of rising production and because the rate of growth of Lima's labor force slowed, from 5.4 percent a year in the preceding two decades to 5.0 percent for 1990–95. Employment in the formal private sector recovered from 39 to 45 percent of the active labor force, just barely below its share in 1970.

Still, public-sector employment was cut so sharply in this period that the informal sector continued to grow despite the improvement of private-sector employment.

The period of economic recovery from 1993 through 1996, well past the initial shock of liberalization and stabilization, provides a good test of the power of the new economic strategy to improve employment conditions. In Lima, salaried employment in the formal sector grew at an annual rate of 3.2 percent (Saavedra-Chanduvi 1998, 27). That rate was much higher than in the previous seven years, but still too low to keep up with the growth of the city's labor force. Employment in the informal sector grew more than twice as fast. Self-employed workers other than professionals and technicians, already one-third of the labor force in 1993, increased by 5.1 percent a year.

The help in opening up new employment opportunities, which everyone expected from industrialization, was frustrated in the 1970–90 period because of all the factors limiting industrial growth itself and possibly also because of a tendency toward a capital-intensive, labor-saving structure of production. The manufacturing sector's share of total employment fell between 1950 and 1980, despite the rise in its share of GDP (Tables 3.1 and 3.2). Long periods of appreciation of the real exchange rate worked persistently to hold down the costs of importing labor-saving capital equipment. The methods of labor protection introduced by the Velasco government may have hurt as well, by increasing the costs of using long-term workers (Chapter 7). A potentially important offset was lost by the lack of any drive to develop labor-intensive industrial exports. Jointly, all these factors held the employment coefficient of industrial production lower than it could have been.

Employment in industrial firms with 100 or more workers rose in the boom of the first years of the García government but fell precipitously from 1988 on. The downtrend continued with little break in the first years of economic liberalization, from 1991 through 1994. At that point, employment in large industrial firms was barely 60 percent of its 1988 peak. It did not recover at all in the period 1994–97, despite the rapid growth of the economy in these years (BCRP 1998b, 66). That stagnation was probably due both to the removal of protection and to changes in labor legislation that made it easier to use subcontracting and to discharge workers. A broader measure of manufacturing employment in all urban areas and in small firms as well as large gives a more positive picture. Employment in manufacturing as a whole increased slightly from 1985 to 1991 (0.5 percent a year) and then by 4.5 percent a year from 1991 to 1994 (Saavedra 1997a, 49–52).

Did liberalization hurt employment in manufacturing? In an absolute sense, clearly not: it increased more rapidly after 1991 than it had in the preceding two decades. Still, the growth of employment was slower than expected on the basis of previous relations between output and employment (Infante 1997). Furthermore, the growth in production itself, although historically high, may have been held below its potential by the steep rise of imported manufactures. Jaime Saavedra has made a heroic attempt to estimate how much employment in manufacturing may have been "lost" (or not gained) because of the increase of imports relative to domestic production. He estimates that manufacturing employment could have risen to a level about 12 percent higher than it actually did if the increase of industrial production had matched the rise of demand for industrial products (Saavedra 1997a).

Rates of open unemployment give another, although weak, indicator of the possible effects of liberalization. Open unemployment is not the core concern: the fundamental problem is the high share of employment in occupations of such low productivity that workers cannot escape from poverty (Hunt 1997; Verdera 1997b). Open unemployment involves far fewer people, but it can vary, from less than 5 percent in 1987 to a range of 8 to 10 percent in the 1990s (Table 5.4).

For young workers, ages 14 to 24, it averaged 16 percent for 1995–97. The pattern over time shows surprisingly little effect from the strong recovery of the economy in the 1990s: open unemployment came down slightly after 1993 but not to the extent that it had during earlier periods of expansion (Infante 1997). That picture probably reflects two combined effects of the new economic strategy: cutbacks of employment in the public sector and increased pressure on firms to hold down labor costs in the face of intensified competition from imports. Liberalization did not create weak employment conditions—they have been woefully weak for a very long time—but its initial effect was to limit the improvement that might otherwise have accompanied the recovery of output.

Wages

Caught between rapid growth of the urban labor force and weak trends of investment and output, workers took a severe beating from deteriorat-

Table 5.4. Open unemployment in urban areas, selected years from 1980 to 1997 (percentage of labor force unemployed)

	Metropolitan Lima	All Urban Areas	
		Total	Ages 14–24
1980	7.1		
1981		6.6	
1987	4.8		
1990	8.5		
1993	9.9	8.5	
1994	8.8		
1995	7.9	8.4	17.4
1996	8.0	7.9	15.1
1997	9.2	8.3	14.6

SOURCES: Infante 1997, 186, for column 1 through 1990; ILO 1996 for column 1, 1993–95; BCRP 1998, 41–42 for 1996–97 estimates for Lima and 1995–97 for all urban areas; Verdera 1997a for all urban areas in 1981 and 1993.

ing real wages through the quarter century from 1965 to 1990. Some governments tried to stop the deterioration either by directly intervening in wage setting or by using currency overvaluation, and at times by subsidizing imports of food as well, to bring the prices of tradable goods down relative to wage rates. The Fujimori government has emphatically rejected direct intervention but in practice has used one of the same policies as the Velasco and García governments: holding down import prices by appreciation of the currency in real terms, favoring an import surplus that has the effect of making real wages higher than they would otherwise have been. Real wages have been helped in the short run at the cost of making it difficult to improve employment conditions.

Real wages in manufacturing increased in the 1950s and early 1960s, stopped growing in the 1965–70 period, then fell 13 percent in the 1970s (Webb 1977, 241; Table 5.5). They reached an intervening peak in the middle of that decade, but this level was unsustainable because it relied on a heavy import surplus: the deficit on current account was equal to 10 percent of GDP. When the country was forced to eliminate that external deficit, real wages fell.

Real wages dropped even more sharply through the 1980s, although a serious problem of measurement has given rise to markedly different estimates. The problem is that official measures of changes in the consumer price index exaggerated the degree of inflation (Escobal and Castillo 1994; Escobal and Aguero 1996). If the official price index is used to deflate nominal wages, real wages seem to have plunged by two-thirds between

Table 5.5. Index of real wages in manufacturing 1965–1980, and two alternative indexes for wages of hourly paid workers in the private sector, 1980–1990

	Manufacturing Wages in Lima (1965 = 100)	Hourly Paid Workers in the Private Sector, National (1980 = 100)	
		Using Official Price Index[a]	Using Geometric Price Index
1965	100		
1970	101		
1975	118		
1980	88	100	100
1985		65	74
1990		34	68

SOURCES: PREALC 1982, 166, for column 1; Saavedra 1997b, 25, for columns 2 and 3.
[a] The consumer price index was subject to considerable distortion in the 1980s; its use to calculate real wages overstates their decrease. The alternative geometric price index adjusts for problems of measurement under conditions of high inflation and gives a more accurate picture of the decrease in this decade (see text).

1980 and 1990. With an alternative index of consumer prices, a "geometric index" designed to reduce distortions associated with high inflation, the fall was closer to one-third. On either basis, wages were clearly much lower in 1990 than in 1980 and almost surely lower than in 1965.

The official consumer price index seems more reliable for changes in the 1990s. Both the official and the geometric indexes indicate that real wages for urban workers rose 12 percent from 1991 to 1994 (Saavedra 1997b, 27). The disquieting side is that 1994 may have been another transitory peak: wages of hourly paid (blue-collar) workers started falling again despite the strong rise of the economy. By 1997, they were back below the depressed level of 1991 (Fig. 5.1).

This apparent contrast between trends in real wages and in production starting in 1995 could be yet another problem of undependable official statistics. The accuracy of the series of average real wages used for Figure 5.1 has often been questioned. Still, pending any new research that changes the picture for 1995–97, the contrast is worth noting as a reminder of the continuing basic weakness of labor markets. It also suggests an interesting connection between real wages and currency appreciation. From December 1990 through December 1994, the real price of foreign exchange fell by 25 percent (Table 8.1). Combined with lower tariffs, that fall brought prices of tradable goods down relative to nominal wages: a change in relative prices that could account for most or all of the rise of real wages for 1991–94. The fall in the real price of foreign exchange then stopped;

Fig. 5.1. Indexes of real wages for hourly paid workers in Lima, for firms with ten or more employees, and of the real minimum wage, 1990–97.

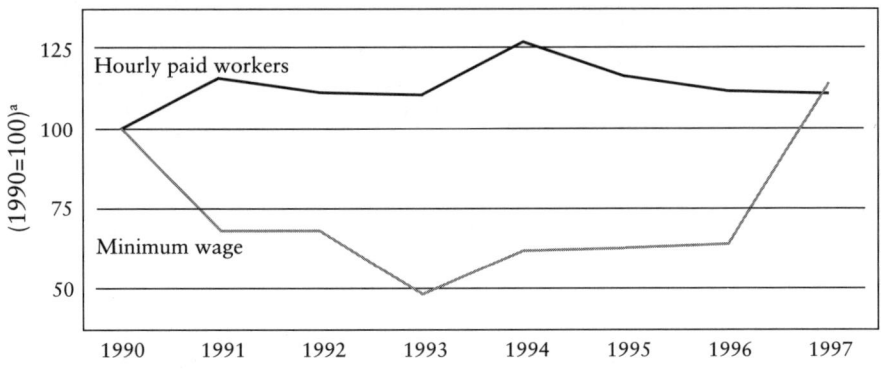

Sources: BCRP 1995, 73; BCRP 1998b, 65.
[a] Data converted to year 1990 from published base of August 1990. (August is a misleading base: it was the month of the Fujishock, in which real wages plunged far below the average for the year.)

the real exchange rate barely moved between December 1994 and December 1997, exactly when, according to the data used for Figure 5.1, real wages stopped rising. The indication that they actually fell instead of holding steady could be a statistical error but does not seem inherently unlikely in a context of continuing basic imbalance between people searching for regular employment and the inadequate opportunities open to them.

Can market forces alone be expected to raise living standards of Peruvian workers at any time in the foreseeable future? That question is serious in light of the record of such a prolonged downward trend. Francisco Verdera explains many doubts and also points to the fundamental question: a sustainable upward trend for real wages requires rising productivity (Verdera 1997a, 1997b). If output per worker cannot be increased, the case is hopeless.

Productivity gains cannot be decreed or guaranteed by any direct choice of economic policy. They become more likely if slower growth of the labor force makes it easier to provide adequate capital per worker, more likely if economic management provides better conditions for sustained growth, and even more likely if better quality education can be offered to more people. Beyond these basic determinants, liberalization of the economy should also be favorable because it puts greater pressure on businesses to search for technological changes that should help raise productivity. To return to higher protection would decrease the possibilities for long-term increases in real wages.

Direct intervention in labor markets could help or hurt according to the form it takes. It could help considerably if it consists of support for on-the-job training in new skills, of active concern for worker safety, of promotional measures to encourage expansion into export markets, and of support for research and development to help firms become more competitive than they could on their own. It could hurt if it consisted of measures that directly raise the cost of labor, as it now does through a host of taxes and forced saving based on wages, or if it consisted of actions like the decrees of the García government to raise all wages arbitrarily.

Direct intervention could help reduce poverty and inequality and would be unlikely to significantly hurt the competitive position of firms if focused on protection of minimum wages as distinct from generalized increases.[3] The Fujimori government maintained minimum wage protection but undermined it by driving the real minimum wage down drastically from 1990 through 1995 (Fig. 5.1). That policy, which seemed to be an expression of the government's determination to emphasize reliance on private market forces, was suddenly reversed in the next two years. In two quick jumps, the minimum wage was raised in real terms, by December 1997, to a level more than double that of December 1995. The jumps were so steep that they may well have caused trouble for some firms. Although the pitiless repression of the preceding five years certainly did call for correction, it would have been less disruptive to start earlier and move more gradually. Still, much better late than never.

Organized Labor

Organized labor has rarely had any great impact either on economic policy in general or on the course of real wages in Peru, although it has at times won major confrontations in particular cases. It was never as potent as in Argentina, Chile, or Venezuela. Organization was discouraged by law

---

3. Debates about the possibility that increases in minimum wages could discourage employment of low-skill workers will never end: the evidence is so mixed that even the most careful analysts disagree. A recent investigation of the consequences for a wide range of developing countries concludes that protection of minimum wages systematically lessens poverty but also that it can have negative effects on employment (Lustig and McLeod 1996).

and by direct repression in some periods, notably the 1920s and again from 1948 to 1956. Unionization was more readily accepted in the late 1940s under the Bustamente government and again during the second Prado government, but the great majority of unions were small and highly local. The major exceptions were the textile workers, bank clerks, and later the particularly aggressive union of school teachers. As of 1962, about 15 percent of the nonagricultural labor force was unionized (Payne 1965, 27–55, 129–31).

The Velasco government changed labor regulations greatly to facilitate organization. More new unions were given legal recognition from 1968 to 1975 than in all Peruvian history (Stevens 1983). By 1970, unionized workers in blue-collar jobs (hourly and daily paid workers), were almost equal to nonunionized workers in Lima's private sector (Table 5.3).

During the economic contraction that followed the deficits of the Velasco government, employment conditions worsened, real wages began to come down, and organized labor made its first nationwide attempts to stem the tide. An impressive general strike in July 1977 seemed to announce a basic change in relations between labor and the rest of the society. The military government that replaced General Velasco returned to direct intervention against strikes and to arrests of labor leaders as a solution (Conaghan and Malloy 1994, 104–6, 148–49). With repression back and employment conditions worsening, organized labor's strength went into a long decline.

Peruvian workers turned away from organization after the 1970s mainly because employment conditions were so poor that their bargaining power was gravely weakened, but perhaps also in some degree because of the changing composition of the urban labor force. As more and more migrants entered from the sierra, they proved to be much less interested than established urban workers in following class-based policies of confrontation. They were not as inclined to view themselves as members of the working class; they considered employment in factories as something temporary, chiefly to accumulate savings to start a store or other small business of their own (Adams and Valdivia 1994). For them, "to be a worker is a somewhat relative matter" (Parodi 1986). Peruvian labor leaders have a tough role to play, in all directions.

The basic strategy of the Fujimori government has not been labor friendly. The limited forms of job security remaining from the reforms of the Velasco government have been dismantled as obstructions to the "flexibility" of labor markets. Flexibility means mostly that firms should not be faced with restrictions on their control of working conditions or their decisions to discharge workers. A series of changes in labor legislation from 1991 through 1995 took away the remnants of earlier protection against dismissal and placed new limits on the scope of labor organization (Verdera 1997b, 17–25). The share of salaried workers in the private sector covered by collective bargaining contracts fell from 21 percent in 1985 to 11 percent by 1994 (Saavedra-Chanduvi and Díaz 1998, table 8).

The changes in labor legislation and decrease in union membership left labor markets in Peru back in much the same unprotected state as they had been a half century before. They may also have had the effect of reducing inequality among wage earners. Unionization had favored relative equality among the workers covered by collective bargaining but widened inequality in the labor force as a whole by raising wages of unionized workers relative to nonunionized. In 1991, 38 percent of the private-sector workers in the top quintile of earnings were covered by collective bargaining, compared with only 10 percent of the workers in the lowest quintile (Saavedra-Chanduvi and Díaz 1998, table 9). As unionization decreased in the 1990s, inequalities among wage earners decreased too. The other side of the coin is that wages fell relative to higher incomes from property ownership.

The High Importance of the Informal Sector

The informal sector is a supremely heterogeneous collection of activities that play many different roles in the economy. It is jointly an escape hatch from legal constraints, an opening for personal independence, and a last-ditch form of survival in a society that has not provided sufficient opportunities for productive employment.

The sector includes a high and still-growing share of all urban workers, some with incomes that are above-average wages for regular employment in the legal private sector but many with abysmal productivity and incomes. These workers and small firms are outside the law in that they are not officially registered, are not covered by the social security system, and can usually avoid any regulation. They necessarily pay value-added taxes on what they buy from the formal sector, but normally not on their earnings.

The question of how many people make their living in the informal sector has received many different answers, according to the particular definitions and measures used. Table 5.6 gives two measures for the share

Table 5.6. Estimates of the percentages of workers in the informal sector and of domestic workers, Lima, 1970–1996

	Informal Workers as Percentages of the Labor Force in Lima[a]		Household Workers as Percentages of the Labor Force in Lima Table 5.3
	Table 5.3	Saavedra	
1970	31.6	—	9.8
1986	—	43.2	—
1990	40.7	46.8	5.1
1995	41.6	50.8	4.7
1996	—	53.4	4.2

SOURCES: Table 5.3; Saavedra-Chanduvi 1998, 27.
[a] Informal workers defined as self-employed excluding professionals, unpaid family workers, and both owners and employees in firms with less than five employees. Domestic workers not included.

of Lima's labor force working in the informal sector, for selected years from 1970 to 1995. Although they differ about levels, their trends provide a useful picture of the sector's growing importance. The series that goes back to 1970 indicates a substantial increase in the number of people involved: they increased at a rate of 7.1 percent a year from then to 1990. The rate of growth then slowed to 5.5 percent a year in the first half of the 1990s, still slightly higher than that of the active labor force.

The higher measures in the second series of estimates reinforce the picture of the sector's continued growth in the 1990s. Even higher percentages are reported for all urban areas (not just Lima), in a helpful multicountry study of the informal sector (Marcouiller, Ruiz de Castilla, and Woodward, 1997, 369). This study uses two measures, the first based on the size of microenterprise and the second on social security coverage. For the first, firms are counted in this sector if they have five or fewer employees. On this basis, the authors estimate that the informal sector included 58 percent of the country's urban labor force in 1985. The second alternative, the share of workers not under social security, gives a still higher measure, 62 percent.[4] With the first definition, Peru's informal sector included a considerably higher proportion of urban labor than did those of either El Salvador or Mexico: 58 percent in Peru, 48 in El Salvador,

---

4. The basic data for Peru in this article come from the Living Standards Measurement Study carried out for the World Bank for 1985–86. One of the papers (Suarez-Berenguela 1988) reviews many different measures and analyses of Peru's informal sector.

and 31 in Mexico.⁵ The productive activities of the sector account for a high proportion of personal services and retail sales as well as considerable industrial production. More than 80 percent of the workers in personal services and retail trade were in the informal sector at the time of the three-country comparative study, either self-employed or unregistered workers and owners in very small firms. In manufacturing, the two main activities for the informal sector are clothing and footwear: the share of informal employment has also been close to 80 percent for both of them (Vega Castro 1989; Marcouiller, Ruiz de Castilla, and Woodward 1997, 373).

A study of the informal sector in Mexico provides a helpful breakdown of its activities, presumably applicable to Peru as well. The categories used are self-employment, informal salaried workers in microenterprise, and workers under contract to firms in the formal sector. In Mexico, the self-employed group as a whole and the contract workers have consistently higher average earnings than workers in formal-sector employment (Maloney 1997, fig. 3). At the other end of the spectrum, hired workers in microenterprise have consistently lower earnings than any other group, far below workers in the formal sector. The Mexican informal sector differs from that of Peru in that its average earnings, taking all groups together, have been higher than those in the formal sector. The reverse is true in Peru, most strongly so for women workers (Marcouiller, Ruiz de Castilla, and Woodward 1997, 377–78).

Many workers are in the informal sector by their own choice, often earning more than they could have under wage employment in the formal sector. Many others are there against their preferences, forced into it by the lack of adequate openings for employment in the formal sector. An intriguing study of the labor market in Lima in 1994 concluded that two-thirds of the workers in the informal sector earned more than they would be expected to earn in formal employment, based on their education and other determinants of wage differentials (Yamada, Felices, Ramos, and Ruiz 1996, 84–85, 151–78). The other one-third were victims of persistently weak opportunities for employment in the formal sector.

---

5. A regional review by the International Labor Office gives a different picture, with closely similar measures of the urban informal sector in nearly all Latin American cities and countries included in the estimates (ILO 1996, 32–33). The only exception is Montevideo, which stands out for a small informal sector. This exception is consistent with evidence that Uruguay has the region's lowest percentage of people in poverty, but the reported near-equality of all the

Informal sectors include positive economic functions that grow at higher levels of income. They also include so many activities with low productivity that one normally expects the sector to lose importance in the course of development. Estimates of the share of informal employment in the United States indicate that its level in 1900 was comparable to that of Latin America now, but the U.S. level fell steadily through the next three decades. Self-employed workers as a share of the labor force fell from 34 percent in 1900 to 23 percent by 1930 (Castells and Portes 1989, 19). Why have the corresponding shares in Peru and much of the rest of Latin America continued to go up?

The most highly publicized study for Peru, by Hernando de Soto, argues that the main reason has been the constraints imposed by excessive regulation. On the face of it, that explanation does not seem relevant for a significant informal sector in the United States at the beginning of the twentieth century or in Peru in the 1950s: neither economy was subject to any extensive regulation at these times. It may be more applicable to Peru in the 1970s and 1980s, when two powerful factors ran into conflict with each other: a rising tide of migration from the country to the cities and a major increase in governmental regulation.

Most migrants have come from communities in which ways of earning a living are bound in traditional family and community relationships. Production is carried out on a self-employed or very small scale basis with a minimum of the accounting, financial, and legal complications of modern society. New migrants look for work and guidance to their predecessors, especially to relatives from the same communities, and carry on much the same activities as they did at home. They re-create in Lima the informal activities they have always known. In this interpretation, the informal sector is largely a cultural phenomenon, by no means explicable in purely economic terms (Golte and Adams 1990; Adams and Valdivia 1994).

De Soto's interpretation did not deny the relevance of such cultural factors but emphasized the obstacles faced by the migrants when they try to gain legal authorization to initiate productive activities in the cities. His analysis gave high credit to the entrepreneurship and productivity of the migrants and contradicted any notion of people who dodge the law to gain unfair advantages. It also documented telling evidence of unnecessary costs and delays imposed by regulation. De Soto helped change the public vision of the sector and even managed—in the face of the chaos of the late

---

others is inconsistent with differences brought out in other international comparisons (García 1993; Marcouiller, Ruiz de Castillo, and Woodward 1997).

1980s—to get the García government to make changes that considerably reduced the costs and delays of starting up a business and transferring property (Bromley 1994).

As regulatory obstacles to property transfers were reduced and all kinds of economic regulation were cut back or eliminated in the first half of the 1990s, the informal sector kept growing. This fact makes de Soto's insistence on the dominant role of regulation much less convincing than it may have appeared at first. It does not weaken the validity of one of his basic points: that the legal and institutional framework of the society included characteristics intended to protect existing privileges at the cost of entrepreneurship and development. The institutional system impeded competition and promoted bribery by imposing useless and costly delays for legal authorizations to enter business activity. The informal sector is in part a response by the poor to the obstacles placed in their path by the privileged classes.

This sector is also an added problem for a society that needs revenue from taxation to deal with a host of pressing problems. Jorge Vega suggests that avoidance of taxation has been a major part of the explanation of the rise of informality from the 1960s on (Vega Castro 1989). Whatever the basic intention, it is exceptionally difficult for the government to collect taxes on sales or earnings (as distinct from taxes on purchases) by independent workers and small firms.

Relative immunity from taxation and treatment as if these activities were in some sense intrinsically outside the domain of systematic social negotiation may be changing. The Fujimori government's determined drive to restore the nation's tax base in the 1990s has included incredible episodes of using army tanks to surround open-air markets of informal sellers, to force them to make payments corresponding to taxes. A more promising path has been to recognize and negotiate with representatives of informal producers and sellers to reach agreements on minimal levels of record keeping and payment of value-added taxes. That approach has both brought some revenue to the government and given people in the informal sector some measure of systematic recognition as an important group with a legitimate voice in the society, without subjecting them to a host of regulations. Most of the regulations criticized by de Soto have been eliminated. The problem may now lie in the inadequate efforts to provide the regulations genuinely needed for public safety, health, reasonable working conditions, and dependable payment of wages.

From a macroeconomic point of view, the growth of the informal sector in the 1970s and 1980s reflected the generalized deterioration of the economy. With a rapidly increasing labor force and a high rate of migration to the cities, people looking for work outran formal job openings. The sector remains for many workers a necessary means of survival, an extralegal but positive answer on the individual level to lack of success at the level of the macroeconomy.[6]

Although the informal sector has provided earnings opportunities and productive activities that raise the supply elasticity of the economy, its growth can be seen as a setback for the organization of labor and for labor's voice in the political system. The self-employed and the people in microenterprise can form organized groups and defend themselves to some degree, but not as workers in the traditional sense. That fact could be adverse for meaningful democracy: organized workers can provide a political force that pulls public attention toward concern for social problems and offsets the common resistance of the business community to taxation for such purposes. The rise of the informal sector may have contributed to the weakening of democracy under the Fujimori government (Graham 1992, 169–99, 204; Cameron 1994). "One effect of the crisis of Latin America in the 1980s was to undermine collective action and encourage the search for individual solutions and strategies of survival . . . the response to the crisis takes the form of multiple individual actions that have the cumulative consequence of destabilizing political institutions without constituting an organized alternative" (Cameron 1994, 190–91).

Coherent political parties and organized labor might have a better chance to thrive if formal-sector employment increased relative to informal. Is that a genuine possibility, or is the long trend toward a greater role for the informal sector likely to be irreversible? Peruvian experience has not yet provided a sustained test, but that of Chile indicates that strong employment conditions can raise the relative role of the formal sector. Direct measures of open unemployment in Santiago make clear a severe worsening of employment conditions from 1973 to 1983, followed by gradual improvement to something close to full employment by 1990. In the first period, the share of labor in the informal sector as a percentage of all nonagricultural activity increased from an average of 25 percent in 1972–73 to 29 percent for 1982–84. In the second period, as open

---

6. William Maloney's examination of alternative explanations of the informal sector in Mexico includes tests for possible queuing to enter formal-sector employment. The tests show that lack of job offers plays a role in sending people into the informal sector but, more important, this sector provides people with positive opportunities, including earnings that compare well with formal-sector employment (Maloney 1997).

unemployment came back down, the share of the informal sector fell in close association, to 24 percent by 1990 (García 1993, 103). That picture points to a possibility for Peru, if economic policies can be focused effectively on providing sustained growth of opportunities for productive employment.

Conclusions

The purposes behind the policies adopted to promote industrialization in Peru from the 1960s on were highly understandable. The problems that followed concerned the methods and underlying context, not the goals. The basic mistake of the particular strategy was that it protected industrialists from any need to raise efficiency, reduce costs, improve product quality, or pursue technological change. If the strategy had aimed in the opposite direction, to help raise profits through competitive export performance rather than through sales to a captive market, the results could have been distinctly better.

It would have been difficult at best to make rapid headway toward creation of a more strongly competitive industrial sector, although not impossible to start. Peru and most other Latin American countries have had to cope with strong comparative advantages in mining and other nonindustrial activities, a high rate of population growth depressing labor markets, and a weak background of education and skills in the labor force. To promote a more competitive industrial sector and stronger employment conditions in the process would have been at best an uphill fight. It might not have succeeded by now even if it had started in the 1960s. To move in the wrong direction was no help at all.

Every day starts with some modest chance to do things differently, although also with the weight of yesterday's mistakes. No economic strategy can correct the massive imbalance of Peruvian labor market conditions in a short time. The hope might be to move systematically in this direction by public policies jointly favorable for improving the competitive strength of the industrial sector, for achieving macroeconomic balance, and for a more labor-intensive structure of production. A new start in this sense should be possible in the framework of an open-economy strategy. The steps taken so far have been promising in some ways but remain inconsistent and inadequate.

6

POVERTY AND INEQUALITY

Peru has no monopoly on high degrees of poverty and inequality, but these stubborn characteristics have deeply marked its history. Adverse structural factors, both economic and social, have been compounded in many periods by unhelpful management of the economy. The 1970s and 1980s were particularly frustrating: despite attempted reforms, poverty worsened compared with both the rest of Latin America and Peru's own past.

Questions of causation are, as always, extremely treacherous. Causation moves in intersecting circles, not straight lines. Poverty can in a sense be explained by low productivity and weak economic growth, but the low productivity of the majority of the labor force is mainly a result of social inequality, of blocked access to education, skills, land, and capital. High inequality in the distribution of income is not a result of outstanding productive contributions by the wealthy minority; it is due mainly to restricted opportunities for the majority (Sheahan and Iglesias 1998). In turn, the tensions of blocked societies make for impatient rejection of restraints on one side and deep fear of change on the other, tensions constantly pulling policies toward inflexible extremes adverse to growth.

For Peru, Adolfo Figueroa concludes that inequality became so extreme that it *created* much of the social violence and many of the economic problems that plague the country. Peru has fallen into a "distributive crisis, which occurs when income inequality surpasses a threshold of social tolerance. . . . Noncontractual incomes expand; the social contract breaks down; and social violence and instability prevail" (Figueroa 1995, 391). Rejecting the frequent argument that economic growth can be assumed to be the solution for inequality, he reverses the sequence: "To resume economic growth, Peru must solve its distributive crisis" (Figueroa 1995, 394).

The fundamental problems can be considered in two separable dimensions: (1) tenacious structural factors that may be subject to gradual correction but that no change of government or of economic strategy can resolve in any direct or immediate way; (2) current economic management and profound differences in understanding how particular policies relate to the complex of factors involved. This chapter is mainly concerned with underlying structural conditions. The first section summarizes social indicators of poverty and inequality, evidence of poverty in terms of income, who makes up the poor population, and what major factors help explain the incidence of poverty. The second section focuses on measures of inequality in the distribution of income, both as compared with other countries and in Peru. The third section discusses possible responses to the structural factors aggravating poverty and inequality, including social programs as well as economic strategies. The effects on poverty and inequality of macroeconomic management in Peru and the major attempts at structural reform under the governments of Velasco and García are examined in the next chapter.

Poverty: Degrees, Trends, and Characteristics

The meaning of poverty shows up most starkly in terms of infant and child mortality, illiteracy, urban slums, and preventable diseases of the poor. Peru's cholera epidemic of the early 1990s was a striking case of social failure, specifically the inability to provide clean water and sanitary facilities for the urban poor (Figueroa 1993, 145–46). Such social breakdowns, and measures of social conditions, are the clearest indicators of extreme poverty. By such measures, poverty in Peru has clearly been higher than average for Latin America.

A second way to measure degrees and changes of poverty is to compare incomes to standard cutoff lines for minimum consumption standards. Such comparisons indicate that the incidence of poverty in Peru was moderately above the average for the region as of 1970 and then worsened relative to the rest of Latin America through the 1980s. In the first half of the 1990s, the percentages of families below lines of poverty and of indigence fell markedly although poverty remained, as of 1994, much higher than a decade earlier.

Degrees of poverty change with economic growth or retreat, but for many people in poverty, the deeper question is their capacity to respond to opportunities, to deal with the particular problems that hold them down (Helwege 1995). The concept of "chronic poverty" included in a study of poverty in Peru in 1994 is one of many efforts to quantify this side of the issue. Households are classified in this category if, besides being below the poverty line in terms of income, they have problems that make it particularly difficult to get out of poverty by their own efforts. The deficiencies considered include illiteracy of the head of the household, children of primary school age who are not in school, and/or extremely poor conditions of health or housing (Elías 1995; Reyes 1995). The attempt is to identify households that are unlikely to escape poverty without direct help, even when employment and other market conditions are favorable. As of 1994, 23 percent of Peruvian households were counted in this category (Table 6.1). For the rural sierra, the incidence was 45 percent.

Infant Mortality and Other Social Measures

As of 1960, Peru's income per capita was fifth highest in the region, 25 percent above the regional median. Its rate of infant mortality, on the other hand, was among the worst: fourth highest of 20 countries, 23 percent above the median (Table 1.1). By 1992, the rate had been brought down greatly but remained even higher relative to the new median for the region. Of twenty countries, only Bolivia and Haiti had worse infant mortality rates in 1992.

The deterioration in infant mortality relative to the rest of the region from 1960 to 1992 could be explained in some measure by worsening relative income. Peru's income per capita fell from 25 percent above the regional median in 1960 to 13 percent below it by 1992. Cross-section

Table 6.1. Estimates of the shares of Peruvian households in poverty, indigence, and chronic poverty, 1970–1994 (percentages of households)

	Estimates by ECLAC		Estimates by CUANTO-UNICEF	
	Peru	Latin America	Peru	
Poverty				
1970	50	40		
1979 or 1980	46	35		
1985 or 1986	52	37	(1985)	38
1990 or 1991	—	41	(1991)	55
1994	—	39	(1994)	48
Indigence (extreme poverty)				
1970	25	19		
1979 or 1980	21	15		
1985 or 1986	25	17	(1985)	15
1990 or 1991	—	18	(1991)	24
1994	—	17	(1994)	18
Chronic poverty				
1991			22	
1994			23	

SOURCES: ECLAC 1994, 158–59; 1997, 194; Instituto Cuánto and UNICEF, 1995, 30, 35.

regressions of infant mortality relative to GDP per capita among nineteen Latin American countries indicate expected levels of 114 per thousand for 1960 and 51 per thousand for 1992. The actual rates in both 1960 and 1992 were one-fourth above the expected norms.[1]

In the country, infant mortality rates have differed enormously among departments and regions. In 1996, the five departments of the sierra shown in Table 6.2 had infant mortality rates that ranged from four to five times the rate in Lima. For all of them, infant mortality came down considerably from levels in 1981, but the rates of decrease for all five were much slower than that for Lima. In that exceptionally costly sense, inequality worsened.

Inequality of access to education was extreme in the early postwar years, but Peru has made considerable progress in this respect (Chapter 2). As of 1960, the school enrollment rate for Peruvian children between six and eleven years old was only 57 percent, below the regional median of 66 percent. By 1980, the enrollment rate reached 84 percent, well above the new regional median of 78 (ECLA 1981, 102). Standards of adult

---

1. These regressions are based on infant mortality rates from UNDP 1995, 162–63, GDP per capita for 1992 from the same source, and GDP per capita for 1960 from IDB 1989, 463. Differences in income levels accounted for only 34 percent of differences in mortality rates in 1960 but 52 percent in 1992.

Table 6.2. Inequalities in rates of infant mortality among departments in Peru, 1981 and 1996

	Rate per Thousand		
	1981	1996	Percentage Decrease
Lima	49.8	18.1	64
Sierra			
Apurímac	110.1	70.9	36
Ayacucho	113.9	70.5	38
Cusco	122.9	79.3	35
Huencavalica	128.7	88.6	31
Puno	110.8	76.6	31

SOURCE: Instituto Cuánto 1994, 270; 1996, 241.

literacy rose markedly too, from 71 percent in 1970 to 87 percent by 1992. In both years, these levels were just slightly below the regional medians (UNDP 1995, 162).

With all the progress in raising school enrollments and reducing illiteracy, educational inequalities among Peruvians remain high. Inequality is important both in terms of the low quality of education in public primary and secondary schools compared with private and in terms of lower coverage in rural than in urban areas. Weakness in the quality of public school education goes beyond questions of financing, to issues of teacher training, motivation for students and for teachers, and organization of the educational system. The cards are stacked systematically against the children of all families—the great majority—who cannot afford to send their children to private schools.

Access to education in rural areas has greatly improved, but regional differences in enrollment ratios remain pronounced. As of 1993, the average number of years of schooling completed for people in Lima was 9.8, more than double the average of 4.1 for rural areas (Instituto Cuánto 1994, 241). Table 6.3 summarizes rates of illiteracy for people over 15 years old, for Lima and the same five sierra departments as in Table 6.2. The vastly higher rates in the sierra departments correspond closely to the picture of extreme inequality for infant mortality. The additional inequality brought out in Table 6.3 is that between men and women, in Lima with its low levels of illiteracy as well as in the sierra with its drastic levels.

The initial rise of *Sendero luminoso* in Ayucucho and its strong grip on the rural sierra in the 1980s had complex roots that cannot be reduced to any single factor (McClintock 1984; Degregori 1989, 1992; Palmer

Table 6.3. Illiteracy rates for people over fifteen years old, in Lima and five departments in the sierra, 1993

	Total	Percentage Illiterate Men	Women
Lima	4.2	1.9	6.2
Sierra			
Apurímac	36.9	21.5	51.5
Ayachucho	32.7	18.0	45.8
Cusco	25.4	14.3	36.4
Huencavalica	34.1	18.7	47.7
Puno	22.2	10.9	32.9

SOURCE: Instituto Cuánto 1995, 264.

1992). The extreme inequality of life opportunities, so acutely adverse for people in the rural sierra, must have played a powerful preparatory role. The additional deep inequalities between educational opportunities for men and women may help explain the striking role that women played in *Sendero*'s violence and in its leadership.

Poverty in Terms of Income Levels

The most familiar measure of the incidence of poverty is the head count of individuals or households whose income falls below a poverty line defined in terms of requirements for minimally adequate consumption. Changes in the poverty head count for Peru are given in Table 6.1 above for two different series of measures. The first, from the Economic Commission for Latin America and the Caribbean (ECLAC), covers as many countries as possible from 1970 on. The second is based on surveys under World Bank guidelines for Peru in 1985, 1991, and 1994. The two sets of estimates cannot be linked directly. They use somewhat different methods and poverty lines, but considering the two patterns of change jointly gives a useful long-term picture. The percentage of households in poverty changed little between 1970 and the mid-1980s but increased greatly between 1985 and 1991. The poverty head count then fell from 1991 to 1994. A subsequent survey for 1996 has given rise to conflicting interpretations: data for a matched panel show a slight rise in the poverty head count, but adjustments for geographical price differences and for differences in consumption patterns suggest a further decrease, from 48.9 to 46.4 percent (Francke 1997a; Saavedra-Chanduvi 1998, 3).[2]

---

2. It seems unlikely that poverty increased between 1994 and 1996: income per capita increased in this period, and the same survey indicates no change in inequality (Francke 1997a).

The ECLAC studies show levels of poverty and indigence in Peru higher than for the region at all dates measured: 50 percent of households in poverty in Peru in 1970 compared with 40 percent for the region and 52 percent in 1986 compared with 37 for the region. These comparisons may be questioned because the ECLAC studies did not use identical standards for setting poverty lines in all countries. Their poverty lines aim at similar standards of minimally necessary nutrition, but they allow for national differences in consumption habits and therefore for different expenditure levels at the boundary line.

An alternative set of comparisons in a World Bank study (Psacharopoulos et al. 1992) corrected for this problem by setting equalized poverty lines for all countries for 1980 and for 1989. This study used poverty lines much lower than those of ECLAC and therefore gives lower poverty head counts for all countries. For Peru in 1980, it gives a poverty head count of 31 percent in urban areas and 46 percent in rural. The relations of measures for Peru to averages for the region remained much the same: the poverty head counts in Peru were higher than for the region for both rural and urban areas in 1980, and the ratio of both rural and urban head counts to those of the region worsened between 1980 and 1989.

Inside Peru, rural areas have invariably been much poorer than urban, both for the country as a whole and in each region. In 1994, poverty in the rural areas of the coast, the sierra, and the selva was in all three cases roughly 80 percent higher than in Lima (Table 6.4). For the urban areas of the sierra and the selva, it was not much higher than in Lima itself. The incidence of extreme poverty differed still more sharply between rural and urban areas. With nearly one-half the households in the rural sierra and selva in extreme poverty, their head counts were nine times as high as in Lima.

Changes in poverty and in extreme poverty between 1985 and 1994 show one common characteristic: in all regions except the selva, urban as well as rural, both poverty and extreme poverty worsened. The exception, the selva, shows a considerable decrease for urban areas and very little increase for rural areas. Income from coca and its derivatives probably played a role in this less-worse trend.

Apart from the selva, the increases in poverty between 1985 and 1994 were remarkably similar for Lima and for the rural areas: a slightly lower percentage increase for the rural coast than for Lima and the rural sierra, and nearly equal for the latter two. In a sense, this picture is an improvement on past history: the relative position of the rural areas did not worsen.

Table 6.4. Estimates of the incidence of poverty and extreme poverty, by major regions, 1985–1994

	Share of Population in 1994	Percentage of Households in Region					
		In Poverty			Extreme Poverty		
		1985	1991	1994	1985	1991	1994
Metropolitan Lima	28	27	48	38	3	10	5
Urban coast[a]	20	42[a]	55	49	11	23	15
Rural coast	20	50	—	66	27	—	32
Urban sierra	17	26	53	42	15	22	12
Rural sierra	20	49	73	68	32	55	46
Urban selva	6	48	—	39	23	—	14
Rural selva	6	68	—	70	44	—	46

SOURCE: Instituto Cuánto and UNICEF 1995, 33–35.
[a] Urban coast excludes metropolitan Lima. The measure given in the source for poverty in 1985 (4 percent) is an error. I would like to thank Gilberto Moncada Vigo, Gerente General of Cuánto, for the corrected figure used here.

With the beginning of economic recovery from 1991 to 1994, the incidence of poverty fell in all four areas that can be compared in Table 6.4. These data indicate a much more pronounced decrease in Lima than in the rural sierra, but a re-examination of the basic information suggests that this result may be wrong. The re-examination focuses on the problem of measuring changes in poverty in areas facing significantly different variations in relative prices and consumption patterns (Francke 1997a). With adjusted consumption baskets, this review concludes that the reductions of poverty in the rural sierra and in the urban sierra as well were both greater than in Lima.

Who the Poor Are, and Why

The leading characteristics associated with poverty in Peru are closely related. Poverty is highest for people in rural areas, for those with low levels of education, and for those whose maternal language is Quechua or other indigenous languages. In terms of economic activity, it is highest for people in agriculture, for workers other than salaried employees, and for independent (self-employed) workers in both rural and urban areas.

Table 6.5 gives two breakdowns for people in extreme poverty in 1994. By far the dominant share—two-thirds of the total—was in agriculture. By occupational category, the two groups most strongly associated with extreme poverty were the self-employed and unpaid family labor,

Table 6.5. Economic activities of people in extreme poverty, 1994

	Percentage of Total
By field of activity	
Agriculture	68
Trade	13
Manufacturing	6
Services	8
Other	5
By occupation	
Hired workers	17
Salaried employees	2
Independent, self-employed, including agriculture	35
Unpaid family labor	44
Other	2

SOURCE: Instituto Cuánto and UNICEF 1996, 28.

in both agriculture and urban activities. Together, these two groups accounted for nearly four-fifths of the people in extreme poverty.

Table 6.6 gives a more detailed picture in terms of the characteristics of heads of households. The most notably high ratios of shares in extreme poverty to shares in the total population (shown in the fourth column) are those for maternal languages other than Spanish, for those with no more than primary education, for hourly paid workers as distinct from salaried employees, and for self-employed and unpaid family workers. In contrast to many studies in other countries, female-headed households were less commonly subject to poverty than were those headed by males: they accounted for 17 percent of all households but only 11 percent of those in extreme poverty.

Perhaps the most important of the many factors determining the structure of poverty has been the society's prolonged failure to provide anything like equal access to education for people in the rural areas. This lack of access has hurt them badly by constraining their mobility, productivity, and earnings potential (Chapter 2). Poverty in agriculture has also been worsened by the rapid growth of the rural labor force, relative to the supply of arable land for them to work on (Chapter 3). Poverty in urban labor, especially for people forced into the informal sector, has been aggravated by persistently weak employment conditions, notably the slow growth of employment in the private sector from 1970 to 1990. This failure in turn is traceable jointly to the particular industrial-

Table 6.6. Characteristics of heads of households for families in poverty and in extreme poverty, 1994

	Percentage of National Households	Percentage of All in Poverty	Percentage of All in Extreme Poverty	Ratio: Share in Extreme Poverty / Share in Total Households
By gender				
Female	17.4	13.5	10.9	0.63
Male	82.6	86.5	89.1	1.08
By maternal language				
Non-Spanish	25.4	36.2	48.0	1.89
Spanish	74.6	63.8	52.0	0.70
By education				
None or primary	49.7	67.2	77.9	1.57
Secondary	33.2	28.7	20.8	0.63
Superior	17.2	4.1	1.3	0.08
By occupation				
Hired workers	15.0	20.6	21.2	1.41
Salaried employees	13.3	5.3	2.2	0.17
Household workers	0.3	0.4	0.3	1.00
Independent	51.1	58.7	65.6	1.28
Unpaid family labor	1.1	1.1	1.7	1.55
Not working[a]	19.1	13.9	8.9	0.47

SOURCE: Adapted from Instituto Cuánto and UNICEF 1995, 41, 49.

[a] Includes all heads of households classified as unoccupied, out of the labor force, and occupation not specified.

ization policies followed in this period and to considerable macroeconomic mismanagement (Chapter 4).

Yet another crucial factor has been discrimination against or disregard for the country's indigenous people. Households headed by people speaking indigenous languages suffer an incidence of extreme poverty that is 89 percent higher than their share in the nation's households (Table 6.6). That striking discrepancy compared with Spanish-speaking households might be explained in several different ways. People speaking indigenous languages have been concentrated in activities that yield low incomes: most in agriculture and many as independent workers or unpaid family labor. Limited access to education has been selectively adverse for people whose maternal language is indigenous. In 1994, 17 percent of the heads of households speaking indigenous languages had no schooling at all, compared with 6 percent for Spanish speakers; only 31 percent reached secondary or higher levels of education, compared with 57 percent for Spanish-speaking households (Instituto Cuánto and UNICEF 1996, 132).

Low levels of education and low-income activities together account for much of the disproportionate poverty of families with non-Spanish maternal languages. Both reflect pervasive discrimination against them: discrimination in the sense of the society's failure to provide anything like equal access to education for rural areas, in social and economic constraints on the employment open to them and in what they are paid in given activities. Their average earnings in paid work have been less than half those of nonindigenous labor. About two-thirds of the gap can be attributed to lower levels of education and to sector of employment, an indication that direct discrimination may account for the other one-third (MacIsaacs and Patrinos 1995, 226–29). Beyond such direct effects, differences in the educational levels and in sectors of activity between indigenous and nonindigenous households themselves reflect discrimination in social provision of educational access and in the scope for personal mobility.

Inequality

Inequality takes many forms, including the distribution of income and assets, access to education and health care, economic mobility and social acceptance, and in its most basic sense differences in opportunities and scope for choices in life (Sheahan and Iglesias 1998). These diverse inequalities are all linked, partly through the pervasive effects of differences in incomes and partly through social decisions. In a society concerned with equalization of opportunities, access to education and to health care could be made considerably more equal than the distribution of income, and changes in this direction could conceivably limit the degree of income inequality in the following generation. Peruvian society has made some progress in this sense but has a long way to go. Preceding details of inequalities in education, sharply different rates of infant mortality according to region, and the earnings differentials adverse to indigenous people all point to radically unequal life conditions. They all feed back into high inequality in the distribution of income.

The first part of this section reviews evidence of degrees of inequality and their changes since the early 1960s. The second part considers the causes and the costs of inequality in Peru, and in Latin America generally.

Measurements of Inequality

Inequalities in terms of social welfare clearly appear in the measures of differential education, literacy, and infant mortality discussed earlier in connection with poverty. Estimates of inequality in the distribution of income are in general consistent with such social indicators, although they are inescapably plagued with difficulties that leave them open to serious question. The difficulties, not just for Peru but for all countries, include deliberate under-reporting of income, refusal of some of the highest income people to participate in household surveys, weak or nonexistent record keeping, and conceptual problems such as changing relative prices for different consumption baskets of different income groups. For developing countries in which income and consumption by poor people may largely take the form of nonmarketed products they raise themselves, and in which wealthy people traditionally keep substantial assets out of the country, all these problems are magnified. It is possible to make a good case for refusing to give much credit to any comparisons of income distribution in developing countries (Lustig 1995, 35–38). Still, heroic investigators and dedicated research institutions keep doing their best to find out as much as they can and to organize the information in reasonable ways.

A study by Shane Hunt of long-term trends in real wages for workers in coastal agriculture and construction, for varying periods from the late nineteenth century up to 1940, brings out an almost total lack of any sustained increases. He estimates that real earnings of workers in sugar fields were slightly lower in 1940 than in 1895, those in rice cultivation had the same level of earnings in 1940 as in 1924, and those in construction fell by one-third in that latter period (Hunt 1977, table 17). In contrast, wages in mining went up steadily, and output per capita increased at a rate of 1.4 percent a year from 1913 to 1950 (Hunt 1996, 65). Stagnation of real wages in agriculture and construction probably meant that inequality was increasing: rising average income for the country as a whole was going to the higher income urban and mining sectors.

An early effort by Richard Webb to create dependable measures for the Peruvian distribution of income in 1961 concluded that the highest tenth of the distribution received 49 percent of all personal income. The income received by the highest tenth was 2.7 times the total received by the lowest 60 percent. For comparison, an average calculated for forty-four developing countries in the same period gave a ratio of 1.7 between the totals going to the upper tenth and the lowest 60 percent (Webb 1997, 7).

A World Bank study comparing changes in the distribution of income for twelve countries, mostly from the early 1960s to the early 1970s, concluded that the share of the poor population in Peru remained low but steady for this period. The share of the poorest 60 percent, at 18 percent in both 1961 and 1971, was close to their shares in Brazil and Mexico but was still the lowest of the twelve countries in both years (Ahluwalia, Carter, and Chenery 1979, 322).

According to Webb's estimates, the top *1* percent of Peru's families received one-fourth of the country's personal income in 1961, or—if the undistributed profits of their corporations are taken into account—31 percent of national income. Alfredo Bryce Echenique (1995) gives a fascinating account, from his family's experience, of what it was like to be on the winning end of this distribution and of how easy it was to stay rich, with the proper inheritance or marriage. Webb suggested that "the rich," perhaps 200 families, received close to one-fifth of national income in the form of property income. He did not consider this group to be closed: rapid economic growth from 1950 (to about 1975), let many people move up. "Most of the largest fortunes today are probably less than two generations old" (Webb 1977, 12).

This study brings out a revealing picture of differential trends among major groups in the period from 1950 to 1966. People in the modern sector (one-fifth of the total labor force in 1961) raised their earnings by 4.1 percent a year. Traditional-sector wage earners in the sierra and in the selva fell far behind with gains of 1.5 percent a year. Incomes of independent peasants with small landholdings—one-third of the labor force in 1961—increased at a rate of only 0.8 percent a year (Webb 1977, 39). This pattern of unequal change took place through a particularly prosperous sixteen-year period, under conditions of a relatively open economy, subject to little regulatory intervention of any kind—much the same kind of economic regime as that restored in the 1990s.

Table 6.7 brings together a series of estimates for later years, most of them from different sources and not safely comparable. Still, although not fully comparable, those for 1961 and for 1971–72 are so close as to suggest a relatively stable degree of inequality in the course of the 1960s. In contrast, the estimates for 1981 and 1985 both indicate considerable improvement. The presumably consistent estimates by the INE for the second half of the 1980s show a remarkable improvement in 1986 but then an equally remarkable deterioration two years later. The estimates for 1991 and 1994 are also comparable between themselves and show a slight improvement between these two years.

118   Searching for a Better Society

Table 6.7. Estimates of the distribution of income in Peru, 1961–1994[a]

	Percentage Shares		Gini Coefficient of Inequality
	Lowest 50 Percent	Highest 20 Percent	
1961 (Webb)	12	64	—
1971–72 (Amat y León)	11	61	0.55
1981 (Deininger and Squire)	—	58	0.49
1985 (INE)	—	—	0.47
1986 (INE)	—	—	0.41
1988 (INE)	—	—	0.50
1991 (Cuánto-UNICEF)	—	—	0.44
1994 (Cuánto-UNICEF)	20	50	0.43

SOURCES: Webb 1977, 6; INE 1989, 79–81; Thorp 1991, 209; Deininger and Squire 1996a, 41; Instituto Cuánto and UNICEF 1996, 46.

[a] Estimates from different sources are not safely comparable to each other, although those from the INE for the 1980s and from Cuánto-UNICEF for the 1990s should be consistent in these periods.

Estimates for the distribution of consumer spending, as distinct from the distribution of income, provide supporting comparisons. Gini coefficients for inequality of spending show a pronounced decrease from 1985 to 1991, from .42 to .38, then a continuing fall to .35 by 1996 (Saavedra-Chanduvi 1998, 7). The Gini coefficients for the distribution of spending are lower than those shown for income inequality in Table 6.7, as they normally should be: spending by lower income people is consistently higher relative to their incomes than spending by upper income groups. The changes in the first years of the liberalization program, from 1991 to 1994, were so slight that it is difficult to be sure of their direction; another set of estimates shows a small decrease in the consumption share of the lowest 40 percent and a small increase for the highest 20 percent (Medina 1996, 82). Although subject to such reservations for the period 1991–94, the trend through 1996 still seems to have been toward slightly lower inequality.

The apparent lack of any worsening of income distribution from 1991 to 1996 runs counter to evidence that in nearly all Latin American countries the first years following economic liberalization have been characterized by worsening inequality (Berry 1997). The main directly favorable factor is clear: unlike many countries that became caught in prolonged economic contractions when they initiated liberalization and adjustment programs, Peru began a dramatic rise in production and income in 1993 and 1994. The underlying causes of that difference are discussed in Chapter 8.

The estimates of inequality for 1991 and 1994 suggest that it remained high relative to developing countries in other regions but has become lower than the average for Latin America. Deininger and Squire (1996b, 584) report an average Gini coefficient for Latin America of .49 for the first half of the 1990s, .38 for East Asia, .34 for the industrialized countries, and .29 for Eastern Europe.[3] If the coefficient of .43 is reasonably accurate for Peru in 1994, it remains on the high side compared with most of the world but below the average for Latin America.

On one level, the conventional measures are, with all their discrepancies and necessary assumptions, reasonably helpful in comparing degrees of inequality. On a second level, they leave out so much that their conclusions can come to seem either useless or misleading. Among the considerations that they leave out are the earnings of the wealthy from their assets outside the country. This stream of concentrated income is omitted from any domestic reporting and is outside the scope of taxation. Another omission is the appreciation of capital assets. Between 1990 and 1994, total wages and benefits fell 15 percent in real terms while the stock market index multiplied five times over. Few stocks are owned by poor people. Earlier restrictions on ways of making profits and on importing new automobiles were taken away almost entirely. The poor do not buy many new automobiles. The apparent decrease in the Gini coefficient from .44 in 1991 to .43 in 1994 helps dispel fears that the distribution of income worsened seriously in this period, but it would be wishful thinking to take it as clear evidence of any fundamental change for the better.

Causes and Implications of Inequality

From a familiar and useful perspective, inequality in Peru can be explained reasonably well in terms of relative supplies of the factors of production. Unskilled labor has been superabundant relative to arable land in agriculture and to skilled labor and capital in nonagricultural activities. These

---

3. The average given by Deininger and Squire for Latin America may be an overstatement. Their calculations exclude estimates for Argentina and Uruguay, two countries that on most evidence have been among the less unequal in the region, for lack of acceptable data on distribution in rural areas. For measures comparing inequality in these and other Latin American countries, although not Peru, see ECLAC 1997, 203–5.

relations exert persistent pressure against earnings of unskilled labor in favor of high relative earnings of the minority with skills and capital. A conceivable correction would have been the development of labor-intensive exports to take advantage of low-cost labor and to improve employment conditions in doing so. That correction has been inhibited by the country's strong comparative advantage in the capital-intensive mining sector and by a development strategy that did not favor export diversification. In such a context, relatively high inequality is not in the least surprising.

From a different perspective, inequality has fundamentally been a matter of how the society functions (Figueroa, Altamirano, and Sulmont 1996). The abundance of unskilled labor relative to opportunities for productive employment did not just happen as a fact of nature. It was in part a consequence of exceptionally rapid population growth in the half century through the 1960s. That growth could have been handled with much less strain if the society had developed anything like reasonably equal access to education for lower income people, both rural and urban, to give more of them the chance to gain the skills needed for higher productivity and personal mobility.

The process could have proceeded much less inequitably and with more sustained growth of national income if more effective taxation of higher income people had provided resources for greater social investment, without the deficit spending and foreign borrowing that led to serious setbacks of economic growth. Higher social investment, more widely distributed, would have meant less poverty, less inequality, and—as Adolfo Figueroa emphasizes—less likelihood of extreme violence. All of this is perhaps a dream world: the society did not function this way. The fact that it did not is an essential part of the explanation of why inequality has remained as high as it has.

Peru does not differ greatly from most Latin American countries in these respects: most have much the same inequalities of basic conditions, and the region correspondingly has the highest average levels of inequality in the world. The basic factor common to almost the entire region has been discrimination against rural populations that are racially different from dominant European-descent urban groups: the indigenous people in the Andean countries and in most of Central America and the Black people in Brazil and the Caribbean (Engerman and Sokoloff 1997). The exceptional cases of relatively egalitarian countries, notably Costa Rica and Uruguay, do not discriminate significantly against their rural populations in provision of educational opportunities or other social programs.

They have relatively equal distributions of income because all groups have reasonably similar access to means of enhancing their productivity and also because an educated population is better able to resist discrimination in public policy decisions, in all dimensions.

The long-term reduction of inequality suggested by the estimates in Table 6.7 may owe something to the widening in access to education from 1960 on, even though much of it remained of doubtful quality. The land reform of 1969 may have been a second contributing factor: it did not directly affect the majority of the rural poor, but it wiped out one traditional base of high incomes and it set the stage for more widely shared improvement whenever agricultural incomes rose in following years. A third factor, with much less positive connotations, is that the rise of illegal coca production and exports in the course of the 1970s and 1980s raised earnings for many in the rural labor force. Finally, the gap between urban and rural earnings was reduced by the drastic deterioration of urban employment conditions and real wages in the 1980s. Decreasing inequality may not be a wholly positive achievement.

Is Adolfo Figueroa's thesis that the extreme violence of the 1980s and early 1990s was caused by "a distributive crisis" contradicted by the measures that cast doubt on any prolonged worsening of inequality? On one level, the conclusion might simply be that the estimates are too uncertain to prove anything one way or the other. Still, it must be said that they do not demonstrate any clear worsening. Perhaps the answer is that the continuing strains of the society might not have led to violence, even with high inequality, if incomes had been rising and poverty falling. What really hurt was that incomes fell and poverty worsened so badly. Furthermore, the collapse of the reform efforts of both the Velasco and García governments must have deepened frustrations with the economic system and contributed to support for *Sendero luminoso* and the MRTA in the 1980s. Figueroa is fundamentally right that the persistently unfair character of the society was responsible for much of the violence, even if the distribution of income did not worsen.

Possibilities for Change

The present orientation of Peruvian economic strategy is bound to change sooner or later: in reaction to previous misdirected intervention, it has gone too far toward an extreme of nonintervention to cope adequately with the country's needs. Dependence on private market forces to this degree could easily worsen inequality and set back progress in reduction of poverty (Bulmer-Thomas 1996a). The economy could be managed more positively for reduction of poverty and inequality, even in the constraints of a basically market-oriented orientation. This section examines briefly three sets of possibilities: reduction of poverty through more sustained economic growth; active use of social programs; and selective intervention to change the structures of production and trade in ways favorable for more egalitarian development.

Economic Growth as a Means to Reduce Poverty

More sustained economic growth could help reduce poverty, although it might also allow increasing inequality. For most Latin American countries, the incidence of poverty fell considerably in response to relatively high economic growth in the 1960s and 1970s, only to rise again in the depressed conditions of the 1980s. For Peru with its somewhat different timing, the major increases in the incidence of poverty in the 1970s and 1980s shown in Table 6.3 were associated with a breakdown of the growth process: GDP per capita fell by one-fifth between 1970 and 1990. The recovery of the economy from 1991 to 1994 cut the incidence of poverty from 55 to 48 percent. If sustained, growth should continue to reduce the proportion of families below the poverty line, but it is one thing to recognize the importance of this relation and something else to rely on it as an adequate solution.

Research based on Latin American data for the 1980s suggests that an increase of 1 percent in income per capita could be expected to reduce the number of households below the poverty line by about 1.6 percent (Psacharopoulos et al.1992, 69–71, A13.4; Morley 1995, 156–57).[4] Pedro Francke adds the important point that the structure of growth can make a considerable difference. For Peru, a given rate of overall growth would be more effective for reduction of poverty if it consisted of equal growth rates among sectors, or even better if it featured relative growth of agricultural income, than it will be if dominated by growth of mining exports (Francke 1996). Francke's emphasis on the question of sectoral composition is highly relevant for Peru and still consistent with the basic point

---

4. This estimate is considerably higher than that of Lynn Squire, based on a study covering all developing regions: an increase of 1 percent in the growth of output per capita was associated with an increased annual reduction of 0.24 percent in the poverty head count (Squire 1993).

that growth can be a powerful way to reduce poverty. But is that relation dependable? At least four qualifications suggest some doubts.

First, particular countries can deviate systematically from regional patterns, period after period, for reasons of their own. The study by Psacharopoulos et al. points out that individual countries—Brazil, Panama, and Peru—had greater poverty in both 1980 and 1989 than the expected levels calculated on the basis of their income per capita. For Peru in 1980, urban poverty (actually calculated for Lima rather than all urban areas) turned out to be 50 percent higher than predicted on the basis of average income.

Second, such relations derived from past periods may be poor guides about what to expect when conditions change in basic respects, as the 1990s certainly have compared with the 1980s. Postwar experience in the United States provides a striking example of changes in such relations. From the 1940s through the 1960s, economic growth was accompanied by falling poverty and lessening inequality, but in the next two decades the picture changed completely. Further increases in average incomes became increasingly concentrated in higher income groups, while real incomes of poorer families fell persistently. Cyclical swings still made a considerable difference, but the degree of inequality associated with a given level of unemployment kept rising through each cycle (Danziger and Gottschalk 1995, 136). Poverty stopped going down, despite economic growth.

Third, attempts to explain poverty levels by rates of economic growth leave out, or divert attention from, questions of differential causation for particular *kinds* of poverty. They do not separate for attention any measures of the kinds of poverty that do not respond readily to growth of output and employment. That point is particularly relevant for Peru: recovery of output from 1991 to 1994 reduced aggregate poverty considerably but failed to reduce the share of households in chronic poverty.

Finally, Adolfo Figueroa's interpretation of circular causation helps make clear that growth itself can be held down by high inequality. Worsening social conflict in the 1980s, including extremely destructive violence, seriously damaged productive capacity and investor confidence. Poverty and inequality, and fears of their consequences, put great pressure on reform governments to adopt short-term measures that were intended to help but often made things worse. It is not just that weak growth limited the possibilities of reducing poverty; extreme poverty and inequality weakened capacity for growth.

Social Programs

The people who most readily rise above the poverty line in response to economic growth are normally those with readily usable skills, awareness, proximity to business activities, and good health. Much poverty in Peru, measured approximately by the high percentages of "chronic poverty" in Table 6.1, involves problems that go beyond creation of employment opportunities. These people need more direct help: in extreme cases, for survival; in most cases, for dealing with the specific difficulties that constrain their earnings potential.

Latin American countries have initiated a great variety of "targeted" social programs in recent years, intended to strengthen people's ability to participate in the productive process (Graham 1994; Grosh 1994; Raczynski 1995). They have been closely associated with the adoption of more market-oriented economic strategies, for two major reasons. One is their emphasis on reducing poverty through raising productivity, through more productive work rather than welfare. The other is that they are conceived as alternatives to traditional measures of support for the poor, measures that involve interference with markets, such as subsidized public utility rates, intervention to raise wages, or generalized food subsidies. The targeted programs are both a way to reduce poverty by increasing productivity and a way to reduce government intervention in the economy.

The García government initiated a series of somewhat similar programs in the 1980s. These programs provided real help for many people, although not for long. For agriculture, they included both extensive credit and support for some prices. For the informal sector, they provided credit for microentrepreneurs. The *Programa de apoyo directo* (PAD) was meant to provide organizational support for the *pueblos jovenes,* and the *Programa de apoyo de ingreso temporal* (PAIT) was designed to create temporary jobs and provide worker training to help find permanent employment.

The most publicized and best financed of these programs, PAIT, provided jobs for three-month periods (for which people could keep reapplying), for 374,000 people from 1985 to 1987. Three-fourths of these workers were women, many without any previous employment and also many who had been household workers in jobs that required long commuting travel for earnings even below PAIT's minimum wage. PAIT gave many of them a chance to work close to their homes and families in the *pueblos jovenes,* usually in jobs that involved cleaning up the areas, painting, road improvements, and other infrastructure. The work helped improve living conditions in the *pueblos jovenes* and opened the way to more independence for many women, although it probably did not accomplish much in the way of training for private-sector employment. The program's main defect was that the governing APRA party used it in heavy-handed style to bolster party support, provide administrative jobs for party members, and undercut autonomous communal organizations (Graham 1992, 180–96). When that government's mismanagement of the economy led to accelerating inflation and forced retrenchment in 1988, it simply abandoned PAIT, with no help for any workers who had depended on it.

The PAD program for direct help to the *pueblos jovenes* put much of its limited financing into showcase projects of little or no value to poor people. The program for credit to microentrepreneurs did much better. It was run by a semiautonomous agency more protected from political interference. It provided credit to approximately 30,000 small producers and traders and achieved an outstanding record of dependable repayment (Graham 1992, 177–78). It did not suffer from the abuses that marred PAIT and PAD, but it too was cut back greatly from 1988 in the general process of retrenchment at that time.

By 1990–91, the drastic cutbacks in social spending in the last year of the García government, combined with the further austerity of the Fujimori stabilization program, brought public social expenditures down to the pitiful level of $21 per capita, including education, public health, welfare programs, and all other social functions—barely 11 percent of the average for Latin America (ECLAC 1997, 95). The new government remained so reluctant to raise social spending that the international financial agencies began to exert pressure, backed with financing, to do something positive. With that encouragement and perhaps also in recognition of the presidential election scheduled for 1995, the government started a strong drive in 1993 to strengthen existing social programs and initiate new ones. Spending on the *Programa de apoyo a la pobreza extrema* doubled from 1993 to 1995. Total social expenditures went up from 2.1 percent of GDP in 1990 to 5.9 percent by 1995; from 16 to 40 percent of government spending. Still, despite these impressive increases, the starting point was so low that the share of GDP devoted to social programs remained less than half the regional average (Table 6.8).

The main organization established in 1991 to attack poverty, *Fondo nacional de compensación y desarrollo social* (FONCODES), did practically nothing for the first two years but came to life in 1993 with a new director, a politically independent business executive. With greatly increased resources, the program initiated many community-based proj-

Table 6.8. Social expenditures relative to GDP and to total government spending, Peru and Latin America, 1990–1995 (percentages)

	Peru	Latin America
Social expenditures / GDP		
1990–91 average	2.1	10.4
1994	4.0	
1995	5.9	
1994–95 average	5.0	12.2
Social expenditures / total government spending		
1990–91 average	15.9	42.1
1995	40	
1994–95 average		48.7

SOURCES: ECLAC 1997, 95, for Peru 1990–91 and all ratios for the region; other measures for Peru from Blanco 1997, 54–55.

ects, with a high level of concentration in rural districts characterized by extreme poverty. That focus on the rural poor may have been at least partly a response to the weakness of rural support for the government at the time of voting on its new constitution (Graham and Kane 1998). Political intervention in the program was evident and became so troublesome that the independent director resigned in protest (Roberts 1995, 105). Still, the political targets included the poor: the program maintained an impressive record of directing most of its resources to "the traditionally marginalized rural population" (Graham and Kane 1998, 76; Francke 1997b).

Targeted social programs invariably have difficulties both with political distortions and with exclusion of some of the poor population. Bolivia and Chile have provided relatively good examples of methods that seem to have kept the degree of political interference lower than in Peru (Graham 1994, 21–81; Raczynski 1995, 207–54). They relied on independent or semiautonomous agencies, preferably under congressional review by a congress more independent than those under the García and Fujimori governments in Peru. The second problem, exclusion of some of the poor, is inherent in the nature of targeting: if the programs set narrow targets to avoid spillovers of benefits to people not in poverty, they can deny help to many people who are. The older style "universal" programs were often inefficient, but they also managed to give help to more people who needed it. In particular, subsidies for specific foods that are highly important to poor people (as distinct from generalized food subsidies that give most of their benefits to families with high consumption) and defense of minimum wages (as distinct from decrees raising wages in general) can do a great deal to help the poor in periods of economic contraction.

Minimum wages in Peru took a severe beating from 1980 to 1996. The Fujimori government cut their level in real terms by one-fifth between 1990 and 1992 and held them at this lower level through 1995 but then implemented two major increases in 1996 and 1997 (Chapter 5). That change could be seen as a retreat from strict austerity or, more positively, as a way to share with at least some of the poor population the gains made possible by the recovery of the economy.

The social programs of the present and earlier Peruvian governments have an uneven record at best (Thorp and associates, 1995). The Fujimori government has probably done more to direct help to rural poor people than has any of its predecessors, with particularly strong efforts to broaden access to education and public health services. Still, the gaps remain considerable. A survey of living conditions in 1994 found that one-third of all the people in extreme poverty had been either seriously ill or were suffering from accidents in the four-week period preceding their interviews; only 23 percent of them had been able to get any medical consultation (Instituto Cuánto and UNICEF 1996, 26).

When social programs are dismissed as *asistencialismo*, the implication is that they may do more harm than good. For some, the objection is that they can foster dependence. For others, they are merely palliatives, meant to forestall any social protest that could force fundamental changes (Schuldt 1997, 138–39). Such criticisms do not seem to give much value to the ways in which social programs can make life more bearable for the poor, but both point to vital questions. Effective social programs need to enlarge the personal capacities of the poor so that they can do more to raise their income levels on their own. The second criticism rightly directs attention to the society itself. Individual capacities can be blocked if the society does not allow people to move freely and the economy does not generate productive opportunities. Peru needs its social programs but also needs to reorient its economic strategy to realize the productive potential of its people.

Influencing Market Forces to Favor Reduction of Poverty

In countries in which the unskilled labor force keeps growing rapidly and in which ownership of assets is highly concentrated, market forces are almost bound to favor high concentration of current income. These forces should become less unfavorable as the growth of the labor force slows and access to mid-level skills becomes broader, but it is possible to do more to favor reduction of poverty by economic policies designed appropriately for that purpose. The basic objectives might be summarized as fostering a labor-intensive growth pattern, with greater access to capital for small entrepreneurs and with greater mobility and access to land for the many people who are still caught in low-income agriculture. None of these objectives needs to conflict with a basically market-determined economic system: the objectives are simply ways to make such a system work more equitably.

A key policy measure discussed earlier in connection with patterns of trade is to favor the development of more diversified, more labor-intensive exports. That development could be encouraged through many variants of tax and credit policies and most powerfully through a consistent effort to keep the exchange rate at levels favorable for a competitive industrial sector. Such a policy would also help Peruvian firms compete against imports without the distorting effect of trade barriers and make it possible to reduce the external deficits associated with any given level of economic activity.

Such a reorientation is more than a remote theoretical possibility: it is exactly the kind of change that converted Chile's open economy from one that was generating increasing poverty to one that proved able to reduce it fairly rapidly. From 1973 to 1983, poverty and inequality increased greatly, partly because of structural changes and partly because the particular model of liberalization established in the 1970s allowed the country's competitive position to deteriorate and led to increased dependence on foreign lending and to a deep depression when external credit was cut off. In response to that collapse, Chile changed its model to promote competitive exports by making exporting more profitable relative to sales in the domestic market. From 1984 on, exports increased rapidly, and better external balance permitted sustained growth, with steadily improving employment conditions. By 1988, both poverty and inequality began to decrease (Sheahan 1997). Peru is faced with deeper problems than Chile was and cannot expect similar results in any such short time, but it can move in much the same direction if helped by a similar policy approach.

A complementary possibility, also chosen in Chile after its return to democracy, is to change the tax structure in ways that increase the relative weight of taxation on property and decrease that on wages. This move would have a direct effect of lessening inequality of post-tax incomes and a possibly more important indirect effect of encouraging producers to use more labor relative to capital. The problem is the question of political influence: successful resistance to such measures by higher income groups has a long and impressive record. Close integration of world capital markets in the 1990s makes it more difficult than ever for individual countries to raise taxes on capital. Most of the actual changes following economic liberalization have gone the other way (Bird and Perry 1994).

A serious effort to reduce discrimination against the indigenous people who constitute the bulk of the poor could conceivably make an even more fundamental change for the better. Discrimination restricts both their personal mobility and the supply flexibility of the whole economy. If discrimination could be lessened, market forces could work more cleanly, in ways favorable for reduction of income inequality. Economic growth alone cannot do much about this factor, although tighter labor markets could make discrimination more costly to businesses. The United States has not made notable progress on such issues despite many years of legislation, judicial action, and strong penalties against firms convicted of discrimination. The resistances are profound.

Conclusions

Poverty has been much higher in Peru than it need have been, primarily because of blocked opportunities for people in agriculture and weak employment conditions in urban activities. The underlying conditions have been to some degree beyond the scope of economic policy: rapid population growth ran into the constraints of arable land and water in agriculture, a strong comparative advantage in mining fostered a capital-intensive structure of exports that has been little help for employment, and discrimination against people of indigenous descent has been a powerful deterrent to their earnings capacity. Social policies left the poor with restricted access to educational opportunities until very recent years, and even now the quality of education available to them remains weak. Economic policies, although sometimes helpful, have gone in perverse directions with remarkable frequency.

Inequality in the distribution of income is nearly impossible to measure in any satisfactory way, but serious attempts to quantify it indicate that it was exceptionally high in the early postwar years, even compared with the rest of Latin America. They also suggest, more hopefully, that it came down somewhat from the early 1960s to the 1990s and from 1991 to 1996. Inequality in social conditions and health may not have improved at all. Infant mortality rates in the sierra, always a high multiple of those in Lima, have not come down nearly as fast as in Lima.

Inequality has many causes, including concentrated ownership of assets and a superabundance of unskilled labor relative to land, skills, and capital. Above all, it is a consequence of restricted opportunities for the poor: of disabling social conditions that have held back both the poor themselves and the growth of the economy. Much the same has been characteristic of the majority of Latin American countries. Most have much the same inequalities of basic conditions, and the region correspondingly has the highest average levels of inequality in the world. The common factor for many, although much less so for Costa Rica and the Southern Cone, has been discrimination against rural populations that are racially distinct from dominant European-descent urban leadership.

Poverty in Peru increased greatly in the 1980s but fell considerably with the revival of the economy from 1992 through 1996. If economic growth can be maintained, poverty should keep falling, aided by somewhat slower population growth and by wider access to education. Still, one-fourth of the country's people remain caught in chronic poverty, related more to structural and personal constraints than to lack of employment opportunities. This poverty did not fall with the economic recovery of the first half of the 1990s; to reduce it requires continuing social effort to correct the constraints involved and some degree of consensus on the need for adequate taxation to finance major social programs without falling back into inflation. Such efforts ask a lot of any society. It may be exceptionally difficult for Peru, just as it is exceptionally needed, because the problems go so deep.

7
STATE-LED DEVELOPMENT, 1963–1990

Given a chance in 1963 to choose a presidential candidate who favored active government intervention to change the country's economy, the people of Peru elected him. Fernando Belaúnde was a most moderate reformer—he provided reassurance along with the promise of change—but the choice was a clear departure from Peru's traditionally conservative, market-determined economic strategy.

The new orientation toward a more active role for the state continued, with many variations, up to its forceful rejection in 1990. The term *state-led development* may suggest more genuine leadership, or more development, than actually occurred. Still, it points to a common intent of these governments and probably of most governments of developing countries all over the world in the first decades after World War II. It could include, it should include, the markedly different focus of state leadership common in East Asia, where governments took very active roles but emphasized building a strongly competitive industrial sector.

State-led development as implemented in Latin America has featured much public investment, extensive public enterprise, pervasive regulation, selective subsidies, and high degrees of protection against competition from imports. It does not logically need to mean, but in practice usually has, a propensity to disregard fiscal and monetary constraints and a strong penchant for holding down the price of foreign exchange. That second side of the orientation responded to structuralist concepts that monetary and fiscal limits were of secondary importance at most and that too much attention to them could block essential structural reforms. The accompanying preference for fixed exchange rates, even in contexts of severe foreign exchange constraints, had several objectives: to encourage investment by keeping down the costs of imported capital equipment, to hold down the consumer price index, and to favor real wages.

Many different reforms were tried out by Peruvian governments from 1963 to 1990, some promising and some decidedly not. The costs to the people of Peru were high. Was that because of the structural reforms themselves or because of the accompanying disregard of internal and external macroeconomic constraints? Surely both in part, but the latter factor was probably the core of the matter. Rising inflation and repeated foreign exchange crises crippled any possibilities of achieving successful transformation of the society. These difficulties could have been greatly moderated by coherent macroeconomic management.

The first section of this chapter reviews the main consequences of state-led development in Peru, with particular attention to its most dramatic versions under the governments of General Velasco and Alan García. The second section concentrates on the basic logic of the heterodox macroeconomic program adopted at the start of the García administration: was it intrinsically a mistake, or did its initial successes point to potentially helpful possibilities? The third section focuses on the Achilles heel of the whole period: external deficits. The last section examines the relations among state-led development, protection, and macroeconomic management.

Variations in the Character of State-Led Development

The differences among policies of succeeding governments from 1963 to 1990 were pronounced and did not follow any well-defined strategy. It

Table 7.1. Index of GDP per capita and rates of inflation for selected years, 1963–1990

	Governments	Index of GDP Per Capita 1963 = 100[a]	Rate of Inflation, Percentage
1963	First Belaúnde administration	100	6
1968	General Velasco	110	19
1975	General Morales Bermudez	126	24
1980	Second Belaúnde administration	126	59
1985	Alan García, first year	112	163
1987	Peak of García programs	128	67
1989	Last full year under García	99	3,371
1990	Transition to Alberto Fujimori	93	7,482

SOURCES: BCRP 1997, 119, for GDP per capita; inflation 1963–75 from IMF 1980, 340–41; for 1980–90 from IDB 1990, 172, and 1997, 263.

[a] Index of GDP per capita converted from BCRP estimates at constant prices of 1979.

was more as if each government tried alternative possibilities, without ever quite finding a set that worked well. The Velasco government has been characterized as a leading example of state capitalism, relying on public investment and ownership as well as high protection and many other forms of intervention (FitzGerald 1979). The following two governments, those of Morales Bermudez and the second Belaúnde administration, cut back on Velasco's reforms and on protection as well, to the point that Belaúnde's government has been characterized as neoliberal (Conaghan and Malloy 1994). The García government then reversed Belaúnde's policies by turning to much more activist use of controls and subsidies and to a complex heterodox program of macroeconomic management intended to stimulate growth and to restrain inflation at the same time.

Granting the importance of such variations, the period from 1963 to 1990 had characteristics that distinguish it from both the country's earlier economic orientation and the 1990s: all of these governments either initiated or maintained relatively active forms of intervention, on the premise that the state had responsibility for shaping the character of the country's development. Collectively, they shared in a process that changed Peru in many ways but also gave it a miserable record of failed growth and worsening inflation (Table 7.1).

The Belaúnde and the Velasco Governments, 1963–1975

Even the conservative administration in office at the end of the 1950s began to adopt modest protective measures, but the Belaúnde government of 1963 was the first to win election for a reformist program including import substitution for industrialization. Belaúnde's program had many other components: he was particularly popular for promises to promote land reform, to open up the country's interior by massive road construction, and to bring under national control the seemingly untouchable foreign company that dominated the oil industry. Once in office, he started on a major program of public works, but congressional opposition blocked any real progress with land reform, and Belaúnde himself backed away from confrontation with the International Petroleum Company (Chapter 2). Protection was easier to sell, and import substitution at last got under way. In a more promising intervention, his administration also introduced the Certex system of fiscal incentives to stimulate new exports (Schydlowsky, Hunt, and Mezzaara 1983; Iguíñiz and Muñoz 1992, 125–30).

The failures to follow through on land reform or take action to limit the power of the foreign oil company proved unacceptable to a surprisingly pro-reformist participant in the political system: the armed forces. Belaúnde was forced out, not because of excessive intervention but because of too little. General Alvaro Velasco removed him in 1968 and took quick action on both land reform and oil. The International Petroleum Company was nationalized immediately, with no loss of time for negotiations over compensation. The sweeping land reform of 1969 is discussed in Chapter 4. These actions were just the beginning of an imaginative set of attempts to establish a new economic system distinct from both traditional capitalism and socialism.

The reforms of the Velasco period were not predetermined by any thought-out program, but they had fairly clear central themes: to foster a cooperative society, to reduce class conflict, to end domination of the society by the traditional elite, and to strengthen national autonomy (Lowenthal 1975; Stepan 1978; McClintock and Lowenthal 1983). The reforms constituted an attempt to implement at long last the ideas elaborated by Víctor Haya de la Torre in the 1920s (Chapter 2).

In the conviction that ownership and control of property were the roots of the country's problems, the Velasco government used land reform to eliminate the traditional haciendas, nationalized the oil industry and most of the largest mines, and created an innovative system intended to make industrial companies share ownership and control with their workers. It attempted many other reforms as well, including efforts to change the educational system, to help workers organize and to protect them from arbitrary discharge, and to help urban slum dwellers gain legal title to their homes. Did all this accomplish anything to change the society?

The reforms did not directly change the distribution of income to any significant degree. They redistributed income among workers in agriculture, and among workers in other sectors as well, but did not reduce the great differences of earnings between sectors. With agricultural incomes so much below those in other sectors, because of lower productivity, redistribution limited to changes among workers in agriculture did not lessen overall inequality (Webb and Figueroa 1975, 111–67).

The land reform did not directly affect the bulk of the rural poor. The hacienda lands were not distributed to the majority of the rural population outside the haciendas: they were converted to cooperatives run by their own former workers and tenants (Chapter 4). Still, the reform may have decreased inequality by wiping out the concentration of incomes that had previously gone to large landowners. Furthermore, it had a significant longer term effect on the rural sector. The subsequent breakup of cooperatives into dispersed individual holdings created a much more equal, probably less concentrated distribution of land ownership than ever before in Peruvian history. Besides lessening inequality in agriculture, that change may have contributed to a gradual decrease in the imbalance between rural and urban poverty.

As of 1970, ECLAC estimates of poverty classified 68 percent of rural households below the poverty line, contrasted to 28 percent of urban (Feres and León 1990, 155). Ten years later, after a difficult period of economic collapse and slow recovery, urban poverty had risen to 35 percent, but rural poverty had decreased slightly, from 68 to 65 percent. This favorable change, modest in absolute but pronounced in relative terms, may well owe something to the breakup of the old haciendas.

Some of the Velasco government's own policies undermined any immediate benefits from the land reform. Prices of food products were held down by increased imports, partly subsidized to reduce inflation and by centralized government buying that closed off alternatives to producers. Worse, macroeconomic mismanagement and foreign borrowing to deal with it created a massive problem of external debt, which led directly to a forced contraction that hurt the rural poor along with everyone else.

Reforms affecting industry and labor had very mixed effects. They stimulated industrial investment, but high protection weakened pressures for efficiency and technical progress. Protection also favored earnings of industrialists and their employees relative to lower income workers in agriculture and in the urban informal sector. This strategy fostered industry dependent on protection and on imported supplies and equipment for its own capacity to produce (Chapter 5).

The government tried to help workers by taking away previous restraints on organization, by introducing regulations that made it practically impossible for firms to discharge anyone who had worked longer than a brief trial period, and by initiating regulations requiring profit sharing intended to build up worker ownership. Many new labor unions were formed; communist-led unions were legalized for the first time. But the regulations that prevented firms from firing workers had the natural consequence of stimulating their efforts to avoid hiring any new ones. For concerns with any possibility of importing labor-saving equipment as a way to escape hiring more workers, the choice was all too easy. The purpose of such protective regulation was clear enough: persistently weak labor markets and low degrees of labor organization had always left workers at the mercy of arbitrary employers. Bargaining was hopelessly one-sided; intervention to make it less one-sided was a natural reaction for a reformist government. The problem was the rigidity of the method: if employers are forbidden to fire any long-term workers, they have an incentive not to hire any.

The same problem may have been aggravated by measures intended to promote shared ownership. Large firms were required to distribute a specified share of profits to their employees in the form of ownership rights. In a few cases, that practice actually began to give workers some share of ownership. The weakness in those cases was the absence of any effective way to make sure that they could gain dependable information about what the firm was doing, or might alternatively do, to give them any toehold for effective participation in decisions. Most often, firms managed to adapt their accounting methods or to set up subsidiaries outside the scope of the regulations to avoid reporting any profits to be distributed.

The government's initial support for popular organizations, including labor unions, increased new possibilities for a participatory society. Most of these organizations survived the downfall of the Velasco government, and many have done their best to help open up the society. In the growing conflicts of the second half of the 1970s, the unions helped lead opposition to the military. Even under Velasco, the new scope for union organization and action quickly ran against the government's preference for dampening down class conflict. Confronted with demands from labor unions that it considered too aggressive, the government responded by sponsoring its own competing unions to undermine them. Similarly, confronted with increasing criticism from the press, the government took the leading periodicals away from their owners and placed them under management by groups that it chose as more cooperative. It also attempted to change the judicial system in ways that demonstrated a conviction that the government's sense of justice was the only one that mattered (Pásara 1983). Military governments may sometimes be reformist, but they rarely welcome ideas contrary to their own.

The Velasco government concentrated on questions of property ownership, foreign investment, and labor–management relations; it did not pay anything like equal attention to problems of internal or external macroeconomic balance. These weaknesses seriously damaged the economy and worsened poverty.

At its start, the government took pride in a determination to prove that military discipline could succeed where civilian governments often fail: to stop inflation by keeping tight control of spending. It was impressively successful for its first two years, but by 1972 government spending began to take off aggressively. The generals placed in charge of nationalized or newly created state firms proved endlessly imaginative at finding reasons for large-scale investment projects. Military spending itself, the many reform programs underway by then, and the deficits of many of the state-owned enterprises added to inflationary pressures. The government reacted in a classically futile way: it prevented public firms from raising their prices to cover increasing costs. The uncovered expenses of the state oil monopoly, Petroperu, were equal to 32 percent of sales by 1974 and to 44 percent by 1975 (Sheahan 1980b, 18). How did Petroperu and the other state firms find the money to cover their deficits? Mainly by borrowing abroad, just as the central government itself was doing to cover its growing fiscal deficit.

On the external side, exports and imports were both subject to contrary forces. Public investment in mining was intended to raise exports, but appreciation of the real exchange rate worked to restrain them for all sectors. Imports could be totally prohibited if a firm asserted that it could replace the product, without any need for concern about costs or quality. Imports increased despite these new restrictions because the rise in government spending stimulated production, and the heavy dependence of the industrial sector on imported supplies and equipment raised demand for imports correspondingly.

In the last three years of the Velasco administration, 1972–75, the balance of payments deficit on current account rose from almost zero to 10 percent of GDP. At first it was financed easily enough by borrowing; Peru began to go deeply into debt. By 1975, foreign lenders began to back off and drove the country into a period of contraction. General

Velasco, handicapped by failing health as well as a failing economy, was eased out by the military and replaced by the much more conservative General Morales Bermudez.

Temporary Retreat: Morales Bermudez and the Return of Belaúnde

With private external credit largely shut off and the International Monetary Fund insistent on tightened restraint, the Morales Bermudez government was forced into the role of a stabilizer-executioner. Although it did not go to the contractionary extremes of the Chilean military in this period, cutbacks in government spending combined with devaluation and with repression of labor drove down real wages and increased poverty.

The long-overdue correction of the exchange rate, combined with more active use of the Certex system of subsidies for new exports and with restraint of domestic demand, enabled the Peruvian industrial sector to break through to significant exports for the first time in its history (Chapter 3). In a comparison of industrial exports for nine Latin American countries, Peru's share was only 2 percent for the period 1970–74; it rose to 11 percent for 1975–79 (IDB 1982, 119). By 1978, the excess imports of 1975 were replaced by a modest export surplus. An increasing surplus the following year, accompanied by rising inflation, should have been a signal to stop devaluation and apply tighter monetary restraint. The government went the other way: both devaluation and rapid monetary expansion continued, and the inflation naturally worsened as well (Sheahan 1987, 265–66).

The Morales Bermudez government did nothing to undermine land reform but rescinded most of the contentious actions of his predecessor in the fields of labor rights and judicial practices and returned to private ownership the news media that the Velasco government had taken over in its last stage. Morales Bermudez also agreed to allow elections and a return to democracy in 1980. This decision may have been in response to growing public antagonism to the military rule in effect from 1968, in despair at failure to control inflation, or simply in fulfillment of repeated promises to give control back to civilians. The election returned former President Belaúnde to office, as if in compensation for his eviction in 1968. This time, he represented the middle-road choice, in opposition to both leftist parties and rightist free-market candidates. As often happens, the middle of the road did not turn out the safest place to be.

The second Belaúnde administration reversed the protectionist orientation of the first: quantitative restrictions on imports were eliminated and a good many tariff rates were cut substantially, although hardly in the all-out style followed by the Fujimori government ten years later. The partial opening up to import competition was intended both to improve efficiency and to slow the gathering forces of inflation. To help with that latter objective, the real exchange rate was allowed to appreciate as well. At the same time, Belaúnde's populist side, spending for grand projects to remake the country, went ahead unchecked. So did the inflation, accompanied once again by rapidly worsening external deficits.

It is unfair to blame the Belaúnde government for all of its economic problems: a devastating earthquake, the damage from an exceptionally severe attack of el Niño, worsening terms of trade, and growing revolutionary violence all made things worse than they might otherwise have been. Just when the government adopted its unfortunate policy of allowing the currency to appreciate in real terms, the world economy slowed under the influence of tightened monetary policies in Europe and the United States. The contraction of world financial markets raised the interest charges for Peru's external debt and then led into the generalized debt crisis that plagued the whole region for the next five years. The courtly president, a natural model for anyone's favorite uncle, was unable to find any effective way to deal with these factors. With production falling but the external deficit and inflation both growing and with external credit practically shut off, the government adopted a policy of fiscal and monetary contraction that drove GDP per capita down by 14 percent in 1983. In Belaúnde's last two years, the economy stagnated while inflation continued to rise.

From Promise to Chaos: The García Government

The García government brought a wave of hope that the economy could be restored to life and that poverty and inequality could be rapidly reduced by turning away from conservative prescriptions to a heterodox style of economic management. Instead of trying to hold down inflation by restraining demand through contractionary monetary and fiscal policies, García promised to stop it by direct controls over wages, prices, interest rates, and exchange rates. In contrast to the long downtrend of real wages under the two preceding governments, he decreed a onetime jump to be followed by specified limits. Instead of bending government support toward the urban sector and industry, he promised to give priority to agriculture and rural development. Instead of the Velasco government's suspicion and hostility toward private business, he promised a policy of systematic *concertación* with business leaders. Instead of using scarce foreign exchange to pay debt service obligations, he made himself a temporary hero by denouncing the creditor countries for taking away the financing needed for growth: debt service payments would be limited to 10 percent of exports, to keep the other 90 percent for imports of productive supplies and equipment. All these measures, along with a charismatic style full of youthful energy, swept even battle-hardened Peruvians into enthusiastic support.

For two years, the García government lived up to much of its initial promise. Then, in a process hauntingly similar to the Velasco government, everything began to come apart (Paredes and Sachs 1991; Paus 1991; Pastor and Wise 1992; Gonzales de Olarte and Samamé 1994).

García's heterodox approach worked well at first, both for reducing inflation and for raising output. The economy had a great deal of excess capacity at the start, as well as external balance, thanks to the contractionary policies followed by Belaúnde in his last years. These advantages permitted a strong response on the output side as soon as García's policies began to stimulate demand. GDP per capita increased by 14 percent between 1985 and 1987, and the rate of inflation decreased (Table 7.1)

The rise in demand was not associated as much with greater spending by the government itself as with two of its reform measures. One was a rapid increase in credit to the agricultural sector, in line with promises to give priority to revival of agricultural production and incomes. The other was its decree raising wages while blocking prices. Under ordinary circumstances, it might have been impossible to get away with such an operation: producers who are squeezed between higher wage costs and controlled prices would be expected to cut back output rather than sustain losses. The García government had an ingenious answer to that problem, or what seemed at first to be an answer. It intervened in financial markets to force down interest rates and thereby reduce financial costs of producers to offset their increased wage costs.

The balancing act that succeeded in the industrial sector did not work for agriculture. Increasing urban incomes and demand quickly began to make price controls for dispersed agricultural producers and markets practically impossible. The government sensibly abandoned control of food prices, which allowed this component of inflation to continue and also had the effect of raising agricultural prices relative to industrial.

Adolfo Figueroa calculates that prices received by small farmers, relative to the prices of their purchases, rose 56 percent between 1985 and 1987 (Figueroa 1995, 378). The supply response proved unexpectedly strong: national income contributed by noncorporate agricultural producers had gone down persistently from 1970 to 1985, but it jumped 30 percent in 1986 and held at that higher level the next year. In 1986, the distribution of income suddenly turned toward greater equality than ever registered in the past (Table 6.6).

For the urban poor, the García government created the initially impressive set of social programs discussed in Chapter 6, programs providing both temporary employment and credit for microentrepreneurs. Along with steeply higher real wages for workers in the formal sector and boom conditions for private business, the strategy looked successful in all dimensions. Underneath that happy surface, three interlinked problems came together to ruin things: the familiar problem of excess spending and renewed inflation, worsening violence, and this government's erratic behavior.

From 1987, spending began to outrun the scope for growth on the supply side; shortages and upward pressure on prices began to spread. The government's reaction was to step up subsidies and hold tightly to fixed prices for the state firms regardless of rising costs. Relative prices of public services and of the oil and gasoline supplied by Petroperu fell to absurdly low levels and created ever-larger deficits financed by ever-greater credit (Cáceres and Paredes 1991, 80–113).

Among the individual economic programs, perhaps the most troublesome turned out to be the initially helpful expansion of agricultural credit: it rose to fantastic amounts, financed by that most explosive of all means, central bank credit. This program became the greatest single contributor to runaway inflation. The government did not greatly increase its own spending but it undercut fiscal balance by tax favors to promote selective economic objectives and compounded the loss of revenue by allowing the administration of tax collection to deteriorate through incompetence and corruption.

Despite all the price controls and subsidies or perhaps rather in response to the way these factors aggravated monetary and fiscal imbalance, inflation jumped in 1988 to seven times the rate of 1987. Faster monetary expansion no longer stimulated real output growth; through its effects on inflation it added to the rout. Output per capita fell 27 percent between 1987 and 1990. The distribution of income, which had improved so promisingly at first, deteriorated back to the high level of inequality at the start.

Macroeconomic imbalance and price distortions would have destroyed this government's economic strategy in any case, but in some ways these factors came to seem among its lesser problems. Worsening violence took an increasing toll of life and production in rural areas and then spread to Lima. The government had pulled back from extreme military repression in its first two years but thereafter allowed it to intensify. *Sendero luminoso* lost many of its members, and many innocent campesinos lost their lives as well. *Sendero* kept replacing its losses with new volunteers, with young people losing hope in the society and increasingly determined to destroy it.

In its relations to the civil society, almost everything that the government did began to take on evidence of duplicity and manipulation. The promising social programs designed to help the urban poor, and initially effective in doing so, were turned into party vehicles of patronage and enforced political support (Graham 1992; Chapter 6). Much the same process corrupted tax enforcement and government administration in general. In a strikingly ill-advised move that poisoned relations with the private sector, García suddenly abandoned his promise of *concertación*. In July 1987, he announced out of the blue a program to nationalize the country's banks and insurance firms. That decision was taken without any consultation with business or congress or, apparently, even his own economic advisers. The attempt was resisted bitterly by employees of the banks as well as by owners and finally rejected by the courts. It brought an abrupt end to any cooperation between the private sector and the government and surely contributed, along with worsening indicators of inflation, to a plunge in private investment (Gonzales de Olarte 1996b, 15). It must also have contributed to the eagerness with which the business community welcomed the extreme version of economic liberalism adopted by the Fujimori government in the 1990s.

Was Heterodox Expansion a Hopeless Mistake?

The García period ended so badly that its initial attempt to combine economic expansion with direct controls to block inflation has had few if any supporters since. Still, it was an attempt to answer a serious problem: the absence of economic growth accompanied by persistently rising inflation. Could it have been continued successfully if García had not veered off and destroyed the cooperation of the private sector by trying to nationalize the banking system?

The ten years of relatively orthodox economic policies under the Morales Bermudez and second Belaúnde governments had been highly disappointing to hopes for either transformation of the society or economic growth. Most of the Velasco period reforms were swept away or greatly watered down, output per capita fell, and by 1985 the rate of inflation was seven times higher than it had been a decade earlier. Some of this weak performance of the more orthodox governments could be explained as a necessary cost of correcting the extreme macroeconomic imbalance at the end of the Velasco government, but much of it could equally well be seen as the result of overly cautious policies, backing away from state leadership of the economy. García's promise to try a new approach, to promote renewed expansion under direct controls to hold down inflation, was clearly welcome to many Peruvians.

Similar heterodox approaches have been common in postwar Latin America. They have often shown striking success for brief periods, never for very long (Dornbusch and Edwards 1991). The very frequency of their repetition rightly suggests that they have some logical appeal, and the short bursts of success also indicate that they could do some good if not pursued too long. They could be a means to break out of a common impasse. That impasse is exactly the kind encountered in Peru: with weak systems of taxation that hold down fiscal revenue, governments that consistently restrain spending to keep it in such narrow limits have very little scope either to answer pressing social needs or to stimulate a depressed economy.

Table 7.2 gives summary indicators of changes in inflation and output per capita during the 1980s for Peru and six other leading Latin American countries. For inflation, these countries divide into two markedly contrasting groups: by 1989, inflation rates were more than 1,000 percent a year in Argentina, Brazil, and Peru, but less than 30 percent in the other four. These differences fit exactly with the countries' different policy regimes in the second half of the 1980s. Argentina, Brazil, and Peru all tried to stop inflation by heterodox policies relying on direct controls, while failing to apply macroeconomic restraint. The other four countries all used serious fiscal and monetary restraint, along with varying degrees of liberalization. The latter prescription clearly worked much better to hold down inflation. The contrast is not as clear for changes in output. Argentina and Peru were at the negative extremes, with per capita incomes

Table 7.2. Comparative rates of inflation in 1980 and in 1989, and changes in GDP per capita, for seven Latin American countries

	Rates of Inflation (% Increase in Consumer Prices)		Percentage Changes in GDP per Capita[a]
	1980	1989	1980 to 1989
Argentina	101	3,079	−26
Brazil	83	1,284	− 5
Chile	35	17	+ 11
Colombia	27	26	+ 13
Costa Rica	18	17	− 6
Mexico	26	20	− 9
Peru	59	3,399	−25
Latin America	—	—	− 9

SOURCE: IDB 1990, 265, and individual country pages.
[a] GDP measured in constant 1988 dollars.

falling by one-fourth. The decrease in Brazil was only 5 percent, less than that for the region as a whole. It was a difficult decade for almost everyone, but most of all for Argentina and Peru.

The appeal of the heterodox approach is almost invariably an initial context of idle productive capacity with weak employment conditions, accompanied by an inherited inflation that is slow to respond to macroeconomic restraint. The inflationary side discourages use of monetary or fiscal expansion, but failure to adopt expansionary policies leaves the economy drifting sideways or down, just as it did in the second Belaúnde administration. In such a context, with no real shortage of productive capacity, it looks possible to raise everyone's incomes by stimulating demand provided that inflation is restrained by direct controls. Price controls may be impossible to enforce for small producers in competitive fields but can usually be applied to larger private and state-owned firms providing basic public services. Alternatively, unilateral controls can sometimes be avoided by group negotiations with business leaders and labor unions, as in Mexico in the late 1980s. Constraints on increases that are not forced by actual shortages can create greater space for activist monetary and fiscal policies.

The crux of the matter is the need to maintain balance between increases in spending and possible increases in output, as well as between increases in imports needed for production and increased exports. The common breakdown comes on the external side, as renewed expansion stimulates imports and frequently pulls potential exports into the domestic market. It helps if a government can start with external balance, as the García government could in 1985. It does not help if wages are suddenly increased by degrees that outrun possible increases in production. That side of the matter undermined the early postwar expansion in Argentina under Perón and equally so that of the García government in Peru. Even wage restraint does not guarantee success. Mexico in the late 1980s used it effectively to prevent inflation from the side of labor costs but still headed into trouble on the external side by allowing prolonged currency appreciation.

It is possible to go off course in so many ways that simple rules—Never run a budget deficit or Never increase the money supply faster than the rate of growth of output—have considerable appeal. A more constructive answer for Peru in 1985 might recognize that the economy had considerable room for expansion and that renewed growth could both reduce poverty and conceivably lessen the appeal of violence. It was not intrinsically misdirected to adopt a heterodox approach. The crucial requirements for avoiding breakdown would have been to shift toward restraint of domestic demand and wages in 1987, in response to the rapid change in balance between demand and productive capacity, and to stop the deterioration of incentives to export. Imports nearly doubled between 1985 and 1987 while exports fell slightly, leading to a record deficit on current account (BCRP 1993, 1). Even if García had not managed to antagonize the private sector, even if price controls had been more tightly enforced, the project was hopeless in the absence of export promotion and demand restraint. With their help, the expansionary process might have been kept going, at a slower pace but without explosion. Without such corrections to face a changing reality, the breakdown became inevitable, and the price to Peruvians was very high.

The Achilles Heel: External Deficits

The economy managed three short periods of growth from 1970 to 1990: in the first half of the 1970s under Velasco, in 1980–81, and from 1985 to 1987. All three were cut off by the same constraints: rising balance of payments deficits on current account, rising external debt, and decisions by lenders to restrict further credit under these conditions. On the most direct level, the cause of aborted growth was the recurring scarcity of foreign exchange (Iguíñiz and Muñoz 1992, 13–30).

Underlying the scarcity of foreign exchange, four fatal characteristics of economic strategy in this period made it almost impossible to achieve sustainable economic growth. First, high levels of protection raised the profitability of domestic sales relative to exports and served as a persisting antiexport bias. Second, periods of growth were led by increasing domestic demand, which raised requirements for imports of equipment and supplies and had the added effect of pulling potential exports of primary products into the domestic market instead. Third, a consistent preference for holding down the price of foreign exchange both fed the demand for imports and held down the profitability of exports. Fourth, the expansionary fiscal and monetary policies that raised demand and stimulated short periods of growth were not revised when demand began to outrun productive capacity.

Figure 7.1 charts the oscillations of the current account balance from 1970 to 1990. Under the Velasco government, it fell from a small surplus in 1970 to a peak deficit by 1975. The Morales Bermudez government restored a surplus by 1979, but under Belaúnde the deficit returned by 1981 to a higher level than under Velasco. The following contraction allowed the García government to start with a surplus in 1985, but it was quickly turned into another deep deficit by 1987.

This explanation minimizes two traditional factors in recurrent foreign exchange crises: adverse changes in the terms of trade and in world financial markets. Falling export prices clearly can cause deficits that are not due to domestic economic policies. They were significant in the second case of aborted growth but not in the first or third cases. The Belaúnde government was hampered by the worldwide debt crisis starting in 1992, but it had already achieved its nonsustainable deficit before that problem arose. The García government met considerable hostility from international lenders after his decision to limit debt service payments to a maximum of 10 percent of export earnings, but that hostility was not what caused its formidable current account deficit. Even with that opposition, the García government managed to borrow enough to raise the country's external debt by more than 50 percent.

Changes in the level of external public debt, and total debt, are summarized in Table 7.3. It does not look as if Peru had been starved of external credit. Rather, credit was too plentiful for the country's good. The increase of 95 percent in total debt from 1970 to 1975 led the way to a costly process. External borrowing can be a real help when it eases

Fig. 7.1. Balance of payments on current account, 1970–90.

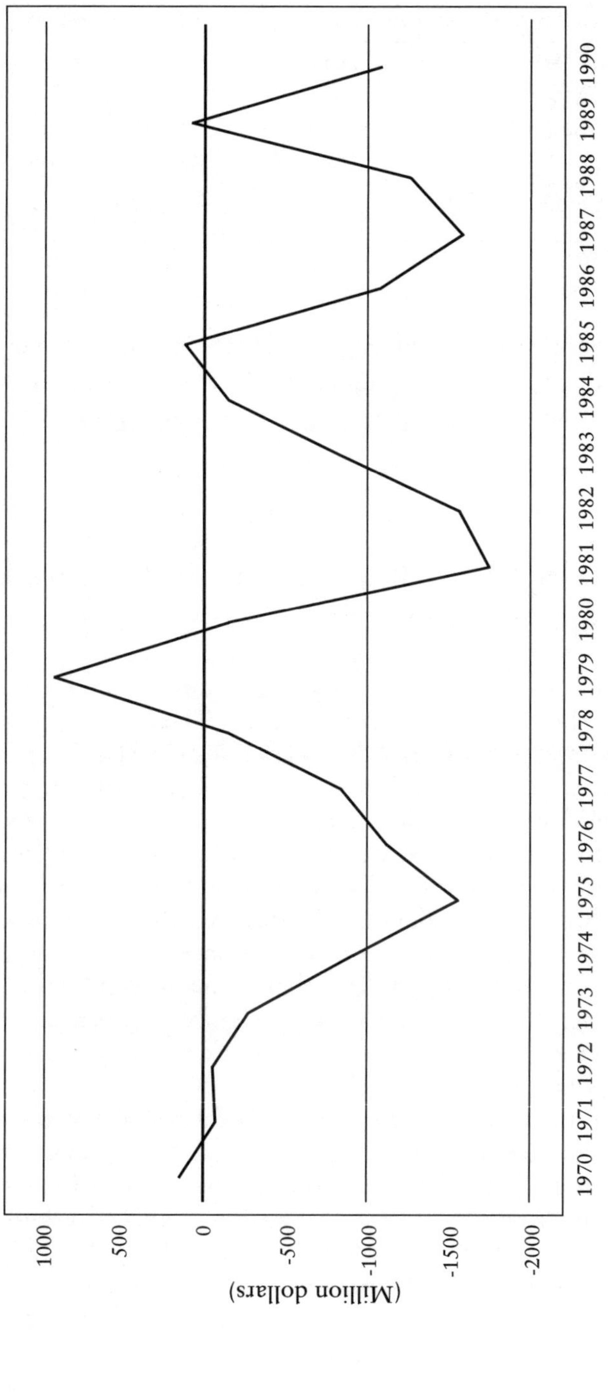

SOURCE: BCRP 1993, 1.

Table 7.3. External debt, public and total, 1970–1990 (millions of dollars)

	Public Debt	Total Debt	Percentage Change in Total	
1970	945	2,712		
1975	3,066	5,288	1970–75	95
1980	6,043	8,723	1975–80	65
1985	10,552	12,876	1980–85	48
1990	17,039	19,262	1985–90	53

SOURCE: BCRP 1993, 107.

constraints on growth, but a seventeenfold increase in external debt over two decades of falling output per capita did little more than facilitate overspending and saddle the country with an ongoing burden adverse to development.

State-Led Development, Import Substitution, and Macroeconomic Management

The quarter century of state-led development from the mid 1960s to 1990 turned out to be painfully difficult for Peru. The problem might be explained in some measure by the idiosyncracies of particular governments, but systematic factors were clearly involved. The strategy of protection to promote import substitution had enough drawbacks to account for much of the difficulty, although it could surely have been implemented in ways to make it more helpful—or less damaging—if macroeconomic management had been even moderately careful. Are there any necessary connections between import substitution and the macroeconomic mismanagement that characterized this period? Is there something fundamentally wrong with the general strategy of state-led development, or were Peru's problems with it instead the consequences of particular characteristics of its economy and policy measures?

In terms of economic logic, decisions to protect particular industries do not imply any need to run fiscal deficits, overexpand the money supply, or overvalue the currency. In terms of political forces and national goals, the connections may be closer. Most of the governments concerned were trying to ensure the support of industrialists and urban labor. Industrialists who depend wholly on the domestic market, unconcerned about exports, can become a potent lobby for expansionary policies. With urban workers pulling in the same direction, a commitment to industrialization became something close to a commitment to expansionary macroeconomic policy. That policy may be highly desirable when it does not push demand beyond the limits of productive capacity, but becomes costly when it does. The absence of concern for safe limits was the undoing of the strategy.

Emphasis on macroeconomic disequilibrium is not meant to suggest that protection itself was irrelevant. It may have brought into being some industries that would otherwise have been delayed and fostered new skills in the process. That potential gain was offset by increased monopoly power for domestic firms shielded from competition, decreased pressure for efficiency, higher costs of production that retarded the development of industrial exports, and favoritism to the "modern" side of the economy at the cost of the lower income traditional side. Restriction of access to imports, for consumers chiefly but also to some extent for producers, aggravated inflationary problems because it prevented switching to lower price alternatives when supplies of particular goods became scarce. The elasticity of supply of the whole economy was held down and squeezed the space available for noninflationary expansion.

Lower and more selective levels of protection could have been consistent with both faster industrialization and reduction of poverty if combined with effective promotion of industrial exports. In this same period, the East Asian countries were industrializing rapidly with considerable protection and with impressively low degrees of inequality (Sachs 1987). It could be done; it was done.

One of the key differences compared with Latin America was that the East Asian countries established relatively equal conditions in the first place, through wide access to education and high levels of education for almost everyone, and in some cases through land reform as well. A second difference is that they did not foster excesses on the side of domestic demand: they could not avoid inflation completely but they kept it low. A third difference is that they bent over backward to push industry into export competition rather than allow it to relax and exploit consumers behind protection. That push toward exports included extensive use of subsidies, direct government help behind the scenes, and an effort to maintain exchange rates favorable for profitable export competition. This strategy was clearly a version of state-led development too, but a version different from the Latin American. Naturally, a great many other factors were involved as well, including a strong work ethic and the absence of significant natural resources pulling comparative advantage toward the primary sector. Still, with all such reservations about the comparison, it seems clear that protected industrialization aimed at the domestic market was an inferior strategy. An efficient and sustained process of state-led development could have helped a great deal; this particular version went in the wrong direction.

Conclusions

The two Belaúnde administrations and those of both Velasco and García were all in their ways responding to dissatisfaction over basic social conditions. They accomplished some changes, most notably land reform and a great expansion of access to education, but none of them gave anything like adequate attention to the need for coherent macroeconomic strategy. They lost the dynamism of 1950–65 without putting anything constructive in its place.

In that earlier period, export incentives and external markets were jointly favorable; increasing income from exports stimulated rising domestic demand and investment; tax revenue increased with income; and fiscal balance helped hold down both inflation and external deficits. In the following quarter century, fiscal and monetary restraint were greatly weakened, the rural sector and potential industrial exporters were hurt by adverse incentives, and pressures of import competition that might have forced attention to efficiency were blocked. The industrial sector responded to the incentives built into the strategy: it focused on the protected domestic market, with little or no attempt to compete in external markets. It never came close to earning the foreign exchange needed for its own imports of equipment and supplies. The more the industrial sector grew, the more nearly impossible it became for the country to maintain external balance.

It should have been possible to get better results from a strategy of state-led development. Greater fiscal and monetary restraint during expansionary periods could have lessened the inflationary consequences: that restraint would have meant postponing some projects and limiting the growth of demand and income in expansionary years, for the sake of sustained expansion over the whole period. Greater emphasis on promoting new exports, and less on protection, could have increased efficiency and relieved bottlenecks on the side of foreign exchange.

The brief but revealing exception of the 1975–80 period under the post-Velasco military government pointed to possibilities that might have made an enormous difference if followed up, but the Belaúnde administration failed to do so. Its costly choice of renewed currency appreciation, intended to check inflation, exactly foreshadowed the preference of the Fujimori government in the first half of the 1990s.

The upsurge of violence in the 1980s added enormously to the problems caused by macroeconomic policies. Besides its toll of death and destruction, the violence undermined confidence in the future of the country. The sustained violence was not just the result of perverse ideology: it grew from the country's history of failure to do anything about the extreme poverty of the rural areas, discrimination against the indigenous population, and inability to generate adequate opportunities for productive employment. These issues were essentially ones of economic and social structure rather than of state-led development as an economic strategy.

The basic structural conditions in Latin America—above all the low levels of and unequal access to education that have done so much to limit personal mobility, productivity, and capacity for technological change—made state-led development more difficult than in East Asia. In the strategy itself, disregard for macroeconomic balance and the orientation toward protection rather than a competitive industrial sector ensured poor results. Latin America desperately needed to get out of the trap of this particular version of state-led development. It did not need to renounce the whole idea of socially determined guidance to shape the character of development.

8

THE 1990S

Reversion to a Relatively Open Economy

Peru's economic strategy took a sharp reverse turn in 1990, back to the main lines of the market-determined regime that the country had rejected in the 1960s. This second reversal was a readily understandable response to the mounting chaos of a state-led development strategy that went badly wrong, but the specific liberalization program chosen raises many questions of balance among goals. It gave much more attention to reintegration with the world financial community, reassurance to private investors, and control of inflation than to employment, equality, structural change, or autonomy.

Most characteristics of the new strategy have remained almost unchanged since its definition in 1990–91, but some, notably its social side, have altered considerably. In the first two years, the government made no serious effort to help the poor cope with the shock of adjustment, but from 1993 on, concern for poverty became something of a crusade, with a stated target to cut it in half by the year 2000. The originally tight restraint on government spending was replaced by a strong growth trend for public investment as well as for social programs. In the critical problem area of exchange rate management, the costly appreciation allowed from 1990 through 1994 was at least temporarily stopped: the real exchange rate was held in a narrow band from then through 1997. The essence of the liberalization strategy remains intact, but these changes help make clear that it need not be a rigid package: it can encompass alternative policies with significantly different consequences.

A truly determined drive to reduce poverty could use two lines of action: social programs directed to improving the personal capacities of the poor and economic policies designed to make the economy function in less inequitable ways. This government has chosen to emphasize social policies and has given them real content. It has resolutely avoided doing anything significant to reshape the operation of the economy to favor reduction of poverty and inequality. That policy leaves open the real possibility that ongoing market forces may pull toward inequality with such strength that they outweigh even a well-supported set of social programs.

The first section of this chapter summarizes the economic and political factors, inside and outside Peru, that dominated the choice of the new strategy in 1990. The second section discusses its logic, its main characteristics, and the halting process of change in some of its methods. The third through fifth sections review the main consequences so far in terms of macroeconomic stabilization, investment and growth, the structure of production, external balance, employment, poverty, and inequality. The last section suggests alternative possibilities in a liberal economic strategy that could make it more favorable for sustained growth, reduction of poverty, and conceivably even reduction of inequality.

Liberalization as Reaction to Previous Failure

"Previous failure" refers to Latin America as a whole, not just Peru. For most of the last half century, the region fell far short of its potential, with a needlessly poor record of erratic growth, inflation, and high inequality. Some individual countries made promising headway even in the difficult decade of the 1980s, but Peru came to stand out instead for its descent into growing poverty and violence. That deterioration created strong pressures for drastic change, but it also limited the scope for independent choice in determining a new strategy.

Through the depressing decade of the 1980s, Peru's increasing violence dominated public fears, fed into discouragement of investment, and aggravated all its economic problems. For the business and financial community, two additional concerns were highly important. One was the conflict between the private sector and the state, as the government under Alan García turned against the private sector in its attempt to take over the banking system and allowed the whole structure of public administration to deteriorate (Gonzales de Olarte and Samamé 1994). The second was the breakdown in relations between Peru and the international financial community, as the government repudiated scheduled debt service even to the main international development institutions.

Many other Latin American countries quietly stopped paying regular debt service in this period with some conflict but no breakdown of relations. The difference for Peru was that the García government raised nonpayment to an issue of aggressively independent principle. That position might have been an admirable example of courage had it been backed up by coherent economic management, including effective export promotion to lessen dependence on external credit. In the event, without either coherence or export promotion, the policy cut Peru off from potential help that might have made the rout of 1988–90 less overwhelming. It also intensified pressure from the private sector to bring Peru back into regular contact with the international financial community.

Inside Peru, the trauma of the 1980s predetermined some of the main priorities for any new administration. The government had to act against inflation and violence, to restore some order to its own operations, and in particular to improve the ability to collect tax revenue. If it was to have any support from the private business and financial sector, it had to re-establish connections with the international financial community. That context dictated a conservative orientation. Still, it left some scope for choice between an answer limited to macroeconomic stabilization and the alternative of thoroughgoing liberalization and between gradual adjustment and the alternative of all-out shock treatment. On both counts, the government started toward the more modest alternatives but was quickly pushed to the opposite extreme by the international financial community.

The International Monetary Fund and the World Bank have always encouraged changes away from protection and regulation but before the 1980s had not normally insisted on them. Their hesitation may have been a reflection of uncertainty about how far it was desirable to go. It may also have been a matter of understanding that interference with national choices for state-led development would involve them deeply in domestic political and social issues (Tanzi 1987). Whatever the earlier reasons for circumspection, in the course of the 1980s the international institutions became progressively more insistent on the necessity of all-out structural reforms. They could more readily do so because the debt crisis made the developing countries more dependent on credit from the international agencies. On the political level, changes toward more conservative governments in the United States and England pulled all these agencies in the same direction. By the time Peru's turn came, earlier reservations about interference had been replaced by insistence on detailed conditions in all directions.

In the same process, the international agencies increased pressure for drastic shock treatments to get rid of distortions in one swoop, as opposed to gradualist reforms. The initially favored candidate in Peru's presidential election of 1990, Mario Vargas Llosa, adopted the same position and promised quick relief from the tangled mess of the past. Fujimori's campaign took the opposite position, in favor of a gradualist program. That promise helped him beat the odds and win the election.[1] Accordingly, before taking office, he chose a team of economic advisers dedicated to such a program. But he also agreed with business and financial leaders that it was essential to restore relationships with the world financial community and took a crucial trip to Washington and Tokyo to that end. His receptions in the two capitals made it clear that he was expected to put through an immediate, all-out liberalization program. That change required a radical reversal of instructions to his economic advisers, followed immediately by their resignations. With a new set of advisers, the opponent of shock treatment quickly implemented the dramatic "Fujishock" of August 1990.

In one decisive step, the government eliminated price controls for private-sector products and increased manyfold the prices of energy and other goods and services provided by state companies: the consumer price index more than doubled in a single day. The chronic traffic jams of Lima's main streets suddenly disappeared, as people, stunned by enormous leaps in bus fares and gasoline prices, retreated from sight. Formerly crowded stores and restaurants were deserted; the city seemed to hold its

---

1. This is not to say that his promise of gradualist reforms was decisive in the election. It was helpful because many people feared a shock program, but it was probably a secondary issue. What counted most was that he embodied all the advantages of a complete outsider—even better, a non-Hispanic outsider—in a context in which the majority of the country was disgusted with traditional parties and leaders.

breath. Soup kitchens sprang up everywhere, manned by volunteers using donated ingredients, with no help from the government. The only clear sign that the government was at all concerned was the presence of open military vehicles, with soldiers holding their rifles, driving slowly through the near-empty streets.

To the surprise of many, the great majority of Peruvians kept going patiently ahead as best they could. Life, and traffic, gradually returned, the mass of the people who were not in a position to raise prices of anything suffered deeper poverty, and the government proceeded with the details of its thorough reversal of the country's economic strategy.

The New Strategy: Logic and Methods

The central themes of the new strategy would have been welcome to Adam Smith. Nearly all regulatory restrictions on business were swept away, and protection against imports was reduced sharply (Rossini 1991; Gonzales de Olarte 1993a; Sheahan 1994). All subsidies and differential tax advantages meant to promote exports or rural development or to protect lower income groups were eliminated. The government stopped entering directly into wage settlements in the private sector, cut the minimum wage deeply, and drastically reduced public-sector wages and employment. State ownership of basic public services was retained at first, with prices raised to levels intended to eliminate deficits; privatization began gradually, after three years, for electric power, telephones, state-owned mines, and the oil industry.

Restrictions on foreign investment were replaced by warm invitations. Fiscal deficits were almost eliminated by holding down government spending while making a strenuous effort to raise tax collections, with a new tax agency, SUNAT, to replace the hopelessly enfeebled office left by the García administration. Tight monetary restraint backed up the drive for fiscal balance. Despite the severe constraints of available tax revenue, the government gave priority to resuming service on external debt. That policy did not leave much revenue available to implement promises to shield the poor from the impact of all the measures that raised prices and reduced employment (Figueroa 1995).

The logic of the process was of course the basic free-market vision of an economic system in which the search for profit is expected to guide firms toward efficiency. Taking away protection was intended to force producers to focus more on cost reduction and quality improvement than had been necessary under the strategy of import substitution. It was also expected to restrain inflation: directly, by allowing buyers to switch to imports whenever domestic prices of particular goods rose above external levels; indirectly, in a more fundamental sense, by increasing the flexibility of the production process through more open access to imported supplies and equipment.

Liberalization was expected to, and did, hurt firms and workers dependent on protection, consumers previously sheltered to some degree by price controls or helped by subsidies, and public-sector workers hit by both lower real wages and massive dismissals. Official statements emphasized the intention to implement emergency social programs, but in practice very little was done in the first two years. That disregard of the poor changed radically from 1993 on. Social programs increased from 2 percent of GDP for 1990–91 to 6 percent by 1995 (Table 6.8). A major set of antipoverty programs got underway, very much influenced by political concerns but still relatively well focused on rural districts characterized by high degrees of poverty (Chapter 6).

Public investment was held down tightly through 1991, but in the course of 1992 it began a steep rise. It increased 13 percent a year for 1992–93 and then 25 percent in 1994 (BCRP 1997, 120, 123). The increase was partly stimulated by aid from international development agencies and perhaps also by increasingly serious worries over the downturn of the economy in 1992. Whatever the mixture of motives, the change was a real help both to begin reconstructing battered public infrastructure and to stimulate economic recovery.

The initially negative impact of liberalization on production and employment was magnified by allowing the currency to appreciate in real terms at the same time that protection was cut back. That costly strategy weakened the benefits of a more open economy. These benefits depend heavily on a country's ability to maintain a competitive position for a wide range of producers, not just for a few primary products. If the price of foreign exchange is too low to enable the more efficient side of the industrial sector to export profitably or to keep the rate of growth of imports from getting out of control, sustained growth becomes very difficult, and diversification of the economy even more so. That issue has been, and remains, a major one.[2]

---

2. Debates over exchange rate policy have not been limited to academics: business groups have been actively concerned and outspoken too (Castillo and Quispe 1996, 81–89). In the

In the severe years of the world debt crisis, developing countries did not have much room for choice in these matters. The tight conditions of world financial markets practically forced them toward an export orientation because external credit was so difficult to obtain. In the last years of the 1980s, a swing back to monetary expansion in the industrialized countries generated a new round of capital flow toward developing countries. That change greatly reduced pressures to promote exports. In 1990, Peru had no immediate need to take measures to make its producers more competitive: if the government could satisfy the international financial community about its purity of intentions and its capacity to implement them, it could count on a substantial inflow of foreign capital. The capital inflows could—and did—pull the real exchange rate toward appreciation. The positive side was that this process helped reduce inflation; the negative side was that it handicapped the development of new exports and set up conditions for rising trade deficits as soon as the economy began to recover.

From 1990 through 1994, the conflict between concern for inflation and recognition of the damage to Peruvian firms led to back-and-forth movement of central bank intervention to guide short-term changes in the real exchange rate, but the basic trend remained strongly downward. The real price of foreign exchange fell by one-fourth between December 1990 and December 1994 (Table 8.1). The balance then changed: the rate stopped falling, but it did not begin to recover. Whether this represented a conscious change of objectives or the accidental result of changing capital flows is not clear. What is clear is that the price of foreign exchange has remained too low for the economy to be able to combine rapid growth with external balance. For individual producers, the low price of foreign exchange has made it difficult either to compete with imports or to develop new exports.

The industrial sector clearly lost its central place in national economic strategy. Industrialists naturally fought back as hard as they could and were able to gain some concessions, but not many. The government's responses to such pressures, coming from everyone, went more toward favors for the financial and mining sectors than for industry (Castillo and Quispe 1996, 115–26). Official statements have been consistent in rejecting consideration of anything resembling "industrial policy." In practice, the exchange rate regime has amounted almost to an anti-industrial policy.

---

first years of the liberalization program, nearly every monthly issue of *Moneda*, the journal of the Banco Central de Reserva, included articles by Peruvian economists and business leaders

Table 8.1. Index of the real exchange rate, 1990–1997

	Index in December[a] August 1990 = 100
1990	105.7
1991	86.5
1992	91.4
1993	88.2
1994	77.4
1995	79.6
1996	79.9
1997	77.4

SOURCES: BCRP 1993, 139; 1998b, 71.

[a] The real exchange rate used is the average of buying and selling rates for the multilateral index calculated by the Banco Central de Reserve del Perú.

Consequences for Inflation, Output, and Investment

Differences among goals have a lot to do with differences among consequences. The new strategy succeeded well in terms of the government's main objectives: in slowing down inflation and restoring full participation in world financial markets as well as leading to a revival of investment and production. It has not yet been as effective in terms of employment, external balance, or structural changes in directions likely to lessen inequality.

Table 8.2 summarizes measures of changes in inflation, output per capita, investment, and external debt. The astronomical rate of inflation for 1990 owed a great deal—more than half—to the Fujishock itself. The release of all controlled prices at once, combined with drastic increases in prices of public services, was in part intended to push the price level so high that demand would fall enough to remove inflationary pressure. It did not work out quite that easily—inflation remained very high through 1991—but then came down by fairly regular steps to 9 percent for 1997. Nine percent is of course a wonderful change for the better, lower than any year in the preceding quarter century, although it is still a considerable handicap for international competition unless offset by correcting the exchange rate.

The adjustment program's initial impact on output was negative, as such programs usually are: output per capita fell steeply in the second

---

debating the forces determining exchange rates, their consequences, and the policies that might (or should not) be used.

Table 8.2. Inflation, changes in GDP per capita and gross investment, direct foreign investment, and external debt, 1990–1997

	1990	1991	1992	1993	1994	1995	1996	1997
Rate of inflation	7,482	410	74	49	24	11	12	9
GDP per capita, percentage change[a]	−5.5	1.1	−3.5	4.6	11.2	5.5	0.8	5.4
Gross investment, percentage change[a]	5.0	13.3	−3.9	13.4	28.9	20.3	−3.1	12.7
Direct foreign investment ($ million)								
Privatizations	0	0	6	168	2,241	547	1,688	145
Other	41	−7	144	519	867	1,501	1,554	1,885
External debt, end year ($ billion)								
Total	22.9	25.4	26.6	27.4	30.2	33.4	33.8	28.5
Public[b]	18.9	21.0	21.5	22.2	24.0	25.7	25.2	18.8

SOURCES: BCRP 1998a, 145–46, 160, 176, 178.
[a] GDP per capita and investment at constant 1979 prices.
[b] Public sector debt is medium and long term, excluding short term.

half of 1990, rose slightly in 1991, then fell again in 1992. At that point, recovery seemed stalled, and criticism of the economic program began to sharpen. Congressional critics took heart and focused attacks on the government for giving in too readily to IMF-World Bank pressures. The president, not given to patient negotiation, responded by closing down the congress (Chapter 2). Although that move provoked denunciation from many people concerned for democracy, the private business sector and the majority of the public responded with approval: the traditional political parties were still in disgrace, and the president had demonstrated both his commitment to the new economic strategy and his capacity to take forceful action. *Todavía es vivo el chino.*

The *auto-golpe* of April 1992 reassured the business and financial community about the stability of the economic program, and that reassurance gained strength in September when the Lima police captured the leader of *Sendero luminoso* and a group of his closest associates. For the great majority of Peruvians, that was an enormous relief.

As hope revived, so did property values, expected returns on investment, and economic activity. Investment rose at almost incredible rates from 1993 through 1995 (Table 8.2).[3] GDP per capita recovered its 1990 level in 1993 and increased a striking 11 percent in 1994. This surge of production was possible, once demand began to rise, because the deeply depressed conditions of the economy at the beginning of the decade had left enormous excess capacity. Even after continuing high growth in 1995, output per capita still remained 12 percent below its level of 1980 (BCRP 1995, 138).

The main driving force for expansion from 1993 on came from the great rise in investment. Internally, the major factor was a striking rise in construction, starting with the public sector and followed quickly by the private. That rise responded to improving financial conditions but above all to the reassurance of decreasing violence, against the background of many years of minimal construction and considerable destruction. The rise in investment included a return of foreign investors, who had been held back for many years by both the violence and the hostility of the Velasco and García governments. Excluding purchases of newly privatized state firms, direct foreign investment rose from nothing in 1991 to $519 million in 1993 and $1,885 million by 1997 (Table 8.2). The inflow for purchases of privatized state firms barely started in 1992–93, then jumped to $2,241 million in 1994, mainly for privatization of the telephone system. Apart from purchases of firms providing basic public services, foreign direct investment concentrated chiefly on newly opened opportunities in mining, for purchases of state-owned mines, for exploration, and for modernization of technology in a sector that had been running downhill for years.

The industrial sector has not attracted as much foreign investment as have mining and public utilities, perhaps because of its disadvantaged position in the new economic strategy. A sample covering forty of the largest domestic industrial firms for the period 1990–93 also showed considerable reserve about investment: only a minority increased their assets in this period (Castillo and Quispe 1996, 99–113). Industrial production was not set back: it rose much more rapidly from 1990 to 1996 than in the preceding two decades (Chapter 5). Still, it lost ground relative to industrial imports, which rose much faster than GDP. For nearly all industries, output increased in absolute terms while falling relative to imports.

---

3. The percentages given in Table 8.2 are based on the measures by the Banco Central de Reserva del Perú as calculated in 1979 prices. Alternative measures by the IDB, calculated in dollar prices of 1990, give different percentage increases but with the same basic pattern.

The External Side

The promising possibilities demonstrated by recovery of output and investment have been accompanied by two weaknesses on the external side. One is financial: rising current account deficits and increased dependence on external capital. The second, a more profound and longer term problem, concerns the structures of production and trade. Liberalization that favors reliance on primary exports, combined with an exchange rate strategy adverse to the competitive position of the industrial sector, has encouraged a capital-intensive style of growth inimical to employment and equality.

In much the same pattern as in preceding populist periods, the government supported its domestic goals by allowing the country to fall into deepening dependence on external capital. The current account deficit increased from 3.8 percent of GDP in 1990 to 7.3 percent by 1995 (Table 8.3).[4] Greater restraint on aggregate demand in 1996, and a surge in exports in 1997, brought it down to 5.2 percent for the latter year. Imports increased at a phenomenal rate: 21 percent a year from 1990 through 1995 or 17 percent through 1997.

Service payments on external public debt have not been a problem in terms of foreign exchange availability, but their cost to the budget severely squeezed financing for social and other domestic programs in 1991–92: payments on the debt accounted for one-fifth of total government spending in these years (Gonzales de Olarte 1997b, table 5a). That problem gradually lessened as government revenue increased with recovery of the economy and as payments on the debt decreased, from $2.8 billion for 1990 to $1.9 billion for 1997 (BCRP 1998a, 180). Going in the opposite direction, external debt of the private sector more than tripled.[5]

Both the causes and the likely consequences of the deficits on current account have been debated endlessly in Peru. Causation from one direction is clear enough, but one direction is rarely enough to explain anything. The rate of increase of imports, the most evidently aberrant factor, can

---

4. These ratios have been brought into question by an ongoing debate over the accuracy of the national accounts (Torres 1993; Cuba 1997; Jiménez 1997). All concerned agree that current measures of GDP in constant 1979 prices are distorted by an out-of-date base and in addition that estimates when converted to dollar terms are overstated.

5. This estimate is an approximation made by subtracting public-sector medium and long-term debt and both long- and short-term obligations of the central reserve bank from totals for all external debt (BCRP 1998a, 178). The remainder was $2.7 billion for the end of 1990 and $8.8 billion for the end of 1997.

Table 8.3. External trade and current account deficits, 1990–1997 (In million dollars, except for last column)

	Exports				Current Account	
	Total	Non-traditional	Industrial[a]	Imports	Dollars	Percentage of GDP[b]
1990	3,321	989	762	2,922	−1,383	−3.8
1991	3,406	994	747	3,593	−1,509	−3.6
1992	3,661	966	706	4,002	−2,101	−5.0
1993	3,516	1,016	692	4,123	−2,302	−5.6
1994	4,598	1,215	788	5,596	−2,648	−5.3
1995	5,589	1,445	946	7,754	−4,306	−7.3
1996	5,898	1,590	1,054	7,886	−3,626	−5.9
1997	6,814	2,043	1,426	8,552	−3,408	−5.2
Rate of growth	10.8	10.9	9.4	16.6		

SOURCE: BCRP 1998a, 164–66, 169.
[a] Industrial exports approximated by subtracting agricultural and fishing products from total for nontraditional exports.
[b] Questions about official measures of GDP have suggested that these ratios are understated. By one set of proposed alternative measures, the ratios may have been as high as 9.0 for 1995 and 7.2 for 1996 (Jiménez 1997, 57).

be explained by the combination of liberalization, increasing aggregate demand and production, and appreciation of the currency in real terms. Liberalization may have been the key causal factor in the first few years but can hardly account for the steepness of the further increases in 1994–95. These increases were more directly linked to the combination of increasing output with appreciation of the real exchange rate.

With the exceptionally rapid growth of output from 1993 through 1995, two warning signals pointed to the need for some redirection of macroeconomic policy. Besides the growing external deficit, the rate of inflation stopped decreasing. The government reacted—a plus in itself, compared with earlier inertia—with a compromise. It cut back the growth of public investment and the economy, while raising the real price of foreign exchange very slightly (2.6 percent in the course of 1995). As a result of the contractionary measures, the growth of GDP per capita stopped in 1996. On the more positive side, the rate of growth of nontraditional exports increased, and that of imports slowed down. In view of the slight upturn in inflation, it might have been dangerous to take further steps to make up for the preceding appreciation. These choices are not easy.

Exports have grown well despite appreciation of the real exchange rate. Their resilience could be explained in part by the process of liberalization: it allowed producers greater access to imported equipment and supplies, at lower prices relative to domestic inputs. Producers were also helped by the return of direct foreign investment into export activities, above all in the mining sector. The high rents available from mining and oil exports make them relatively immune to the negative effects of an exchange rate that remains adverse for industrial exports (Schuldt 1994, 54–73).

The problem is that export growth remains dominated by traditional products, particularly the capital-intensive minerals sector. Through 1994, although total exports were growing 7 percent a year, the rate of growth for industrial exports (as estimated in Table 8.3) was less than 1 percent. That picture changed for the better in 1995–97 as the exchange rate stopped appreciating. It is clearly possible to do better than return to the traditional pattern of comparative advantage under conditions in which the advantages are inimical to industrial exports. Without a sustained redirection of its trade and exchange rate strategy, the country is likely to be restricted to a primary exporter's role adverse to diversification, to learning, to development of human resources, and to employment. Mining is not the leading sector one would choose if one were concerned with inequality or with human development.

Social Consequences

Very nearly all liberalization programs in Latin America have been marked by worsening inequality and some with worsening poverty as well (Berry 1997). The Peruvian program had a depressing start too but then led to a considerable reduction of poverty between 1991 and 1994, with a slight decrease in measured inequality (Chapter 6). Those results, not great but better than experience elsewhere, were due mainly to the striking rise of output that began in 1993, helped in some degree by active social programs beginning that year.

The initial emphasis of the liberalization program, dominated by concerns for acceptance by the international financial community and for inflation, ensured that social objectives would at least temporarily take a back seat. These objectives certainly did for the first two years, in terms of both direct social programs and employment and earnings (Figueroa 1995). From 1993, the government began to implement new social programs on a large scale. That change could be seen as a defensive measure to ensure continued acceptability of economic liberalization. To at least some of the proponents of these programs, they are more than that: they are serious attempts to help neglected groups and disadvantaged people gain skills, awareness, and new opportunities for their lives. They could help a great deal, if they are not submerged in a swamp of political manipulation, but they leave open a fundamental question. Is the new economic orientation itself structured in ways that are likely to be favorable for the reduction of poverty and inequality?

The interrelated factors most important for that question have been central themes throughout this book: the effects of the strategy on employment and earnings, on the capacity of the economy to achieve sustained growth, and on the competitive position and technological dynamism of the country's producers. Success in each of these respects should reinforce success with the others in the long run, although in the short term some conflict with others.

A more competitive set of industrial producers would improve the possibilities for sustained growth and thereby increase opportunities for productive employment. The troublesome side of the process is that a drive for competitive strength places increased pressure on firms to economize on the use of labor. The balance between adding workers to raise production as markets grow and cutting jobs whenever the marginal productivity of labor fails to offset its cost could go either way in a particular period. The question becomes what might be done to make the balance positive for employment without undermining the search for increasing efficiency.

The most fundamental ways to achieve this result would be to reduce inequalities in access to education, to raise the quality of public education, and to improve access to health care for lower income people. Even the most conservative liberalization programs could support progress on these issues, subject to one basic problem: if tax rates are kept low to favor private investors, that policy restricts the scope for social spending within the constraint of fiscal balance. Increasing tax revenue with fiscal reforms and recovery of the economy have given the country more room for choice but do not determine the outcome. Rising incomes do not guarantee generosity.

Employment conditions, miserable long before economic liberalization, turned somewhat better in the recovery of 1993–95 (Table 5.3). Formal employment in the private sector began to rise more rapidly than the labor force, in contrast to their relationship from 1970 to 1990. Still, the ratio of employment growth to output growth was lower than in earlier recovery periods (Infante 1997). Real wages, which started to rise when inflation came down and output increased, turned back down again from 1995 through 1997 (Figure 5.1).

The growth of employment has been slower than it could have been because imports have been kept cheaper and exports less profitable than they could have been with a more competitive exchange rate. Firms have been forced to hold down employment more deeply than they need have done or than economic efficiency would call for them to do at a competitive exchange rate.

The structure of employment changed markedly in these years, in ways that on balance favored reduction of wage differentials. Employment in firms with over 100 workers, where wages had averaged much higher than in small and medium-sized firms, fell relative to employment in the latter. Perhaps in part for this reason, earnings of younger workers rose relative to those with more experience (Saavedra 1997b). In the opposite direction, earnings advantages of workers with more education increased relative to those with less, as did earnings of employees paid by the month relative to those of workers paid by the hour. Still, where the common effect of liberalization in most countries has been to widen inequality of labor earnings, the balance in Peru went slightly the other way.

A major additional factor working toward lower poverty in this period is that agricultural output rose even more strongly than did the economy as a whole. Thanks to the great decrease in land ownership concentration made possible by land reform, that output growth had more positive connotations for reduction of poverty than it would have had in earlier Peruvian history.

Rural poverty and inequality as well must also have been reduced to some degree by the surge of social programs that started in 1993. Although they have been very much politically oriented, the largest program, FON-CODES, has been well focused on rural areas characterized by high degrees of poverty (Graham and Kane 1998; Francke 1997b). That and related investment in rural infrastructure, particularly extensive road building, helped spread the positive consequences of the rise in national income. The incidence of poverty in the rural sierra fell by four percentage points between 1991 and 1994 and one percentage point farther by 1996 (Table 6.4; Francke 1997a). Still, the incidence remained much higher than it had been in 1985.

Urban poverty was gratuitously worsened by the ruthless way in which minimum wages were forced down from 1990 through 1995 (Figure 5.1). That policy changed radically in 1996 and 1997: real minimum wages were suddenly raised back above their (pitiful) level of 1990. That change helped some of the lowest income workers without contradicting the basic sense of liberalization. An open economy can thrive perfectly well with rising minimum wages, as the Chilean economy has done ever since the return to democracy in that country.

In terms of social institutions, job protection for workers was practically eliminated in the name of labor market "flexibility" (Verdera 1997b). Labor unions have continued to lose strength, as they did in the previous decade (Chapter 5). Other nongovernment organizations have stayed very much alive and worked hard to help the poor in the awful conditions of 1990–92. The main problem of these organizations has been the government's disinterest in, or distrust of, any independent channels of social concern. They have not been repressed, just ignored.

Two Alternatives Among Many Possibilities

Compared with the deterioration of the 1980s, the economy has functioned much better under economic liberalization. If compared instead with the hopes of the early postwar years for a better society, both less unequal and more self-determined, the new strategy can be seen as a defeat. Liberalization is not oriented toward either of these goals. Still, countless details of ongoing policy choice can change its consequences, as some already have. The following comments are limited to two issues that stand out as particularly important: possibilities for changing the structures of production and exports to favor both sustained growth and better employment conditions; possibilities for creating more diversified economic activity and employment openings in regions characterized by high rural poverty.

More rapid growth of opportunities for productive employment could be favored by changes in the structure of production oriented toward a stronger export position for Peruvian industry, as well as for nontraditional agricultural exports, with less dependence on the capital-intensive and now again largely foreign-owned mining sector. Ideally, such possibilities could be greatly improved by more effective concern for productivity, innovation, and product quality. That fundamental level of behavior cannot be determined by economic policy, but it could be promoted more actively. On one side, it could be favored by government-supported efforts to encourage research and development, to improve knowledge of and access to new technologies and foreign markets, and to help train workers in new skills. On a second side, it could be favored by policies that reward success in diversified export competition more strongly relative to production of standardized products for established domestic markets. The first side is the more fundamental, but it is not likely to accomplish much if the second side leaves weak incentives for changes of producer interests and behavior.

A great many specific variables, beyond those of sustainable growth and structures of production, could affect the possibilities for improving employment conditions. One variable under active debate is the heavy weight of taxes and required social contributions based on wages. Whether paid by employers or by workers, both add to labor costs and thereby discourage demand for workers (Hunt 1997; Verdera 1997a). To reduce them would imply the need for different sources of financing for the associated social programs and for the government; they are inextricably involved in general issues of public finance. The tax system as a whole has become more successful in generating revenue, partly by changed tax laws and partly by creating a far more effective collection agency (Gonzales de Olarte 1997b).[6] The balance of taxation has moved toward more reliance on regressive taxes, chiefly on value added. That outcome is a natural result of the reorientation of economic strategy toward dependence on private investors: it has been general throughout Latin America (Bird and Perry 1994). Still, it proved possible in Chile, once democracy was restored, to raise taxes on profits to finance new social programs. Economic liberalization need not imply regressive taxation.

A second set of alternatives in a liberalized economic strategy concerns rural poverty and the inadequacy of access either to land or to alternative opportunities that keeps poverty so persistent. These problems probably cannot be answered in any reasonably sufficient way for a long time to come. There is too little arable land for the people remaining in agriculture (Chapter 4). Better incentives for nontraditional agricultural exports could help to some degree, especially with the wider diffusion of land ownership that was the outcome of the land reform. Agriculture itself cannot be a sufficient answer: the most direct and probably most efficient way to reduce rural poverty would be to diversify economic activity in these regions. That strategy would run against all Peruvian history and would

---

6. Between 1990 and 1996, the number of registered taxpayers increased five times over, from 287 thousand to 1.6 million. That number remains modest for a country with a labor force of seven million (Gonzales de Olarte 1997b, 24–25, table 4).

not be easy under either liberalization or nonliberalization. Still, some of the relevant structural factors are becoming more favorable, and the rural-oriented social programs of the Fujimori government have surely been helpful too. How could the process be strengthened?

The necessary condition of diversification in rural areas is that the labor force be at least moderately well educated and able to respond to new opportunities. Postwar change in Peru has included a fairly successful effort to provide access to primary education and to reduce illiteracy in rural areas, although not as yet to improve the quality of public education (Chapter 2). The Fujimori government has gone farther than any others in providing rural schools, and FONCODES has done a good deal to help improve transportation and other infrastructure in rural areas. It remains uncertain how much is being accomplished in terms of training relevant to the skills that would be needed for any serious development of new economic activities. Real headway may require that at least some new industries be given direct support for on-the-job training in regions characterized by high poverty. Social programs to improve productive potential could be combined with support for small- and medium-sized firms that respond to the advantages of lower cost labor. The great key, if there is any such thing, would be to strengthen employment conditions for the country as a whole and in the process to increase the incentives for firms to locate where labor is least expensive. The generalized weakness of employment opportunities acts as a drag on development in rural areas.

The government could also help stimulate economic activity in poor regions by decentralizing public-sector activities and interests. Decentralization would mean allowing more local choice in taxation and spending, with less pull of resources toward the capital area and more two-way relations between regions and the national government in general (Gonzales de Olarte 1997c; Guillén 1997).

Conclusions

Economic liberalization as implemented in Peru has been in many respects a positive change from the miserable record of the 1980s. The start of the recovery in 1993 probably owed as much to the end of any serious revolutionary threat from *Sendero luminoso* as it did to the new economic strategy, but the latter helped to set the stage and sustain the recovery. That help included success in bringing down inflation, restoring control of public finances, and carrying through a trade liberalization program that puts more pressure on firms to pay attention to costs, quality, and technological change. It would be only fair to add that state-led industrialization might also have restrained inflation, maintained fiscal balance, and promoted technological advance, if it had been guided by a coherent program that included such objectives. The problem in Peru was that none of its various versions of state-led industrialization accomplished any such results.

The particular model of economic liberalization program adopted in Peru has had avoidable weaknesses. It has not been as helpful for employment as it could have been, it has not favored diversification of production and exports, it has allowed rising current account deficits that required slowing growth in 1996 despite weak employment conditions, and it has deepened dependence on foreign capital. The exchange rate regime has undermined the competitive position of producers of tradable goods. It makes producers overeconomize on employment and keeps the structure of exports biased against the industrial sector.

The social side of the new economic orientation has improved considerably, after a dismal start in 1990–92. The incidence of poverty decreased notably from 1991 through 1994. Private-sector employment grew faster than it had through the preceding two decades. Inequality as measured by the distribution of income remained practically unchanged, in contrast to the worsening experienced in many other countries after economic liberalization. Still, poverty remains higher than it was a quarter century ago. This particular strategy has been more helpful than harmful, but it seems inadequate to cope with the scale of Peru's problems.

9

INTERACTIONS

Goals, Structure, and Strategy

For Peru, the future looks much more hopeful in 1998 than it did at the beginning of the decade. It is not that the main problems of the past have by any means been resolved, just that after many years in which practically everything kept going from bad to worse some important factors have turned more positive. These factors include major aspects of current macroeconomic policy and performance and some, although by no means all, of the country's more fundamental problems at the level of structural conditions. The positive changes do not as yet include any effective solution to the twin problems of high inequality and social conflict.

The most important structural conditions working against equality and reduction of poverty have been the pressure of rapid growth of the population and the rural labor force running against the limits of scarce land, inadequate opportunities for productive employment outside agriculture, and highly unequal access to education, skills, and health care. These conditions have been changing slowly, but they still mean that the normal operation of market forces works to hold back earnings of the majority of the country's workers, rural and urban, relative to earnings from higher skills and capital.

The first section of this chapter reviews relations between social goals and economic strategy. The second section summarizes the main changes in Peru's economic structure over the last half century which have particularly close bearing on the possibilities for more inclusive economic growth. Do these changes suggest that the return to a liberal economic strategy in the 1990s is likely to have any better consequences than it did in its earlier incarnation? Is the country just going through cyclical alternation between two strategies that both give unsatisfactory results, or is it on a promising path to a better future?

The third section considers Peru in the general context of the common movement of Latin American countries away from state-led development to more completely market-determined economies. Good studies of the consequences point to many likely problems and in particular to increasing inequality (Bulmer-Thomas 1996b; Berry 1997). Peru seems something of an exception in that available estimates of the distribution of income suggest that it has remained much the same, without any clear-cut worsening. What accounts for the apparent difference from experience in other Latin America countries? What can Peru, and what can the rest of Latin America, do to promote more nearly equal economic growth?

The fourth section concludes with a brief consideration of the constraints on the choices of economic policy by individual countries in the present international context. That context clearly leaves less room for independent national policies than in the past. It does not rule them out.

Social Goals and Economic Strategy

The dimensions of economic and social performance considered in this study can be divided into four groups: (1) the classic economic variables of growth, income per capita, ability to restrain inflation, and external balance; (2) questions of poverty, the distribution of income, and differential access to both education and political voice; (3) the capacity to promote a competitive and dynamic industrial sector, able to compete successfully in world markets; (4) effects of economic strategy on the chances for enough mutual acceptance among competing interests to hold the society together without political repression and without paralyzing degrees of mistrust among the business sector, labor, the rural sector, and the government.

Such objectives involve many conflicts and tensions; some goals have wide support; for others, agreement is much more doubtful. The Peruvian groups best placed to gain from the prosperity of the 1950–65 period—with good economic growth, low inflation, and external balance—presumably considered that the country's liberal economic strategy was successful, both for themselves and the society as a whole. In fact, antagonism toward that system was so great that it was rejected by democratic reformists favoring state-led industrialization, by revolutionary idealists, and even by the Peruvian military. From one point of view, that rejection was a mistake: by 1990, after a miserable quarter century, a majority supported the decision to return to the liberal economic strategy. From another point of view, both the initial rejection and the return were outcomes of conflicting goals and frustrations in a society handicapped by adverse structural characteristics but trying to achieve, along with higher incomes, an inclusive development and a self-determined future.

The democratic choice of state-led development in the 1960s was a response to widespread dissatisfaction with many aspects of the economy and the society. In the rural sector, the main issues were access to land in the face of its scarce supply and concentrated ownership, lack of resources for investment or education or public health, prolonged poverty that showed little improvement even in periods of economic growth, local political domination by large landowners, and long-entrenched discrimination against the indigenous population (Chapter 4). In the urban sector, an implicit coalition of groups in favor of modernization and social change wanted to break away from patterns of control by the traditional elite of property owners and financial interests allied with foreign investors. Industrialists hoped that protection would give them assured profits and room for growth, workers frustrated by weak employment conditions and by repression of labor organizations hoped that protected industrialization would help answer both problems, and a rising class of professionals expected that both government and industry would provide new openings for upward movement (Chapter 5). Beyond such interest-group objectives, socially conscious people throughout the society became more impatient with the liberal economic strategy as they became more aware of the country's high degrees of poverty and inequality (Chapter 6).

Some of these tensions were attributable to basic structural conditions of the economy and society rather than to the country's liberal economic orientation. The latter had clearly not been a solution and in some ways made things worse. Exporters, mainly mine owners and large landowners, were clearly identified with concentrated wealth and with foreign investment. In a context of highly unequal land ownership and superabundant rural labor, even good export growth was no great help for the rural poor. Imports of industrial products were seen as holding down possible domestic production and employment. The industrial sector was unable to export or to keep up with technological change in the outside world. Foreign investment was perhaps even less popular than imports. The antagonisms common everywhere at that time were aggravated by the highly visible privileges of the foreign company dominating the Peruvian oil industry, foreign leadership in mining production and exports, and foreign ownership of basic transportation and communications.

Peruvian social conditions under the open-market economic strategy contributed greatly to support for radical movements determined to overturn the society. The extensive reforms of the Velasco government were meant both to destroy control by the traditional elite and to undercut the radical left: especially by land reform but in addition by changes in working conditions and social institutions. From the point of view of the Peruvian military as well as that of the modernizing groups directly interested in economic change, a fundamental argument against the liberal economic model was that it failed to provide any answer to the resentment and revolutionary thrust nurtured by extreme inequality. The liberal model worked well enough for macroeconomic stability and growth, but not for resolution of the central tensions of Peruvian society. Why expect it to work out any better now?

Structural Changes and Their Implications

Five important characteristics of the economy and the society have changed to some degree over the last half century, in ways that could make the consequences of a market-determined economic system different now: (1) land ownership and relations of rural labor to arable land; (2) the rate of growth of the labor force; (3) the character of external trade and financial conditions; (4) greater access of the poor to education and political voice; and (5) learning from experience about economic remedies that do not work.

Land ownership has changed fundamentally, in ways favorable both for lessened inequality and for production. As discussed in Chapter 4, the changes were made in two contrasting steps. First, the reforms of the Velasco government swept away the old haciendas and with them the traditional (if already weakening), economic and political dominance of large landowners. Second, the cooperatives that were created on the formerly private haciendas, with the appealing theme of fostering a more cooperative society but without effective attention to their ability to function in economic terms, gradually broke down and gave way to a new wave of individual ownership. The concentration of land ownership decreased to what is probably the least unequal structure in Peruvian history. The dynamics of individual ownership could lead to a return toward greater concentration in the future, but for the time being any gains in agricultural incomes are likely to be more evenly distributed than in the past. The heightened pressures for efficiency in land use built into individual ownership on modest scales should help raise the rate of growth of the food supply, the component of national output that is of greatest direct importance for the people in poverty.

In a less favorable change, the ratio of the agricultural labor force to the supply of arable land has worsened. Between 1960 and 1992, the labor force in agriculture increased by 56 percent. The supply of arable land increased too, but more slowly (Chapter 4). By 1991, the supply of arable land per capita was only 43 percent of the average for Latin America. More nearly equal individual land holdings imply greater pressure to use the land intensely and less inequality in rural earnings, but the small size of nearly all holdings means that it is almost impossible for people in rural areas to escape from poverty other than by finding nonagricultural employment.

The second characteristic that has changed, the rate of growth of population and the labor force, should be favorable for reduction of poverty and inequality (Chapter 2). The fertility rate—an average of 6.2 children per adult woman as of 1970—was close to the highest in Latin America at that time. By 1995, it had come down to 3.1 (World Bank 1997, 225). That change should mean less stressful lives for many women and less downward pressure on wages from the increase of people looking for employment, although it may take a long time to have much effect on the latter: the change does not remove the legacy of existing excess labor forced into low-productivity activities. In the 1990s, with less than half the labor force in Lima able to find regular wage employment in the formal private sector, market forces remain unfavorable for sustained growth of real wages (Chapter 5).

The third characteristic, the structure of the country's external trade, began to show promise of improvement in the second half of the 1970s: industrial exports started to increase more rapidly than output and more rapidly than total exports. That new promise for employment prospects and learning potential was choked off again by adverse policy changes in the 1980s. Comparative advantage in the sense of the sectors most favored by open trade continues to center on mining and fishing, the first a capital-intensive sector with exceptionally high foreign ownership and both relatively weak from the point of view of stimulus for innovation or technological change (Chapter 3).

The promising growth of industrial exports in the second half of the 1970s was associated with one of the rare periods, the only sustained period, in which the real exchange rate moved steadily in favor of exports. Populist economic strategies rightly got the blame for turning incentives back in the wrong direction in the 1980s, but the new economic strategy of the 1990s failed to improve things in this respect. To allow the value of the currency to be determined by market forces while applying monetary policies that reinforced an inflow of capital has been one of the strategy's most damaging features from the point of view of employment, poverty, and potential for sustained growth.

Current issues of external financial balance include two problems that were not serious for the open economy of the 1950–65 period: external debt and the volatile capital flows associated with financial liberalization. External borrowing was not a significant feature of the 1950–65 period: fiscal and monetary restraint kept the growth of aggregate demand and of imports roughly in line with that of productive capacity; requirements of rising imports for production were financed mainly by growth of exports. Excess spending in the first half of the 1970s upset the balance and almost doubled the country's external debt in these five years (Table 7.3). Further increases in the debt in the 1980s left the economy with a heavy continuing burden, even after renegotiation to reduce debt service in the 1990s. That changed context reduces income available for domestic needs, cuts down the scope for public-sector financing, and makes national policy more subservient to pressures of external creditors.

The second problem associated with external financial balance has been the increased volatility of international capital movements, coupled at times with a passive strategy that allows them to determine exchange rates. In the first half of the 1990s, a strong capital inflow helped reduce inflation and stimulate investment, but it also made foreign exchange too abundant in the sense that its price stayed too low for the industrial sector to be reasonably competitive.

The fourth set of characteristics, access to education and political voice, has changed for the better. Previously high illiteracy has been greatly reduced, and school enrollment ratios have risen markedly for both rural and urban poor (Chapter 2). Still, illiteracy in the poorest region, the rural sierra, remains much higher than in Lima and higher for women than men. And the most difficult problem to correct, the weak quality of public school education at the primary and secondary levels, continues to fortify inequality between the majority who cannot afford private schools and the minority who can.

Market-based economic strategies can be expected to work somewhat more equitably and possibly more productively as well, if public awareness and political voice can call attention to specific problems and generate pressure to correct them. Public awareness of economic issues has increased a great deal in recent decades, stimulated particularly by the reform regime of General Velasco. Activist nongovernment organizations have proliferated, and they should help lessen the harshness of the new market orientation if and when the government decides to listen to them. Two-way communication with the public has not been the strong point of the present government, but that government will not last forever. The new context of heightened public awareness could in time contribute to a more inclusive economic strategy.

Perhaps the most fundamental change, carrying pain as well as hope with it, has been a gradual breakdown of social and political domination by the traditional elite. The election of a non-Hispanic president for the first time in the history of the country was a striking demonstration. Before that, the land reform played a major role by eliminating the old haciendas. Throughout the period after World War II, a massive movement from the countryside into the city has undermined Lima's privileged position as an island of culture and income. That process has been marked by an extreme degree of urban deterioration as the old protective boundaries were overrun (Matos Mar 1988). With all its strains, this process constitutes a reduction of barriers: a lessening of the degree to which the indigenous people had been excluded from the center of Peruvian society (Figueroa, Altamirano, and Sulmont 1996, 79–81; Mendez 1996). The process has been traumatic but can also be seen as a long-delayed approach to an integration of Lima with the country of Peru.

In terms of potential for economic growth as well as a different balance of social forces, one of the most evident changes has been the spread of independent small-scale producers in the informal sector, outside traditional business circles. That growth has its negative implications—it is in part a low-income alternative forced by the lack of opportunities for productive employment, and it has contributed to the weakening of organized labor and established political parties—but it also constitutes an opening toward a more flexible economy. The capacity of the economy for effective supply-side response is stronger than it was back in the more orderly, more elite-dominated world of the past.

Fifth and last, the open economy may have a better chance of positive results than it did in the pre-1960s because people can, and sometimes do, learn from the past. Like so many other potentially helpful factors, this one brings with it a new problem: Peru took such hard blows from its versions of state-led development that many leaders of business and government have gone overboard in the opposite direction. Anything that conveys the least hint of direct government action to shape the way that the economy operates is under grave suspicion: the argument of the slippery slope, or the infamous camel's nose in the tent, comes up as quickly in public discussions in Peru as in university faculty meetings in the United States. This attitude provides a measure of safety against repeating errors, but it can also block desirable changes.

With so many differences in the basic context, the return to a relatively open economy could give better results than the same strategy did in the period 1950–65. In terms of supply flexibility and potential for growth, the consequences should be favorable. That result is important in itself, but it was not the weakness of the market-oriented strategy in the first place. The weakness was the system's gross inequity and exceptionally widespread poverty, combined with slow technical learning and with dependence on exports of primary products and on foreign investment.

In the present context, the Peruvian public is much more aware of what is going on and why, although for the time being so grateful to escape the devastating excesses of the 1980s that it has been willing to put up with favoritism to conservative financial interests. More widespread access to education and much less concentrated land ownership are important changes that may lessen the inequality of the system, but the main underlying forces making for poverty and inequality remain: inadequacy of opportunities for productive employment, the worsening scarcity of arable land for the agricultural labor force, the quality of education available to the poor, discrimination against the indigenous population, and the concentrated ownership of financial assets. The return to the former strategy in its present version could be more positive in the domain of production and economic growth but could still remain highly unequal. Whether it does depends on alternatives open to public choice, particularly on what is done to redirect market forces toward effective external competition, to foster more rapid growth of productive employment, and to provide more favorable conditions for diversification of production and employment in areas characterized by extreme rural poverty (Chapter 8).

Economic Liberalization, Poverty, and Inequality: Peru and Latin America as a Whole

The reality of unnecessary poverty and of inequality based on blocked opportunities for the poor more than on achievements by the wealthy has contributed greatly to pressures for radical change in Latin America. These pressures seem to have lessened in the current period, but the problems that created them have not been corrected. The more liberal economic strategy now adopted in almost all countries has mixed implications for poverty, inequality, and autonomy. It may reduce poverty by favoring more sustained growth, but integration with world financial markets directly favors incomes of wealthier groups in the financial sector and weakens the power of socially oriented governments to introduce changes adverse to private investors. A return to a structure of production determined by current comparative advantage can mean, as it does at present for Peru, reliance on capital-intensive exports that are not optimal for employment, for stable earnings of foreign exchange, or for the development of a more competitive industrial sector.

Both economic logic and the experiences of other countries make clear that the new strategy can worsen poverty and inequality: "market-friendly policy shifts have been systematically associated with an abrupt and significant deterioration in income distribution" (Berry 1997, 6–7). Victor Bulmer-Thomas analyzed the implications of a comprehensive set of factors involved and reached much the same conclusion (Bulmer-Thomas 1996a). In contrast to the common experience, the estimates of inequality available for Peru indicate that the distribution of income did *not* suffer any significant deterioration. Why not? Are the estimates misleading? To the extent that the Peruvian experience has been different, should that difference be attributed to its particular historical context, or does it point to general reasons that economic liberalization *need not* have systematic negative effects on equality?

The estimates available for Peru, like all such estimates, are subject to question. They indicate that the distribution of consumer spending became less unequal between 1991 and 1996. Inequality in the distribution of income remained practically unchanged, though with more likelihood of a slight decrease than of any increase (Chapter 6). Against this picture, it is essential to note that property values (not counted as income) increased greatly relative to wages; earnings from assets abroad—rarely held by low-income people—are almost never reported; upper income groups gained more from reduction of high tariffs and elimination of restrictions on imported consumer goods than lower income groups that could never afford such purchases anyway; and the country's handful of ultra-rich families is almost certainly under-represented in the household surveys used to make estimates of distribution. Similar problems plague the estimates for other countries too. It seems fair to conclude that the actual distribution of income is probably more concentrated than available estimates reveal, in Peru and everywhere else, but that the changes in Peru under liberalization have not been as negative as the similarly measured changes in the majority of other Latin American countries studied by Berry and Bulmer-Thomas. The question remains, why not?

Any adequate answer would need to explore all the related factors acting on all the countries compared, but at least one central difference is evident: the striking growth of the Peruvian economy from 1993 through 1995, with its extraordinary leap in investment. Rising investment ratios are favorable for real wages through their effects on productivity and possibly also through stimulus to employment (Paus and Robinson 1997). Most of the countries that carried out liberalization in the 1970s and 1980s experienced at best more modest increases in investment and GDP, often with worsening labor market conditions. Why did Peru differ in this respect?

It did not differ in the first two years: neither investment nor the liberalized economy as a whole looked at all promising until after the dramatic events of 1992. By all indicators at the time, both poverty and employment conditions worsened. Through 1992, Peru would not have looked like an exception but rather a confirmation of the conclusion that liberalization aggravates inequality.

The turnaround to economic expansion and reduction of poverty from 1993 was not an automatic consequence of liberalization. It was stimulated by a combination of four specific factors: two extra-economic events in 1992 and two partial redirections of economic and social policies. Of the two special events, the first was a gratuitous, unnecessary setback to democracy but at the same time a reassurance to the private sector: the dissolution of congress suppressed this channel for criticism of the adjustment program and centered power in the hands of a president determined to keep the economic program intact. The second was the capture of the leadership of *Sendero luminoso* and the effective end of its threat to the structure of the society. Those two events, against the background of a new economic strategy that brought inflation more nearly under control and restored connections to the international financial community, opened the way to a wave of investment based on much greater confidence in the future.

The two redirections of policy that supported revival were a sharp increase in public infrastructure investment and a wave of social programs directed at reduction of poverty. The previously tight restraint on government spending was relaxed enough to allow public investment to rise in real terms by 14 percent in 1992, 13 percent in 1993, and 25 percent farther in 1994 (Chapter 8; BCRP 1997, 120). At the same time, the country's previously dormant social programs suddenly came to life with new leadership and greatly increased financing (Chapter 6). In contrast to Chile under its initial liberalization program, with cutbacks of social spending and no action to prevent unemployment from rising and staying far above historical levels, Peru's economic and social policies were at least partially redirected toward promotion of investment and reduction of poverty. Liberalization in the sense of reduced protection and regulation has mixed effects that could be negative for investment and production for long periods. It does not ensure economic revival. In Peru's case, the combination of historical accident, increased government spending, and major social programs put the economy back in motion. Liberalization then began to help by holding down inflationary pressures from the side of supply and by encouraging the rapid growth of private investment.

Economic liberalization can be adverse for equity in many respects. It takes away restraints on ways to make profits while discouraging legislation and regulation to protect workers. It constrains taxation of property and investment income and lessens national autonomy in financial management. It can easily make government economic policies subservient to the interests of private investors, both domestic and foreign.

Nothing in this analysis of the particular Peruvian case is intended to suggest that liberalization carries with it any built-in protection against increasing inequality or, conversely, that it is bound to make things worse. The analysis is intended to emphasize a different conception: that the otherwise likely trend toward worsening inequality can conceivably be offset by combining it with coherent economic policies directed to that end. Such policies need to include state action to reduce inequalities in education, skills, mobility, and access to capital and land, and to reshape market forces to make them more favorable for employment, for technological progress, and for a more competitive industrial sector. Such a strategy would require many revisions of the excessively passive liberalization strategy originally adopted in 1990–91.

Liberalization strategies can be implemented in different ways with very different consequences. Changes in tax structures, the pattern of government spending, programs to improve education and productivity, labor legislation, monetary policy and interest rates and management of exchange rates can do a great deal to make liberalization less inequitable. A particularly crucial question is whether the government tries to promote employment and sustained growth by doing what it can to make the industrial sector more competitive. The purest versions of liberalization rule out any selective policies to this end, but it is perfectly possible to use more activist versions to preserve its advantages while providing more help for employment and reduction of poverty.

The potential of economic liberalization for harmful consequences and for better results is exemplified by the experiences of Chile under its three contrasting versions (Sheahan 1997). The first model was almost exactly the same as that adopted in Peru in 1990–91. In Chile, the Pinochet government held to this version from the start of generalized economic liberalization in 1975 to the collapse of the economy in the depression of 1982–83. The main consequences included worsening poverty and inequality, a successful reduction of inflation, a temporary spurt of growth, and worsening external deficits. The strategy left the economy vulnerable to a profound depression when external credit stopped flowing in.

For Chile, the solution was to adopt a new version of the strategy to get out of its depression and establish the basis for sustainable growth. That new model, emphasizing capacity to compete in export markets, achieved a high and fairly steady rate of growth without any worsening of external balance or dependence on external credit and with rapidly rising employment to the point at which unskilled labor at last became scarce enough to make market forces work in favor of increasing real wages. With employment and wages both rising, poverty began to come down seriously, and even inequality fell slightly. The new democratic government in 1990 took the next step: it added a wide range of social programs both to provide direct support for the poor and to increase their skills and capacity to respond to opportunities (Graham 1994; Raczynski

1995). With that combined social and promotional strategy, Chile in the 1990s has come as close as any Latin American country has ever come to a model of economic growth that has a good chance to be both sustainable and reasonably inclusive.

Peru has such a severe problem of inadequate employment opportunities that it would even in the best of cases take longer than Chile to reach conditions in which a shortage of unskilled labor could turn market forces in favor of steadily increasing real wages. It has other handicaps as well: it has not yet built up the institutions and skills of government administration achieved in Chile, and despite all the progress of the last two decades, access to education of decent quality remains highly unequal. Peru has a tough road ahead. To delay starting on it has high costs for the poor.

Limits on the Scope for Choice

What prevents more Latin American countries, including Peru, from changing their liberalization strategies toward something like the more successful version of liberalization that Chile turned to when its original model worked out so poorly? The reasons may include fears of promotional policies of any kind and of the increased taxation that might be needed to maintain effective social programs. They may also include fears that foreign investors or the international financial community as a whole might turn against countries in which governments are perceived to be backsliding from full liberalization. Even without any strong external criticism, integration of world financial markets has made capital flight much easier than it used to be. The increased mobility of capital means that the scope for independent national choice of economic policies has been seriously reduced.

This tightened constraint on independent national policies has both advantages and disadvantages. Countries can get into deep trouble entirely on their own. It might help considerably if multilateral restraints served to limit rising fiscal deficits, external borrowing for projects unlikely to be productive, and the regulations that mainly serve to protect a privileged minority. International pressures can also help when they constrain authoritarian governments, as they did when the Pinochet government was tempted to reject the results of the referendum against it in Chile in the 1980s. Autonomy is not a sacred principle: it can be a value or a scourge, depending on who is running the country for what purposes.

The main disadvantage of integration in world financial markets is that it can be adverse to changes aimed chiefly at reduction of poverty and inequality. If a democratic society with a coherent economic strategy were considering more progressive taxation or any other social policy likely to dismay private investors, a liberalized economic system could easily become a serious obstacle. If international investors decide that a government is going in directions harmful to their interests, they can exercise what amounts to almost a veto power by withdrawing capital (Mahon 1996). Still, even though isolation is neither possible nor desirable, countries can either surrender autonomy or defend it: it remains feasible to choose different paths and get different results.

The strongest defense against economic shocks from either worldwide changes in international financial conditions or country-specific adverse decisions by international investors would be to keep tight limits on external current account deficits and the need for external financing. That objective requires the ability to keep domestic saving rising at rates close to those of investment and exports rising at rates close to requirements for imports. A necessary condition for success is to avoid exchange rates that undercut the competitive position of domestic producers. Is it actually possible to control the exchange rate in a liberalized economic system, when changing capital flows can often dominate demand and supply of foreign exchange?

In a fundamental sense, no government has complete control of exchange rates. If the international financial community decides that the Indonesian or Mexican currency is hopelessly overvalued and starts to sell it relentlessly, even high levels of foreign exchange reserves may fail to stem the tide. International investors, for the most part a herd of sheep, catch on slowly and then over-react: to stop a panic once it starts can take all the resources of the IMF and world creditor countries combined. When the evidence of overvaluation is less clear, as in Brazil in late 1997, a determined government can fight back by raising domestic interest rates so high that international lenders are tempted to stay. That partial solution—cutting back production and employment to increase returns to owners of capital—is not uncommon but hardly appealing for any country concerned with poverty and inequality.

Latin American countries with liberalized economic systems have taken a variety of paths to deal with these problems, not always with success. Argentina has been an example that appeals to the hearts of international investors. It has chosen a fixed nominal exchange rate, under a currency board that leaves no options to the government. That action makes the economy highly dependent on capital flows: if these are favorable, the economy booms; if they turn the other way, interest rates rise steeply while output and employment fall. Mexico chose another variant that stayed in place from 1987 to 1994: raising the nominal price of the dollar slowly while allowing the real rate to fall. That process broke down, as have similar methods in many other countries, when the current account deficit continued rising so steeply that international creditors stopped moving capital in and tried—all at once—to go the other way. Chile has done better since 1983 to keep the current account deficit from rising dangerously and so has been relatively immune to such crises. These different choices have different consequences: countries are not helpless, even after liberalization.

Chile's relatively successful path evolved by making changes away from a particularly inegalitarian version of liberalization strategy that did not attempt to promote employment or exports. The changes included a switch from a nominally fixed exchange rate in 1983 to a policy of aggressive devaluation, fiscal incentives to promote new exports as well, lower interest rates, and (in the 1990s) moderate restraints on capital inflows in the form of selective taxes and monetary reserve requirements (Ffrench-Davis and Labán 1995; Sheahan 1997). No economy can be totally insulated from world financial markets—Chile still suffers temporary shocks when the markets fluctuate—but the shocks have been much less severe than is common in other developing countries. More important, the country achieved a striking change in producer behavior, toward far more successful competition in world markets than ever before. In the process, the labor market has moved from deep unemployment to conditions approaching full employment. It would be impossible for Peru to make so much progress so quickly—its existing employment conditions are so much worse—but it is difficult to see why it could not move in the same direction.

Chile can follow a more activist version of liberalization than Peru is yet willing to risk and keep a higher degree of autonomy, partly because it has demonstrated for so many years a capacity for fiscal and monetary discipline and partly because its democratic government has combined social activism with consensus seeking through joint negotiation with business and labor. Chile had the good fortune to build up autonomy in the 1980s without the handicap of capital inflows working against a competitive exchange rate, because world capital markets were so tightly constrained in this period. Finally, most of all, it has demonstrated that a promotional version of liberalization can combine economic growth with relatively inclusive economic and social policies.

Are There Any Answers?

The first question that led to this study was What caused Peru to get into such deep trouble in the 1980s and early 1990s? The second question was Does the return to a more completely market-determined economic strategy in the 1990s provide an answer to the problems that caused all the trouble in the first place? An implicit third question is What do these experiences in Peru contribute to understanding the many economic strains of Latin America through the last half century and the chances for doing better with reliberalized economic systems?

The happy character of these questions is that they lead in so many directions that the search for answers can go on forever. This study seemed at times likely to go on forever or as nearly so as human life permits. It does not propose final answers, just personal interpretations and, with luck, helpful information on many of the issues.

To the first question, the direct causes of breakdown in the 1980s were the external deficits built into the economic model being followed, systematic disregard of macroeconomic constraints, and the growing strength and violence of *Sendero luminoso*. The economic failures and the violence reacted on and greatly aggravated one another. The main problem underlying the economic failures was the misdirected character of the country's (and Latin America's) strategy of state-led development. It was misdirected not because state leadership through active intervention was itself a mistake but because of the particular form it took: it made good sense to try to promote more modern and more dynamic industrial sectors, capable of innovation and continuing technical progress, but to shut out contact and competition with the outside world was a prescription going in exactly the opposite direction. Protection made profits more a matter of political negotiation than of productive effort or innovative imagination. Besides its bias against exports, it made inflationary pressures worse because it handicapped the supply elasticity of the productive system and prevented buyers from turning to imported alternatives when particular domestic prices increased. Still, these factors do not constitute the causes of the country's basic problems: they were more in the nature of perverse reactions to persistent underlying strains.

The fundamental problems behind the country's democratic choice of state-led development in the 1960s were its exceptionally high degrees of poverty and inequality, frustrated opportunities for employment and for social mobility, concentrated ownership of land and other assets, and correct conviction that its traditionally market-determined open economy worsened inequality, undermined the capacity for self-determined development, and intensified social conflict.

Beneath those problems, in turn, the key structural conditions that made market forces work perversely were the rapid growth of population and the labor force relative to land and capital, the country's prolonged failure to provide access to decent education for the majority of its people, and the disdain for and discrimination against the indigenous rural population. When unskilled labor becomes superabundant relative to skills, land, and capital, market forces inexorably favor worsening inequality. Discrimination then makes the consequences worse.

The multilevel character of the basic problems might be seen as similar to a partially buried pyramid: relatively simple macroeconomic issues on the surface, midlevel questions of economic strategy and structural obstacles below them, and major social-economic forces yet deeper. Any answer to the second question—whether economic liberalization helps or hurts—needs to distinguish with care exactly what levels are intended. Furthermore, to complicate the task, liberalization itself is not a static set of policies: it can evolve either helpfully or not. Peru's version started near the least helpful extreme, but it has moved, insufficiently, in more promising directions.

If understood as including concern for macroeconomic balance as well as efficiency, liberalization should help at the surface level of the pyramid: help to maintain better rates of economic growth, with less inflation, than Peru experienced in the 1970s and 1980s. It could also, through increased contact and competition with the outside world, create greater pressures for technical progress and improving productivity. Even on this level, Peru's version has the serious weakness discussed in so many contexts in this study: overliberalization for capital flows and exchange rate management has made it nearly impossible to maintain high rates of growth without excessive current account deficits and has handicapped the industrial sector unfairly—as well as lowered efficiency—by making imported manufactures artificially cheap and the profitability of exporting artificially low.

This particular defect of Peru's liberalization strategy can be remedied without disavowing liberalization itself and in practice has been made somewhat less harmful since the end of 1994 by stopping continued appreciation of the real exchange rate. It would help to repair the damage if the exchange rate could be moved to levels at which the industrial sector could compete more fairly and beyond that to take promotional measures to encourage industrial production in regions of high rural poverty. To make real headway on the latter objective requires improving rural education and supporting effective on-the-job training, investment in social infrastructure, and some degree of decentralization of government itself. The set of social programs developed by the Fujimori government from 1993 to the present must be helping to build up the necessary conditions on the side of capacity for response to new employment opportunities; the failure so far has been on the side of not doing enough to promote such opportunities.

At the deepest levels of the pyramid, the problems have been inadequate access to decent education for the majority of the population, concentrated ownership of property and land, discrimination against indigenous people in both social policies and private employment, and intense social conflict rooted in these basic inequalities. Peru has accomplished real progress on some of these problems, particularly through wider access to education, the land reform and following spread of individual ownership in agriculture, and strengthened social investment in rural areas of high poverty.

Economic liberalization should provide a more favorable background of growth without inflation, and will when it is modified to favor more effective competition by the industrial sector. On the negative side, it favors increased concentration of privately owned assets, discourages progressive taxation, and makes national policy choices more subservient to the interests of the international financial community. The main factor that will decide the balance for effects on poverty and inequality is the way that liberalization affects opportunities for productive employment and sustainably increasing real wages. If compared with the two preceding decades, it has been a considerable improvement. If compared with the needs of Peru, the improvement has been totally inadequate. It is no answer to any goals of creating employment conditions strong enough to generate progressively rising real wages, technological changes favorable to a competitive industrial sector, reduction of inequality, or the creation of an inclusive social consensus.

Latin America as a whole seems committed for the time being to a strategy of economic liberalization, although with numerous differences in the details. As in Peru, it could very well work out in many countries to favor higher rates of economic growth with lower inflation than they achieved under the strategy of state-led development through protected industrialization. It could fall flat, through failure to move beyond dependence on primary exports and external credit or failure to provide wide access to education and to generate sufficient growth of employment opportunities.

The future looks better for Peru, and for many other countries in Latin America, than it did in the 1980s. It looks better in the sense of more favorable underlying possibilities, not in the sense that successful development is bound to occur if countries just keep following their current versions of economic liberalization. Most of them, including Peru, need to change and could change their economic strategies to bring more people into the development process, to increase the capacity of lower income groups for productive participation, and to share the gains more equally.

References

Adams, Norma, and Néstor Valdivia. 1994. *Los otros empresarios: Etica de migrantes y formación de empresas en Lima.* 2d ed. Lima: Instituto de Estudios Peruanos.
Ahluwalia, Montek S., Nicholas G. Carter, and Hollis B. Chenery. 1979. "Growth and Poverty in Developing Nations." *Journal of Development Economics* 6:299–341.
Alberts, Tom. 1983. *Agrarian Reform and Rural Poverty: A Case Study of Peru.* Boulder, Colo.: Westview Press.
Alegría, Ciro. 1967. Reprint. *El mundo es ancho y ajeno.* Santiago, Chile: Ediciones Wirocha. Original edition 1941.
Altimir, Oscar. 1982. "The Extent of Poverty in Latin America." World Bank Staff Working Paper, no. 5222. Washington, D.C.: World Bank.
Alvarez, Elena. 1983. *Política económica y agricultura en el Perú, 1969–1979.* Lima: Instituto de Estudios Peruanos.
———. 1993. "Coca Production in Peru." In Peter H. Smith, ed., *Drug Policy in the Americas,* 72–87. Boulder, Colo.: Westview Press.
———. 1998. "Sustainable Alternative Development in the Andes: The Case Studies of Bolivia and Peru." Report prepared for the adjunct program of the North-South Center of the University of Miami. First draft, March.
America's Watch. 1992. *Peru Under Fire: Human Rights Since the Return to Democracy.* New Haven: Yale University Press.
Amsden, Alice. 1989. *Asia's Next Giant: South Korea and Late Industrialization.* New York: Oxford University Press.
———. 1994. "Why Isn't the Whole World Experimenting with the East Asian Model to Develop?" *World Development* 22:627–33.
Arguedas, José María. 1973. Re-edition. *Los ríos profundos.* Oxford: Pergamon Press. Original edition 1958.
Arregui, Patricia McLauchlan de. 1993. "Empleo, ingresos y ocupación de los profesionales y técnicos en el Perú." Lima: GRADE, *Notas para el debate,* 9.
———. 1994. "La situación de las universidades Peruanas." Lima: GRADE, *Notas para el debate,* 12.
———. 1995. "Dinámicas de transformación de los sistemas educativos en América Latina: El caso del Perú." In Jeffrey M. Puryear and José Joaquín Brunner, eds., *Educación, equidad y competitividad en las Américas: Un proyecto del diálogo interamericano,* 203–52. Washington, D.C.: Organization of American States.

Barraclough, Solon, ed. 1973. *Agrarian Structures in Latin America.* Lexington, Mass.: Lexington Books.
BCRP (Banco Central de Reserva del Perú). 1993. *Perú: Compendio estadístico del sector externo, 1970–1992.* Lima: BCRP.
———. 1995. *Nota semanal,* no. 42 (October 27).
———. 1996. *Memoria 1995.* Lima: BCRP.
———. 1997. *Memoria 1996.* Lima: BCRP.
———. 1998a. *Memoria 1997.* Lima: BCRP.
———. 1998b. *Nota semanal,* no. 32 (August 28).
Berry, Albert. 1990. "International Trade, Government, and Income Distribution in Peru Since 1870." *Latin American Research Review* 25, no. 2:31–59.
———. 1997. "The Income Distribution Threat in Latin America." *Latin American Research Review* 32, no. 2:3–40.
Bird, Richard, and Guillermo Perry R. 1994. "Tax Policy in Latin America: In Crisis and After." In Graham Bird and Ann Helwege, eds., *Latin America's Future,* 167–84. London: Academic Press.
Blanco Oropeza, Carlos. 1997. "Presupuesto público y gasto social." *Moneda,* no. 105:54–57.
Bromley, Ray. 1994. "Informality, de Soto Style: From Concept to Policy." In Cathy A. Rakowski, ed., *Contrapunto: The Informal Sector Debate in Latin America,* 131–51. Albany: State University of New York Press.
Brown, Michael F., and Eduardo Fernández. 1991. *War in the Shadows: The Struggle for Utopia in the Peruvian Andes.* Berkeley and Los Angeles: University of California Press.
Bryce Echenique, Alfredo. 1995. Re-edition. *Un mundo para Julius.* Lima: PEISA. Original edition 1970.
Bulmer-Thomas, Victor. 1994. *The Economic History of Latin America Since Independence.* Cambridge: Cambridge University Press.
———. 1996a. "Conclusions." In Bulmer-Thomas 1996b, 295–314.
———, ed. 1996b. *The New Economic Model in Latin America and Its Impact on Income Distribution and Poverty.* New York: St. Martin's Press.
Bureau of the Census (United States). 1975. *Historical Statistics of the United States: Colonial Times to 1970.* Washington, D.C.: Bureau of the Census.
Caballero, José María. 1977. "Sobre el carácter de la reforma agraria." *Latin American Perspectives* 4.
———. 1981. *Economica agraria de la sierra Peruana: Antes de la reforma agraria de 1969.* Lima: Instituto de Estudios Peruanos.
Cáceres, Armando, and Carlos E. Paredes. 1991. "The Management of Economic Policy." In Paredes and Sachs 1991, 80–113.
Caller, Jaime, and Rosario Chuecas. 1989. *Estratagia de desarrollo industrial: Algunas reflexiones.* Lima: Fundación Friedrich Ebert.
Cameron, Maxwell A. 1994. *Democracy and Authoritarianism in Peru: Political Coalitions and Economic Change.* New York: St. Martin's.
———. 1997. "Political and Economic Origins of Regime Change in Peru: The Fifteenth Brumaire of Alberto Fujimori." In Cameron and Mauceri 1997, 37–69.

Cameron, Maxwell A., and Philip Mauceri, eds. 1997. *The Peruvian Labyrinth: Politics, Society, Economy.* University Park: Pennsylvania State University Press.

Carrión, Julio F. 1994. "The 'Support Gap' for Democracy in Peru: Mass Public Attitudes Towards Fujimori's Self-Coup." Paper presented at the International Congress of the Latin American Studies Association, Washington, March.

Carter, Michael A., and Elena Alvarez. 1989. "Changing Paths: The Decollectivization of Agrarian Reform Agriculture in Coastal Peru." In William C. Theisenhusen, ed., *Searching for Agrarian Reform in Latin America,* 156–87. Boston: Unwin Hyman.

Carter, Michael A., Bradford B. Barham, Dina Mesbah, and Denise Stanley. 1993. "Agro-Exports and the Rural Resource Poor in Latin America: Policy Options for Achieving Broadly Based Growth." University of Wisconsin-Madison, Agricultural Economics, Staff Paper Series, no. 364.

Castells, Manuel, and Alejandro Portes. 1989. "World Underneath: The Origins, Dynamics, and Effects of the Informal Economy." In Alejandro Portes, Manuel Castells, and Lauren A. Benton, eds., *The Informal Economy: Studies in Advanced and Less Developed Countries,* 11–37. Baltimore: Johns Hopkins University Press.

Castillo Ochoa, Manuel, and Andrés Quispe Martínez. 1996. *Reforma estructural y reconversión empresarial: Conflictos y desafíos.* Lima: Cuadernos desco, no. 21.

Conaghan, Catherine M., and James Malloy. 1994. *Unsettling Statecraft: Democracy and Neoliberalism in the Central Andes.* Pittsburgh: University of Pittsburgh Press.

Corden, W. M. 1984. "Booming Sector and Dutch Disease Economics: Survey and Consolidation." *Oxford Economic Papers* 36:359–80.

Cotler, Julio. 1978a. *Clases, estado, y nación en el Perú.* Lima: Instituto de Estudios Peruanos.

———. 1978b. "A Structural-Historical Approach to the Breakdown of Democratic Institutions: Peru." In Juan J. Linz and Alfred Stepan, eds., *The Breakdown of Democratic Regimes: Latin America,* 171–206. Baltimore: Johns Hopkins University Press.

———. 1983. "Democratic and National Integration in Peru." In McClintock and Lowenthal 1983, 3–38.

———. 1995. "Political Parties and the Process of Democratic Consolidation in Peru." In Scott Mainwaring and Timothy R. Scully, eds., *Building Democratic Institutions: Party Systems in Latin America,* 323–53. Stanford: Stanford University Press.

Cuba, Elmer. 1997. "El recálculo del PBI y sus consequencias." *Moneda,* no. 102:52–54.

Danziger, Sheldon, and Peter Gottschalk. 1995. *America Unequal.* Cambridge, Mass.: Harvard University Press.

Davies, Thomas M., Jr. 1974. *Indian Integration in Peru: A Half-Century of Experience, 1900–1948.* Lincoln: University of Nebraska Press.

Deere, Carmen Diana. 1990. *Households and Class Relations: Peasants and Landlords in Northern Peru.* Berkeley and Los Angeles: University of California Press.

Degregori, Carlos Iván. 1989. *Qué difícil es ser Dios.* Lima: El zorro de abajo.

———. 1990. *El surgimiento de Sendero Luminoso: Del movimiento por la gratitud de la enseñanza al inicio de la lucha armada*. Lima: Instituto de Estudios Peruanos.

———. 1992. "The Origins and Logic of the Shining Path: Two Views." In Palmer 1992, 33–58.

———. 1994. "Shining Path and Counterinsurgency Strategy Since the Arrest of Abimael Guzmán." In Tulchin and Bland 1994, 81–102.

Deininger, Klaus, and Lyn Squire. 1996a. Database File for "A New Data Set Measuring Income Inequality." Annex to Deininger and Squire 1996b, by Internet.

———. 1996b. "A New Data Set Measuring Income Inequality." *World Bank Economic Review* 10, no. 3:565–91.

De Soto, Hernando. 1989. *The Other Path: The Invisible Revolution in the Third World*. New York: Harper. Original Spanish edition 1985.

Diamand, Marcelo. 1973. *Doctrinas económicas, desarrollo e independencia*. Buenos Aires: Paidos.

Díaz Alejandro, Carlos. 1984. "Latin America in the 1930s." In Rosemary Thorp, ed., *Latin America in the 1930s: The Role of the Periphery in World Crisis*, 17–49. New York: St. Martin's.

Dornbusch, Rudiger, and Sebastian Edwards, eds. 1991. *The Macroeconomics of Populism in Latin America*. Chicago: University of Chicago Press.

Durand, Francisco. 1997. "The Growth and Limitations of the Peruvian Right." In Cameron and Mauceri 1997, 152–75.

Eckstein, Shlomo, Gordon Donald, Douglas Horton, and Thomas Carol. 1978. "Land Reform in Latin America: Bolivia, Chile, Mexico, Peru, and Venezuela." World Bank Staff Working Paper, no. 275.

ECLA (Economic Commission for Latin America, United Nations). 1981. *Statistical Yearbook for Latin America, 1980*. Santiago: ECLA.

ECLAC (Economic Commission for Latin America and the Caribbean, United Nations). 1994. *Social Panorama of Latin America, 1994*. Santiago: ECLAC.

———. 1996. *Social Panorama of Latin America, 1995*. Santiago: ECLAC.

———. 1997. *Social Panorama of Latin America, 1996*. Santiago: ECLAC.

Edwards, Sebastian. 1989. *Real Exchange Rates, Devaluation, and Adjustment: Exchange Rate Policy in Developing Countries*. Cambridge, Mass.: MIT Press.

Edwards, Sebastian, and Alejandra Cox Edwards. 1987. *Monetarism and Liberalization: The Chilean Experience*. Cambridge: Ballinger.

Elias, Lidía. 1995. "Estudios sobre la pobreza en el Perú: Bibliografía comentada." In Jeanine Anderson et al., *Medición de la pobreza en Lima metropolitana: Metodología y resultados*, 23–74. Lima: Centro de Investigación de la Universidad del Pacífico and Taller de Políticas y Desarrollo Social.

Engerman, Stanley L., and Kenneth L. Sokoloff. 1997. "Factor Endowments, Institutions, and Differential Paths of Growth Among New World Economies: A View from Economic Historians of the United States." In Stephen Haber, ed., *How Latin America Fell Behind: Essays in the Economic Histories of Brazil and Mexico, 1800–1919*, 260–304. Stanford: Stanford University Press.

Escobal, Javier, and Jorge Agüero. 1996. "Ajuste macroeconómico y distribución del ingreso en el Perú, 1985–94." In Moncada and Webb 1996, 41–59.

Escobal, Javier, and Marcos Castillo. 1994. "Sesgos en la medición de la inflación en contextos inflacionarios: El caso Peruano." Lima: GRADE, *Documento de trabajo,* no. 21.

FAO (Food and Agriculture Organization of the United Nations). 1962 to 1995. *Production Yearbook.* Rome: FAO.

Feres, Juan Carlos, and Arturo León. 1990. "Magnitude de la situación de la pobreza." *Revista de la cepal,* no. 41:143–52.

Ferrando, Delicia, and Carlos E. Aramburú. 1996. "The Fertility Transition in Peru." In José Miguel Guzmán, Sashiela Singh, Germán Rodríguez, and Edith A. Pantelides, eds., *The Fertility Transition in Latin America,* 414–36. Oxford: Clarendon Press.

Ffrench-Davis, Ricardo, and Raúl Laban. 1995. "Disempeños y logros macroeconómicos en Chile." In Pizzaro, Raczynski, and Vial 1995, 77–92.

Figueroa, Adolfo. 1984. *Capitalist Development and the Peasant Economy in Peru.* Cambridge: Cambridge University Press.

———. 1988. "Productividad agrícola y crisis económica." *Economía* 11, no. 22:9–34.

———. 1993. *Crisis distributiva en el Perú.* Lima: Pontificia Universidad Católica del Perú.

———. 1995. "Peru: Social Policies and Economic Adjustment in the 1980s." In Lustig 1995.

———. 1997. "Equidad, inversión extranjera y competitividad internacional en Perú y América Latina." Paper presented at meeting of the Latin American Studies Association, Guadalajara, Mexico, April.

Figueroa, Adolfo, Teofilo Altamirano, and Denis Sulmont. 1996. *Social Exclusion and Inequality in Peru.* Geneva: International Institute for Labour Studies and United Nations Development Programme Research Series, no. 104.

FitzGerald, E. V. K. 1979. *The Political Economy of Peru, 1956–78: Economic Development and the Restructuring of Capital.* Cambridge: Cambridge University Press.

Flores Galindo, Alberto. 1987. *Buscando un inca: Identidad y utopía en los Andes.* Lima: Instituto de Apoyo Agrario.

Foxley, Alejandro. 1983. *Latin American Experiments in Neoconservative Economics.* Berkeley and Los Angeles: University of California Press.

Francke, Pedro. 1996. "Tipos de crecimiento y pobreza: Una aproximación." In Moncada and Webb 1996, 137–56.

———. 1997a. "Evolución de la pobreza entre 1991 y 1996." *Moneda,* no. 101:30–38.

———. 1997b. "FONCODES: ¿Llega a los pobres?" *Moneda,* no. 103:44–47.

García, Norberto E. 1993. *Ajuste, reformas y mercado laboral: Costa Rica (1980–1990), Chile (1973–1992), México (1981–1991).* Santiago: PREALC.

Glewwe, Paul. 1988. "The Distribution of Welfare in Peru in 1985–86." World Bank, Living Standards Measurement Study Working Paper, no. 42.

Golte, Jürgen, and Norma Adams. 1990. *Los caballos de Troya de los invasores: Estrategias campesinas en la conquista de la gran Lima.* Lima: Instituto de Estudios Peruanos.

Gómez, Rosario. 1994. "Agroexportación no tradicional: Un desafío." *Informe de Coyuntura, premier pemestre 1994*, 102–20. Lima: Universidad del Pacífico.
Gonzales de Olarte, Efraín. 1991. "Una economia bajo violencia: Perú, 1980–1990." Lima: Instituto de Estudos Peruanos, *Documento de trabajo*, no. 40.
———. 1993a. "Economic Stabilization and Structural Adjustment Under Fujimori." *Journal of Inter-American Studies and World Affairs* 35, no. 2:51–80.
———. 1993b. "La descentralización en el Perú: Diagnóstico y propuesta." Lima: Instituto de Estudios Peruanos, Programa de Educación, *Documento de discusión*, no. 13.
———. 1994. *En las fronteras del mercado: Economía política del campesinado en el Perú.* Lima: Instituto de Estudios Peruanos.
———. 1995. "La descentralización en el Perú: Diagnóstico y propuestas." Lima: Instituto de Estudios Peruanos, paper presented at the seminar *Concertación y liderazgo*, May.
———. 1996a. *El ajuste estructural y los campesinos.* Lima: Instituto de Estudios Peruanos.
———. 1996b. "Inversión privada, crecimiento y ajuste estructural en el Perú, 1950–1995." Lima: Instituto de Estudios Peruanos, *Documento de trabajo*, no. 81.
———, ed. 1996c. *The Peruvian Economy and Structural Adjustment: Past, Present, and Future.* Miami: North-South Center Press.
———, ed. 1997a. *Ajuste estructural en el Perú: Modelos económicos, empleo y descentralización."* Lima: Instituto de Estudios Peruanos.
———. 1997b. "Economía política del adjuste estructural en el Perú: Posibilidades y limitaciones." Lima: Consorcio de Investigación Económica.
———. 1997c. "La descentralización en el Perú: Diagnóstico y limitaciones." In Gonzales de Olarte 1997a, 223–51.
Gonzales de Olarte, Efraín, and Lilian Samamé. 1994. *El pendulo Peruano: Política economica, gobernabilidad, y subdesarrollo, 1963–1990.* 2d ed. Lima: Instituto de Estudios Peruanos.
Gootenberg, Paul. 1991. "Population and Ethnicity in Early Republican Peru: Some Revisions." *Latin American Research Review* 26, no. 3:109–57.
———. 1993. *Imagining Development: Economic Ideas in Peru's "Fictitious Prosperity" of Guano, 1840–1880.* Berkeley and Los Angeles: University of California Press.
Graham, Carol. 1992. *Peru's APRA: Parties, Politics, and the Elusive Quest for Democracy.* Boulder, Colo.: Lynne Reinner.
———. 1994. "Introduction: Democracy in Crisis and the International Response." In Tulchin and Bland 1994, 1–20.
Graham, Carol, and Cheikh Kane. 1998. "Opportunistic Government or Sustaining Reform? Electoral Trends and Public Expenditure Patterns in Peru, 1990–1995." *Latin American Research Review* 33, no. 1:67–104.
Grosh, Margaret E. 1994. *Administering Targeted Social Programs in Latin America: From Platitudes to Practice.* Washington, D.C.: World Bank.
Guillen Marroquín, Jesús E. 1997. "La última oportunidad de la descentralización en el Perú: Entre la parálisis y los nuevos consensos." In Gonzales de Olarte 1997a, 107–33.

Helwege, Ann. 1995. "Poverty in Latin America: Back to the Abyss?" *Journal of Inter-American Studies and World Affairs* 37, no. 3:99–124.
Hunefeldt, Christine. 1997. "The Rural Landscape and Changing Political Awareness: Enterprises, Agrarian Producers, and Peasant Communities, 1969–1994." In Cameron and Mauceri 1997, 107–33.
Hunt, Shane J. 1977. "Real Wages and Economic Growth in Peru, 1900–1940." Boston University Center for Latin American Development Discussion Paper, no. 25.
———. 1985. "Growth and Guano in Nineteenth-Century Peru." In Roberto Cortés Conde and Shane J. Hunt, eds., *Latin American Economies: Growth and the Export Sector, 1880–1930*, 255–318. New York: Holmes and Meier.
———. 1996. "Peru: The Current Economic Situation in Long-Term Perspective." In Gonzales de Olarte 1996c, 11–57.
———. 1997. "Peru's Employment Problem." Paper prepared for the PAPI project, USAID, Lima. Published in Spanish as *El problema del empleo en el Perú*. Lima: CONFIEP and USAID.
IDB (Inter-American Development Bank). 1997 and earlier years. *Economic and Social Progress in Latin America, 1997 Report* and earlier reports. Washington, D.C.: IDB.
Iguíñiz, Javier, and I. Muñoz. 1992. *Políticas de industrialización del Perú: 1980–1990*. Lima: Cuadernos DESCO.
ILO (International Labor Office). 1996. *Informe: Panorama laboral, '96*. Lima: Regional Office of the ILO.
IMF (International Monetary Fund). 1980. *International Monetary Statistics, 1980 Yearbook*. Washington, D.C.: IMF.
———. 1983. *International Monetary Statistics, 1983 Yearbook*. Washington, D.C.: IMF.
———. 1992. *International Monetary Statistics, 1992 Yearbook*. Washington, D.C.: IMF.
INE (Instituto Nacional de Estadística). 1989. *Evolución de la economía Peruana*. Lima: INE.
Infante, Ricardo. 1997. "Reactivación y empleo urbano: 1990–94." In Gonzales de Olarte 1997a, 157–88.
Instituto Cuánto. 1990 through 1996. *Perú en números: Annuario estadística*. Lima: Instituto Cuánto.
Instituto Cuánto and UNICEF. 1995. *Retrato de la familia Peruana: Niveles de vida*. Lima: Instituto Cuánto.
———. 1996. *Retrato de la familia Peruana: Ingresos*. Lima: Instituto Cuánto.
Isbell, Billie Jean. 1992. "Shining Path and Peasant Responses in Rural Ayacucho." In David Scott Palmer, ed., *Shining Path of Peru*, 59–81. New York: St. Martin's.
Jacobsen, Nils. 1993. *Mirages of Transition: The Peruvian Altiplano, 1780–1930*. Berkeley and Los Angeles: University of California Press.
Jain, Shail. 1975. *Size Distribution of Income: A Compilation of Data*. Washington, D.C.: World Bank.
Jiménez, Félix. 1997. "Sobre la equivocada información oficial del PBI." *Moneda*, no. 102:44–57.

Kay, Bruce H. 1997. "Fujimori Populism and the Liberal State in Peru, 1990–1995." *Journal of Inter-American Studies and World Affairs* 38, no. 4:55–98.

Kay, Cristóbal. 1982. "Achievements and Contradictions of the Peruvian Agrarian Reform." *Journal of Development Studies* 18.

Kirk, Robin. 1991. *The Decade of Chaqwa, Peru's Internal Refugees*. Washington, D.C.: U.S. Committee for Refugees.

Krugman, Paul. 1991. *Geography and Trade*. Cambridge, Mass.: MIT Press.

Lago, Ricardo. 1991. "The Illusion of Pursuing Redistribution Through Macropolicy: Peru's Heterodox Experience, 1985–1990." In Dornbusch and Edwards 1991, 263–323.

Lastarria-Cornhiel, Susana. 1989. "Agrarian Reforms of the 1960s and 1970 in Peru." In William C. Thiesenhusen, ed., *Searching for Agrarian Reform in Latin America*, 127–55. Boston: Unwin Hyman.

Londoño de la Cuesta, Juan Luis. 1995. *Distribución del ingreso y desarrollo económico: Colombia en el siglo XX*. Bogotá: Tercer Mundo, el Banco de la República, y Fedessarollo.

Lowenthal, Abraham, ed. 1975. *The Peruvian Experiment: Continuity and Change Under Military Rule*. Princeton: Princeton University Press.

Lustig, Nora, ed. 1995. *Coping with Austerity: Poverty and Inequality in Latin America*. Washington, D.C.: Brookings Institution.

Lustig, Nora, and Darryl McLeod. 1996. "Minimum Wages and Poverty in Developing Countries: Some Empirical Evidence." Brookings Discussion Papers in International Economics, no. 135.

Macario, Santiago. 1964. "Protectionism and Industrialization in Latin America." *Economic Bulletin for Latin America*, 69–90.

MacIsaac, Donna, and Harry Anthony Patrinos. 1995. "Labor Market Discrimination Against Indigenous People in Peru." *Journal of Development Studies* 32, no. 2:218–33.

Mahon, James. 1996. *Mobile Capital and Latin American Development*. University Park: Pennsylvania State University Press.

Mallon, Florencia. 1983. *The Defense of Community in Peru's Central Highlands: Peasant Control and Capitalist Tradition*. Princeton: Princeton University Press.

Maloney, William F. 1997. "Labor Market Structure in LDCs: Time Series Evidence on Competing Views." University of Illinois at Urbana-Champaign, duplicated.

Marcouiller, Douglas, Veronica Ruiz de Castilla, and Christopher Woodward. 1997. "Formal Measures of the Informal Sector Wage Gap in Mexico, El Salvador, and Peru." *Economic Development and Cultural Change* 45, no. 2:367–92.

Matos Mar, José. 1984. *Desborde popular y crisis del estado: El nuevo rostro del Perú en la década de 1980*. Lima: Instituto de Estudios Peruanos.

McClintock, Cynthia. 1981. *Peasant Cooperatives and Political Change in Peru*. Princeton: Princeton University Press.

———. 1984. "Why Peasants Rebel: The Case of Peru's Sendero Luminoso." *World Politics* 37:48–84.

———. 1985. "After Agrarian Reform and Democratic Government: Has Peruvian Agriculture Developed?" In F. LaMond Tullis and W. Ladd Hollist, eds., *Food, the State, and International Political Economy*. Lincoln: University of Nebraska Press.

McClintock, Cynthia, and Abraham Lowenthal, eds. 1983. *The Peruvian Experiment Reconsidered.* Princeton: Princeton University Press.
McCormick, Gordon H. 1992. *From the Sierra to the Cities: The Urban Campaign of the Shining Path.* Santa Monica: RAND Corporation.
Medina A., Andrés. 1996. "Pobreza, crecimiento y desigualdad: Perú 1991–1994." In Moncada and Webb 1996, 61–93.
Melmed-Sanjak, Jolyne S., and Michael R. Carter. 1991. "The Economic Viability and Stability of 'Capitalised Family Farming': An Analysis of Agricultural Decollectivization in Peru." *Journal of Development Studies* 27, no. 2:190–210.
Méndez, Cecilia G. 1996. "Incas Sí, Indios No: Notes on Peruvian Creole Nationalism and Its Contemporary Crisis." *Journal of Latin American Studies* 28, no. 1:197–225.
Meyer, David R. 1983. "Emergence of the American Manufacturing Belt: An Interpretation." *Journal of Historical Geography* 9, no. 2:145–74.
Ministerio de Agricultura. 1990. *Lineamientos de política agraria, 1990–1995.* Lima: Ministerio de Agricultura.
Moncada, Gilberto, and Richard Webb, eds. 1996. *¿Cómo estamos? Análisis de la encuesta de niveles de vida.* Lima: Instituto Cuánto and UNICEF.
Morley, Samuel A. 1995. *Poverty and Inequality in Latin America: The Impact of Adjustment and Recovery in the 1980s.* Baltimore: Johns Hopkins University Press.
Obando, Enrique. 1994. "The Power of Peru's Armed Forces." In Tulchin and Bland 1994, 101–24.
O'Donnell, Guillermo. 1973. *Modernization and Bureaucratic-Authoritarianism: Studies in South American Politics.* Berkeley: University of California, Institute of International Studies.
Palmer, David Scott. 1986. "Rebellion in Rural Peru: The Origins and Evolution of Sendero Luminoso." *Comparative Politics* 18:127–46.
———, ed. 1992. *Shining Path of Peru.* New York: St. Martin's.
Papanek, Gustav F., and Oldrich Kyn. 1987. "Flattening the Kuznets Curve: The Consequences for Income Distribution of Development Strategy, Government Intervention, and Income and the Rate of Growth." *Pakistan Development Review* 26, no. 1:1–54.
Paredes, Carlos E., and Jeffrey D. Sachs, eds. 1991. *Peru's Path to Recovery: A Plan for Economic Stabilization and Growth.* Washington, D.C.: Brookings Institution.
Parodi, Jorge. 1986. *Ser obrero es algo relativo.* Lima: Instituto de Estudios Peruanos.
Pásara, Luis. 1983. "When the Military Dreams." In McClintock and Lowenthal 1983.
———. 1989. *La izquierda en la escena pública.* Lima: Fundación Friedrich Ebert.
Pastor, Manuel, Jr., and Carol Wise. 1992. "Peruvian Economic Policy in the 1980s: From Orthodoxy to Heterodoxy and Back." *Latin American Economic Review* 27:3.
Paus, Eva. 1991. "Adjustment and Development in Latin America: The Failure of Peruvian Heterodoxy, 1985–90." *World Development* 19, no. 5:411–34.
Paus, Eva, and James Robinson. 1997. "The Implications of Increasing Economic Openness for Real Wages in Developing Countries, 1973–90." *World Development* 25, no. 4:537–47.

Payne, James L. 1965. *Labor and Politics in Peru: The System of Political Bargaining.* New Haven: Yale University Press.

Pike, Fredrick. 1967. *The Modern History of Peru.* New York: Praeger.

Pizzaro, Crisóstomo. 1995. "La primera reforma tributaria durante el gobierno de transición: Concertación y debate." In Pizarro, Raczynski, and Vial 1995, 93–118.

Pizzaro, Crisóstomo, Dagmar Raczynski, and Joaquín Vial, eds. 1995. *Políticas economicas y sociales en el Chile democrático.* Santiago: CIEPLAN and UNICEF.

PREALC (Programa Regional del Empleo para América Latina e el Caribe). 1982. *Mercado de trabajo en cifras, 1950–1980.* Santiago: PREALC.

Psacharopoulos, George, Samuel Morley, Ariel Fiszbein, Haeduck Lee, and Bill Wood. 1992. *Poverty and Income Distribution in Latin America: The Story of the 1980s.* Washington, D.C.: World Bank, Latin America and the Caribbean Technical Department Report, no. 27.

Quiroz, Alfonso W. 1993. *Domestic and Foreign Finance in Modern Peru, 1850–1950: Financing Visions of Development.* Pittsburgh: University of Pittsburgh Press.

Raczynski, Dagmar. 1995. *Strategies to Combat Poverty in Latin America.* Washington, D.C.: Johns Hopkins University Press for the Inter-American Development Bank.

Ramos, Joseph. 1986. *Neoconservative Economics in the Southern Cone of Latin America, 1973–1983.* Baltimore: Johns Hopkins University Press.

Remmer, Karen. 1990. "Democracy and Economic Crisis: The Latin American Experience." *World Politics* 41:315–35.

Reyes, José. 1995. "Medición de la pobreza en Lima Metropolitana: Metodología y resultados." In Jeanine Anderson et al., *Medición de la pobreza en Lima metropolitana: Metodología y resultados,* 113–222. Lima: Centro de Investigación de la Universidad del Pacífico and Taller de Políticas y Desarrollo Social.

Roberts, Kenneth M. 1995. "Neoliberalism and the Transformation of Populism in Latin America: The Peruvian Case." *World Politics* 48, no. 1:82–116.

Roberts, Kenneth M., and Mark Peceny. 1997. "Human Rights and United States Policy Toward Peru." In Cameron and Mauceri 1997, 192–222.

Rossini, Renzo G. 1991. "Liberalización comercial y establizacion económica." In *Liberalización del comercio exterior en el Perú.* Lima: Fundación Friedrich Ebert, Tercer Foro Economico.

Rudolph, James D. 1992. *Peru: The Evolution of a Crisis.* Westport, Conn.: Praeger.

Saavedra, Jaime. 1997a. *Liberalización comercial e industria manufacturera en el Perú.* Lima: Consorcio de Investigación Económica, *Investigaciones breves,* 2.

———. 1997b. "Quienes ganan y quienes pierden con una reforma estructural: Cambios en la dispersión de ingresos según educación, experiencia y genero en el Perú urbano." GRADE, *Notas para el debate,* 14:9–77.

Saavedra, Jaime, Roberto Melzi Ríos, and Arturo Miranda Blanco. 1997. "Financiamiento de la educación en el Perú." Lima: GRADE, *Documento de trabajo,* 24.

Saavedra-Chanduvi, Jaime. 1998. "What Do We Know About Poverty and Income Distribution in Peru, with Emphasis in Its Links with Education and the Labor Market." Report prepared for the LAC-Sector Units of the World Bank.

Saavedra-Chanduvi, Jaime, and Juan José Díaz. 1998. "Changes in Labor Earnings Dispersion in Peru: The Roles of Skills and Institutions." Lima: Grupo de Análisis para el Desarrollo.
Sachs, Jeffrey. 1987. "Trade and Exchange Rate Policies in Growth-Oriented Adjustment Programs." In Vittorio Corbo, Morris Goldstein, and Mohsin Khan, eds., *Growth-Oriented Adjustment Programs*, 291–325. Washington, D.C.: International Monetary Fund and World Bank.
Sánchez-Albornoz, Nicolas. 1974. *The Population of Latin America: A History*. Berkeley and Los Angeles: University of California Press.
Schiefelbein, Ernesto. 1997. "Financing Education for Democracy in Latin America." In Carlos Alberto Torres and Adriana Puiggrós, eds., *Latin American Education: Comparative Perspectives*, 31–64. Boulder, Colo.: Westview Press.
Schuldt, Jürgen. 1994. "La enfermedad holandesa y otros vicios de la economía Peruana." Lima: Universidad del Pacífico.
———. 1995. *Repensando el desarrollo: Hacía una concepción alternativa para los países Andinos*. Quito: Centro Andino de Acción Popular.
———. 1996. "Observaciones críticas generales al texto de Daniel M. Schydlowsky." In Schydlowsky and Schuldt 1996, 57–91.
———. 1997. "Economía política de la transición: Hacia una nueva modalidad de acumulación en el Perú, 1990–2000: Perspectivas y alternativas." In Gonzales de Olarte 1997a, 121–55.
Schydlowsky, Daniel M. 1996. "El contexto histórico de la recuperación económica peruana." In Schydlowsky and Schuldt 1996, 13–56.
Schydlowsky, Daniel M., Shane Hunt, and Jaime Mezzara. 1983. *La promoción de exportaciones no tradicionales en el Perú*. Lima: ADEX.
Schydlowsky, Daniel M., and Jürgen Schuldt. 1996. *Modelo económico Peruano de fin de siglo*. Lima: Fundación Friedrich Ebert.
Schydlowsky, Daniel M., and Juan Wicht. 1979. *Anatomía de un fracaso económico*. Lima: Universidad del Pacífico.
———. 1983. "The Anatomy of an Economic Failure." In McClintock and Lowenthal 1983, 94–143.
Seers, Dudley. 1979. "Patterns of Dependence." In José Villamil, ed., *Transnational Capitalism and National Development*, 95–111. Brighton: Harvester Press for the Institute of Development Studies, University of Sussex.
Seminario de Marzi, Bruno, and César Bouillon Buendía. 1992. *Ciclos y tendencia en el Perú*. Lima: Universidad del Pacífico.
Sheahan, John. 1980a. "Market-Oriented Economic Policies and Political Repression." *Economic Development and Cultural Change* 28:267–91.
———. 1980b. "Peru: Economic Policies and Structural Change, 1968–1978." *Journal of Economic Studies* 7:3–27.
———. 1987. *Patterns of Development in Latin America: Poverty, Repression, and Economic Strategy*. Princeton: Princeton University Press.
———. 1993. "Las exportaciones no tradicionales, el tipo de cambio, y el futuro de la economía Peruana." *Moneda*, nos. 62–63:62–67.
———. 1994. "Peru's Return Toward an Open Economy: Macroeconomic Complications and Structural Questions." *World Development* 22, no. 6:911–23.

———. 1997. "Effects of Liberalization Programs on Poverty and Inequality: Chile, Mexico, and Peru." *Latin American Research Review* 32, no. 3:7–37.
Sheahan, John, and Enrique Iglesias. 1998. "Kinds and Causes of Inequality in Latin America." In Nancy Birdsall, Carol Graham, and Richard Sabot, eds., *Beyond Tradeoffs: Market Reforms and Equitable Growth in Latin America,* 29–61. Washington, D.C.: Brookings Institution and IDB.
Smith, Michael L. 1992. "Shining Path's Urban Strategy: Ate Vitarte." In Palmer 1992, 127–47.
Squire, Lyn. 1993. "Fighting Poverty." *American Economic Review* 83, no. 2:377–82.
Starn, Orin. 1995. "Maoism in the Andes: The Communist Party of Peru—Shining Path and the Refusal of History." *Journal of Latin American Studies and World Affairs* 27:399–431.
Stein, Steve. 1980. *Populism in Peru: The Emergence of the Masses and the Politics of Social Consent.* Madison: University of Wisconsin Press.
Stepan, Alfred. 1978. *The State and Society: Peru in Comparative Perspective.* Princeton: Princeton University Press.
Stern, Steve J., ed. 1987. *Resistance, Rebellion, and Consciousness in the Andean Peasant World: 18th to 20th Centuries.* Madison: University of Wisconsin Press.
Stevens, Evelyne Huber. 1983. "The Peruvian Military Government, Labor Mobilization, and the Political Strength of the Left." *Latin American Research Review* 18, no. 2:57–93.
Stokes, Susan C. 1991. "Politics and Latin America's Urban Poor: Reflections from a Lima Shantytown." *Latin American Research Review* 26, no. 2:75–101.
Suarez-Berenguela, Ruben M. 1988. *Informal Sector, Labor Markets, and Returns to Education in Peru.* Washington, D.C.: World Bank Living Standards Measurement Study Working Paper, no. 32.
Tandeter, Enrique. 1993. *Coercion and Markets: Silver Mining in Colonial Potosí, 1692–1826.* Albuquerque: University of New Mexico Press.
Tanzi, Vito. 1987. "Fiscal Policy, Growth, and Design of Stabilization Programs." In Ana María Martirena-Mantel, ed., *External Debt, Savings, and Growth in Latin America.* Buenos Aires and Washington, D.C.: Instituto Torcuato di Tella and International Monetary Fund.
Távara, José. 1996. "Comentarios" to presentation of "El nuevo marco regulatorio." *Boletín de opinión* (Consorcio de investigación económica) 29:54–55.
Tello, Mario. 1989. "Políticas de estabilización en el Perú y el sector externo: 1989." *Economía* 12, no. 23:45–58.
———. 1990. *Exportaciones y crecimiento económico en el Perú, 1950–1987.* Lima: Fundación Frederich Ebert.
———. 1993. *Mecanismos hacia el crecimiento económico: El enfoque de la organización industrial en el sector manufacturero Peruano, 1970–1987.* Lima: Pontificia Universidad Católica del Perú.
Thorp, Rosemary, ed. 1984. *Latin America in the 1930s: The Role of the Periphery in World Crisis.* New York: St. Martin's.
———. 1987. "Trends and Cycles in the Peruvian Economy." *Journal of Development Economics* 27:355–74.

———. 1991. *Economic Management and Economic Development in Peru and Colombia*. Pittsburgh: University of Pittsburgh Press.
Thorp, Rosemary, and associates. 1995. *Challenges for Peace: Towards Sustainable Social Development in Peru*. Washington, D.C.: Inter-American Development Bank, Social Agenda Policy Group.
Thorp, Rosemary, and Geoffrey Bertram. 1978. *Peru 1880–1977: Growth and Policy in an Open Economy*. New York: Columbia University Press.
Torres, Raúl. 1993. *Evaluación del nivel del PIB*. Lima: Centro de Estudios Regionales Andino, Bartholemé de las Casas.
Trevor-Roper, H. R. 1967. *Religion, the Reformation, and Social Change*. London: Macmillan.
Tulchin, Joseph, and Gary Bland, eds. 1994. *Peru in Crisis: Dictatorship or Democracy?* Boulder, Colo.: Lynne Reinner.
Tullis, F. LaMond. 1970. *Lord and Peasant in Peru: A Paradigm of Political and Social Change*. Cambridge, Mass.: Harvard University Press.
UNDP (United Nations Development Program). 1995. *Human Development Report, 1995*. New York: Oxford University Press for the UNDP.
Vega Castro, Jorge. 1989. *El sector industrial informal y las políticas de liberalización del comercio exterior en el Perú: El caso de las industrias de confecciones y de calzado*. Lima: Instituto de Investigación y Docencia.
Vega-Centeno, Máximo. 1988. "Desarrollo industrial y exportaciones industriales." *Economía* 11, no. 21:9–40.
———. 1989. *Crecimiento, industrialización, y cambio técnico: Perú 1955–1980*. 2d ed. Lima: Pontificia Universidad Católica del Perú.
———. 1993. *Desarrollo económico y desarrollo tecnológico*. Lima: Pontificia Universidad Católica del Perú.
Verdera, Francisco. 1994. "El mercado de trabajo de Lima Metropolitana: Estructura y evolución, 1970–1990." Lima: Instituto de Estudios Peruanos, *Documento de trabajo, 59*.
———. 1997a. "Los limites del ajuste: La falta de absorción de empleo asalariado en el caso Peruano." In Gonzales de Olarte 1997a, 189–221.
———. 1997b. "Mercado de trabajo, reforma laboral y creación de empleo: Perú, 1990–1995." Lima: Instituto de Estudios Peruanos, *Documento de trabajo, 87*.
Vicens Vives, Jaime. 1965. *Manuel de la historia económica de España*. 4th ed. Barcelona: Ediciones Vicens Vives.
Webb, Richard. 1977. *Government Policy and the Distribution of Income in Peru, 1963–73*. Cambridge, Mass.: Harvard University Press.
Webb, Richard, and Adolfo Figueroa. 1975. *Distribución del ingreso en el Perú*. Lima: Instituto de Estudios Peruanos.
Williamson, Jeffrey. 1996. "Globalization and Inequality, Then and Now: The Late 19th and Early 20th Centuries Compared." National Bureau of Economic Research, Working Paper no. 5491.
World Bank. 1983. *World Tables*. 3rd ed. Washington, D.C.: World Bank.
———. 1981. *World Development Report, 1981*. Baltimore: Oxford University Press for the World Bank.
———. 1988. *World Development Report, 1988*. Baltimore: Oxford University Press for the World Bank.

———. 1990. *World Development Report, 1990*. Baltimore: Oxford University Press for the World Bank.
———. 1997. *World Development Report, 1997*. Baltimore: Oxford University Press for the World Bank.
Yamada Fukusaki, Gustavo. 1996a. "La problemática del empleo en el próximo quinquenio." In Yamada Fukusaki et al. 1996, 19–87.
———. 1996b. "Pobreza y empleo en el Perú: Los aportes de las ENNIV 1985–1994." In Moncada and Webb 1996, 23–40.
Yamada Fukusaki, Gustavo, Guillermo Felices Saavedra, Marlon Ramos Li, and José Luis Ruiz Pérez, eds. 1996. *Caminos entrelazados: La realidad del empleo urbano en el Perú*. Lima: Universidad del Pacífico, Centro de Investigación (CIUP).

Index

Acción Popular, 31
aggregate demand, 135, 141, 145–46, 163–66, 178
agriculture
  credit, 68–69, 124
  labor force and land, 19–20, 25, 46–49, 57–61, 78–80, 112–13, 173, 177
  production, 46–48, 57, 64–70, 74, 141–42, 167
  See also exports; food supply; incentives; land; rural poverty
Alegría, Ciro, 62 n. 1
Alliance for Progress, 32
APRA *(Alianza popular revolucionaria Américana),* 28–33, 44, 125
Argentina, 44, 95, 119 n. 1, 143–45, 186
Arguedas, José María, 62 n. 1
autonomy. *See* independent development
Ayacucho, 77–78, 109–10

balance of payments, 53, 84–85, 137, 145.
  See also current account; external deficits
banks and financial sector, 37, 43, 69, 142–43, 150, 159, 181
Belaúnde Terry, Fernando, 8–10, 31–33, 63, 66, 82–83, 138–39, 143–44, 150–51
Bolivia, 107, 126
Brazil, 24, 44, 117, 120, 123, 186
Bustamente y Rivero, José Luis, 30–31, 96

Cajamarca, 63
Cantuta, La, 77
capital flows, 159, 178–79, 185–89
Central America, 44, 120
Certex (export subsidy program), 53, 134, 138

Chile, 95, 102–3, 126, 128, 168–69, 183–85, 187
class conflict, 81, 134–37, 189
coastal region, 18–19, 111–12, 116
coca, 19, 58, 73–74, 111, 121
Colombia, 23–24, 37, 44
communal action groups (nongovernmental organizations), xii, 32, 157, 168, 179
comparative advantage, 45–46, 63, 74, 80, 82, 85, 103, 120, 129, 149, 165, 178, 181
competition, 86–87, 91, 101, 139, 149, 188–89
competitiveness of the industrial sector, 49–55, 85–88, 95, 103, 128, 131, 135, 149–51, 163, 166, 171, 181, 184
congress, 34–38, 126, 142, 161, 183
conscripción vial, 29
cooperatives, 63–64, 67, 135, 177
copper, 12, 41, 43–44
Costa Rica, 24, 120, 130
Cuba, 24, 76
currency based on silver, 42
current account (external), 92, 137, 145–47, 163–64, 171, 186–87, 189

debt (external), 10, 85, 135–40, 145–48, 155, 157, 161, 163, 178
democracy, 14, 16, 27, 34–38, 63, 87, 102, 138, 161, 183–87
dependence on primary exports and external finance, 4, 11–12, 49, 55, 83–84, 178, 180, 183, 186–87, 190
de Soto, Hernando, 100–101
devaluation. *See* exchange rates
discrimination, 13–14, 24–27, 114–15, 120–21, 129, 175, 190

diversification of production and exports, 45–56, 158, 163, 171
Dutch disease, 41–42

East Asia, 85–86, 131, 149, 151
economic growth, 5–7, 42, 48–49, 122, 133, 143, 145–46, 160–61, 182–83, 189. *See also* GDP
economic strategy
  before 1960s, 2, 27–28, 40–44, 117, 175
  redirection in 1960s, xi–xii, 2–3, 8, 12–14, 32–34, 82, 133–34, 175
  state-led development, xi–xii, 2, 8–12, 33–34, 84–88, 131–51, 171, 175, 180, 188–91
  liberalization, xii, 11, 15–16, 34–38, 69, 80, 88, 90–91, 118, 121–22, 142–43, 153–58, 164–68, 170–71, 181–91
education
  access, 4, 11, 21, 39, 46, 52, 72, 105, 108–9, 112–15, 120–21, 127, 129–30, 149–51, 166, 170, 179
  higher education (professions), 26, 46
  public and private, 21–27, 109, 166
  quality, 21–24, 27, 79, 94, 109, 179
efficiency, 44, 49, 64, 82, 135, 149–50, 157, 166–67, 177, 189
employment, 11–12, 45–49, 56, 71–80, 88–92, 97, 102–3, 113, 121, 124, 135, 151, 158, 166–68, 170–71, 177–78, 182, 185, 187, 190
engineers (science and scientists), 24, 26, 46, 86
entrepreneurship, 81, 86–87, 100–101
exchange rates, 42–44, 52–55, 68, 70–72, 85–88, 92–94, 128, 132, 137–39, 145–46, 151, 158–60, 163–65, 167, 171, 178–79, 186–90
exports
  agriculture and fishing, 11–12, 41, 53, 70–73
  growth, 31, 41, 52–55, 70–73, 163–65
  industrial and other nontraditional, 40, 50–55, 70–73, 120–28, 138, 164–65, 169, 178
  See also dependence on primary products; incentives for exports
external deficits and external credit, 3, 53, 82–85, 120–28, 132, 137, 139, 144–48, 156, 159, 163–64, 186, 188.
  See also balance of payments; current account

factor proportions, 45–46, 90, 119–20, 130. *See also* agriculture; comparative advantage
fertility rates, 19, 177
Figueroa, Adolfo, 106, 121, 123
financial sector. *See* banks
fiscal deficits, 8, 53, 68, 120, 137, 148, 157
FONCODES *(Fondo nacional de compensación y desarrollo social)*, 125–26, 167, 170
food supply, 57, 64–68, 78–79, 177
foreign investment and ownership, xii, 13, 31–32, 34–38, 40, 42–43, 89, 137, 157, 161–62, 165, 168, 175–76, 178, 185–86
Fujimori, Alberto, 9, 34–38, 69, 82, 87, 92, 96, 101–2, 125–27, 139, 142, 151, 156, 161, 170, 190
Fujishock (August 1990), 94, 156–57, 160

García, Alan, 9–10, 21, 31, 33, 35, 54, 67–69, 76, 87, 90, 92, 95, 101, 121, 124–25, 132–33, 139–45, 150, 155, 162
GDP (Gross Domestic Product)
  measurement problems, 47–49, 163 n. 4
  per capita levels, 5, 40, 133, 139, 141, 162
  sector differences, 46–49, 122
  See also economic growth
gold and silver, 12, 40–41, 44
gold standard, 42–43
guano exports, 12, 41–42
Guzmán, Abamael, 77–78

Haya de la Torre, Raúl, 29–31
health care (public health), 107, 124, 127, 166
heterodox macroeconomic policies, 133, 139–45. *See also* macroeconomic management
human capital (human resources), 4, 20–24, 165–66
human rights, 35–38, 76

illiteracy, 4, 20–21, 107, 109–10, 179
IMF (International Monetary Fund), 138, 155–56, 161, 186
imports
  growth and structure, 42, 45, 49, 68, 84–85, 88, 158, 162–64
  import substitution and industrialization, 2, 4, 32, 42, 49, 91, 137, 148–50
incentives
  for agricultural production, 64, 66–70, 79–80
  for employment, 79, 90, 128–29, 163, 169
  for exports, 42–43, 50–55, 72–74, 85–86, 134, 137, 145, 149–50, 159, 188–89
income distribution. See inequality
independent development, 2, 15, 42, 134, 153–54, 168, 185–89
indigenous communities, 20, 32, 61–64, 100
indigenous people, 14, 18–20, 24, 61–64, 75, 112–15, 151
industrialization (industrial sector), 2, 11–12, 25, 32, 40–46, 81–103, 113–14, 148–50, 159, 162–63, 171, 188–89. See also diversification; exports; manufacturing
inequality
  causes, 4, 7, 11, 13, 24–25, 42, 45, 56, 58, 97, 115, 119–21, 127–30, 135, 180–83, 186
  consequences, 1, 4, 14, 25, 31, 37–38, 58, 61, 75, 78–80, 105–6, 120–21, 189
  kinds and measurement, 6, 108, 115–19, 129–30, 141–42, 165, 171, 181–82
  possibilities for reduction, 120–29, 135, 141, 165–70, 183
infant mortality, 5–6, 58–59, 106–9, 116, 130
inflation, 3, 33, 35, 42, 68, 132–33, 137–44, 149, 158–61, 183, 188–89
informal sector, 89–90, 97–103, 113, 124
innovation (productivity and technological change), 4, 15, 25, 45–46, 49–50, 86, 94–95, 103, 135, 162, 168–69, 171, 178, 180, 188–89
interest rates, 139–40, 186–87
International Petroleum Company, 32, 43, 134, 176

international trade (structure), 39–56, 83–84, 178. See also diversification; exports; imports
investment, 66, 69, 84–85, 87, 135, 137, 142, 155, 161–62, 182–83

labor
  agricultural, 11, 19, 45, 57–61, 177
  distribution among activities, 19–20, 59, 89–90, 112–13
  labor supply and employment opportunities, 20, 45, 89–90, 103, 127–28, 189
  legislation (job security), 90, 95–97, 134–36, 138, 168, 183–84
  organization (unions), 32, 38, 81, 95–97, 102, 136, 168, 175
  skilled and unskilled, 45, 50, 52, 119–20, 127–28, 185
  See also employment; wages
land
  arable land supply, 11, 19, 45, 59–60, 129, 169, 177
  land-owning elite, 24, 32, 61–64, 71 n. 5, 77–79, 175–79
  ownership structure and reform, 31–32, 39, 51, 58, 61–67, 70–76, 79, 121, 128, 134–35, 167, 169, 176–77, 180
Latin America
  democracy and repression, 34–35, 102
  economic strategy, 2, 12–13, 43–44, 82, 132, 143–44, 154, 174, 186–88, 190–91
  exports, 72, 138
  innovation and structural change, 24, 54
  internal divisions (poverty and inequality), 4, 24, 61, 107–8, 111, 118–24, 130, 165, 169, 174, 181–82
Leguía, Augusto, 29
Lima, 18–19, 28, 59, 108–12, 130, 142, 156–57, 179

macroeconomic balance and management, 10–11, 68, 86, 101–3, 114, 132–33, 139, 141–45, 148–51, 155, 164, 188–89. See also heterodox macroeconomic policies
manufacturing, 46–55, 82–88, 90–91. See also diversification; exports; industrial sector
Mariátegui, José Carlos, 28

market forces, 10–11, 42, 94–95, 122, 127–29, 154, 177–81, 189
Marxism (Marxists), 30, 75–78
Mexico, 35, 44, 99, 117, 144–45, 187
microentrepreneurs, 89, 99, 102, 124–25, 141, 180
migration (rural to urban), 11, 20, 32, 59, 76, 79, 100, 179
military
 political intervention and repression, 29–31, 33–36, 76–77, 96, 142
 reformist governments, 9, 31–33, 134–38
mining sector, xii, 11–12, 39, 47–48, 87, 103, 116, 120, 122, 129, 134, 137, 157, 159, 162, 165, 168, 176
mobility (economic and social), 25–27, 39, 45–46, 113–15, 120, 127, 129, 175, 179–80, 189
monetary policies, 141, 143, 145, 150, 178, 184, 187
Morales Bermudez, General Francisco, 9, 133, 138, 143, 146, 150–51
MRTA *(Movimento Revolucionario Túpac Amaru)*, 14, 76, 80, 121

National Democratic Front (1945–48), 30–31, 36
nationalizations and public firms, 8, 10, 37, 134, 137, 142–43
natural resources, 39–42, 149. *See also* copper; gold and silver; guano; oil
neoliberal policies. *See* economic strategy; liberalization

Odría, General Manuel, 9, 31
oil, 12, 32, 41, 43, 134, 141, 165. *See also* International Petroleum Company
ownership concentration, 39, 61–64, 119, 127, 134, 180, 189–90. *See also* land; ownership structure

PAD *(Programa de apoyo directo)*, 124–25
PAIT *(Programa de apoyo de ingreso temporal)*, 124–25
Pasto, 64
Pérez Godoy, General, 31–32
political institutions (governments and parties), 9, 27–38, 44, 102
population, 18–19, 45, 59, 66, 103, 129–30

populism and populists, 9, 29–32, 37–38, 139, 163, 178
poverty
 causes, 56, 60–61, 65, 75–80, 88, 91, 105–6, 112–15, 129–30, 137–38, 149, 167, 180–81
 meaning and measurement, 5, 18, 106–15, 121, 130, 135, 171
 possible remedies, 79–80, 95, 122–29, 167, 169–70, 177, 183
Prado, Manuel, 9, 31
prices
 controls, 30, 68, 95, 133, 137, 139–41, 144–45, 156–58, 160
 index (problems of measurement), 92–93
 relative prices, 42, 68–70, 88, 93–94, 112, 116, 135, 140–42, 156–57, 165
primary product exports. *See* dependence on primary exports
private sector, 34–36, 140–42, 145, 148, 155–56, 161–63, 175
privatizations, 9, 157, 161–62
productivity. *See* innovation; productivity; technological change
Programa de apoyo a la pobreza extrema, 125
protection against imports, 2, 4, 9–10, 82–87, 95, 103, 135, 137, 139, 146, 149–50, 157, 171, 183, 188. *See also* tariffs and quotas
public sector (employment and investment), 2, 9, 30–31, 66–67, 89–91, 132–33, 153–54, 157–58, 164, 183

quality of products and exports, 86–88, 103, 158

regions within Peru (regional development), 18, 21, 60, 79, 111–12, 169–70, 181, 190
regulation of business, 100–101, 136, 157, 183, 185
República Aristocratica, 27–29, 38
rural areas
 discrimination against, 4, 7, 19–21, 24–25, 109–10, 113, 130, 144–50
 poverty, 18, 57–58, 60–61, 78–80, 108–12, 126–27, 135, 151, 158, 167, 169–70, 175–77, 190

Sánchez Cerro, Luis M., 29, 44
Schuldt, Jürgen, 13
Schydlowsky, Daniel, 13
science and scientists. *See* engineers
sectoral distribution of employment and production, 46–49
selva (jungle areas), 18, 111–12, 117
Sendero luminoso (Shining Path), xi, 14, 33, 36, 69, 74–78, 87, 109–10, 121, 142, 161, 170, 183, 188
services sector, 47–49, 99, 113
sierra, 18, 21, 58–59, 63–64, 77, 107–11, 117, 130, 179
social programs (social investment), 79, 120, 141–42, 153–54, 158, 165–67, 169–70, 183–85, 190
social values and goals, xii, 12–16, 25–26, 115, 124–27, 129–30, 148–51, 165, 168, 174–76
Southern Cone countries, 24, 34, 44, 130
Spain, 25–26, 39–40
state-led development. *See* economic strategy
structural factors and development, 7, 10–12, 51–52, 56, 151, 173–74, 189
subsidies, 53, 67–69, 92, 124, 126, 135, 141, 149, 157–58

tariffs and quotas, 32, 44, 69–70, 82–84, 93, 139

tax revenue and structure, 42, 101, 119–20, 128–30, 141–43, 155, 157, 166, 169, 183–87, 190
terms of trade, 139, 146
textiles, 43, 54
Thorp, Rosemary, xii, 30–31

United States, 14, 25, 45, 59, 74, 76, 100, 123, 129, 139, 156
universities, 26, 77–78
urbanization, 20, 44
Uruguay, 99 n. 5, 119 n. 1, 120

Vargas Llosa, Mario, 34, 156
Velasco Alvarado, General Juan, 8–10, 21, 32, 63, 82, 87, 90, 92, 96, 121, 132–38, 140, 143, 146, 150, 162, 176, 179
violence, 2, 14, 33–34, 58, 63, 66, 69, 74–78, 88, 123, 139, 141–42, 151, 155

wages, 23, 56, 91–95, 97, 99, 109–10, 113–14, 124–25, 139–41, 145, 157, 167–68, 182, 190
women (education and incomes), 4, 21, 109–10, 113–13, 124–25, 179
World Bank, 155–56, 161

John Sheahan is professor of economics, emeritus, at Williams College. His previous publications include *Promotion and Control of Industry in Postwar France* (1963), *The Wage-Price Guideposts* (1967), *An Introduction to the French Economy* (1969), *Patterns of Development in Latin America: Poverty, Repressions, and Economic Strategy* (1987), and *Conflict and Change in Mexican Economic Strategy: Implications for Mexico and Latin America* (1992).